Praise for Michael Dirda and *Readings*

"Dirda's mix of gentle, self-effacing humor and persistent passion for literature is like a welcome pleasure from a different time. . . . Regardless of the subject, the author's tone of voice is alternately serious and playful, measured and invariably wise."
—Richard Burgin, *St. Louis Post-Dispatch*

"A generous and subtle critic. . . . Dirda clearly sees his mission as one of enticing as many as he can to read—and love—the literary classics and serious works of history and biography. His obvious relish for books allows him to exhort without sounding self-important and without making reading difficult works seem like taking medicine. . . . Equally unusual is Dirda's preference for wit and style over 'issues.' . . . Dirda prizes wryness and detachment rather than zeal."
—Ben Schwartz, *The Atlantic*

"Dirda can be as funny as Dave Barry (though Dave Barry with a good thesaurus and personal knowledge of Marcus Aurelius). And he can break your heart, as in the beautiful, poignant, 'Listening to My Father,' Dirda's tribute to his steelworker father."
—Elizabeth Hand, *The Magazine of Fantasy and Science Fiction*

"Delightful wit and zestful insight. Anyone who loves books is bound to love Dirda. Highly recommended."
—Henry Carrigan, *Library Journal*

"The first thing I turn to in the Sunday morning's *Post* is Michael Dirda. I am certain that I am going to be surprised, entertained, informed, and intrigued by his autobiographical reminiscences, which are enlivened by a self-deprecating wit, by his fascinating and occasionally hilarious accounts of the search for bibliographical treasures in secondhand bookshops, and by his reflections on books that I have never read but now realize I must, and insights into books I know but now wish to reread." —Bernard Knox

"Michael Dirda's love of reading is a highly contagious virus. One cannot be immunized against it; one cannot be cured; one can only be grateful to catch it." —Anne Fadiman

Readings

Illustration by Susan Davis

MICHAEL DIRDA

Readings

Essays & Literary Entertainments

W. W. Norton & Company
New York London

Library of Congress Cataloging-in-Publication Data

Dirda, Michael.
    Readings : essays and literary entertainments / Michael Dirda.
        p.   cm.
    ISBN 0-253-33824-7 (alk. paper)
    I. Title.
    PN4874.D475 A25 2000
    814'.6—dc21   00-033598
    ISBN 978-0-393-32489-1

W. W. Norton & Company, Inc.
500 Fifth Avenue, New York, N.Y. 10110
www.wwnorton.com

W. W. Norton & Company Ltd.
Castle House, 75/76 Wells Street, London W1T 3QT

 2 3 4 5 6 7 8 9 0

To My Mother and Sisters
and in Memory of My Father

Contents

Preface

From the start, I imagined the essays in this book as "literary entertainments." The pieces themselves were intended to take up serious issues, but the approach was to be resolutely personal, lighthearted most of the time, occasionally wistful or nostalgic. Showing her usual perspicacity, my then-boss Nina King eventually gave in to my shameless entreaties and agreed to let me try this experiment in playful journalism for half a year or so. My first column was published in January 1993 on page 15 of the *Washington Post Book World,* and seven years later it still appears there once a month.

In every way, *Book World* has been immensely accommodating and generous. So long as I touch on books, reading, publishing, or collecting, I have been permitted to be highly personal (the portrait of my father), utterly fanciful (parodies of various literary genres), fairly serious (my "advice to graduates" address), or a blend of all these (the notorious Florida midlife crisis piece). I've written columns in the shape of diaries, plays, and memoirs; there have been essays on forgotten novels, soft-core pornography, *The Tale of Genji,* and the joys of book-hunting; at holidays I've recommended current books and old favorites; during the summer I've advised on beach fiction. In short, "Readings"—as the feature is called—has been a catch-all, a chance for me to talk about some of the books I love. Happily, there have been a great many.

The voice, I hope, is my own, though I may have learned by imitating the dulcet tones of others. As a very young teenager with a library card, I checked out the genial, easygoing essays of Clifton Fadiman. In college I discovered the distinctive prose of Cyril Connolly (*The Unquiet Grave*), M. F. K. Fisher (*The Art of Eating*), Ezra Pound (*Literary Essays*), and Randall Jarrell (*Poetry and the Age*). Even later, I read (and sometimes tried to palely emulate) the journalism of Joseph Mitchell, Janet Flanner, Kenneth Tynan, Joseph Epstein, Guy Davenport, Robertson Davies, Brigid Brophy, H. L Mencken, Desmond MacCarthy, G. K. Chesterton, Anthony Burgess, Gore Vidal, Virgil Thomson, John Updike, W. H. Auden, Robert Phelps, Hunter Thompson, A. J. Liebling, Joan Didion, and William Gass. Each of these writers transformed magazine reportage or casual piece work into something stylish, personal, and artful.

I also learned—I hope—from the essays of my colleagues at the *Post*, especially the late Henry Mitchell (gardener, dog-lover, and wise man) and my fellow critic Jonathan Yardley. Most important of all, I talked books for a dozen years with my good friend David Streitfeld, long the premier publishing reporter in the country but now, alas, covering digital technology and Silicon Valley. Let me also mention other friends at *Book World* past and present: K. Francis Tanabe, Ednamae Storti, Marie Arana, Elizabeth Ward, Mary Morris, Jennifer Howard, Jabari Asim, Michele Slung, Robert Wilson, Brigitte Weeks, Curt Suplee, William McPherson, and, not least, the late and much-missed Reid Beddow. Equally missed is Susan Davis, who provided wonderful pictures for my essays. Bobbye Pratt assisted me in the *Post*'s library, and Rudy McDaniel of the University of Central Florida kindly offered his computer expertise. John Gallman and Jane Lyle of Indiana University Press contributed encouragement, sage counsel, and expert editorial advice. Above all, my wife Marian and our children Christopher, Michael, and Nathaniel have periodically reminded me that people are more important than books.

In an introduction to an omnibus volume of his fiction, P. G. Wodehouse once advised his admirers to go slowly, to ration the stories over several weeks, lest his idiosyncratic prose start to pall through sheer excess. May I beg the same indulgence? Don't rush through these essays all at once. Dip into the book at random. Browse. Trust the gods of serendipity. As Randall Jarrell once proclaimed, Read at whim!

Michael Dirda
dirdam@washpost.com

Readings

The Crime of His Life

The weed of crime, according to the Shadow, bears bitter fruit. But not always. One afternoon some thirty-five years ago, a 13-year-old boy was lingering in the book section of O'Neil's department store, surreptitiously turning the pages of *Tarzan the Untamed*. The Grosset & Dunlap editions of Lord Greystoke's adventures ($1.50 each) cost too much to actually buy, except on the rarest and flushest of occasions, but no store officials seemed to care if an obviously devoted student of the apeman simply stood there, in that quiet corner, and read through an entire novel in the course of a lazy summer day.

I was to meet my mother, bargain shopper extraordinaire, out in the parking lot at 5 P.M. Rather to my surprise I finished that Burroughs masterwork with half an hour to spare, examined the various Hardy Boys selections and found I knew them all, then looked disdainfully at the pricey Scribners Illustrated Classics (Parent-Approved Kiddie Lit) and even glanced through one or two of the deluxe leatherette Bibles. A bit antsy by now, I started to roam through the store when, near the cash registers, I spotted a virgin stand of paperbacks. Having recently lost sleep over a Pyramid edition of *The Insidious Dr. Fu Manchu*—and shuddered hopefully for days at the prospect of thuggees crouching in Ohio oaks—I raced toward the wire rack, thinking that maybe, just maybe, the announced sequel might be there, even now awaiting my trembling fingers. But, it turned out, I would need to defer to another day the company of that satanic archfiend with a brow like Shakespeare's.

Instead I discovered that the revolving rack was stocked entirely with plastic bags, each containing three coverless paperbacks and each bag priced at some ridiculously low figure like 25 cents. I now realize that the store had stripped the paperbacks and sent the covers back for credit. Instead of discarding the mutilated books, which was what the law requires, O'Neil's had decided to sell them at a reduced package rate. None of this profiteering would have mattered to me then. All I cared about was the opportunity to buy three paperbacks cheap.

It didn't take me long, however, before I saw my problem. Edward S. Aaron's *Assignment: Ankara,* the latest Sam Durrell spy thriller, was in one bag; the funny-sounding *Which Way to Mecca, Jack?* by someone named William Peter Blatty was in another (years later Blatty was to become famous for his novel *The Exorcist*). I certainly didn't want to shell out cash for any more bags than was absolutely necessary.

At this point you need to know that I have always carried a pocket knife.

Picturing myself as the suave Cary Grant of *To Catch a Thief,* I stealthily slit the top edge of two bags, matched up my treasures, and slid them together into a package that already contained something called *The Lifetime Reading Plan,* by one Clifton Fadiman. Then, while covering the untimely rip with my trembling palm and already beginning to sweat like Peter Lorre in *M,* I plunked down a quarter at the checkout, smiled wanly at the cashier, and ran out into the parking lot. There I fully expected to hear the sound of approaching sirens, the baying of hounds.

Instead my mother, little knowing that she was driving the getaway car, pulled up in our newish '59 Ford. I jumped inside, panting, and we sped off—to another store, where she and my sisters just had to look for some arcane item of girl's clothing. I stayed in the car.

Not having actually stolen anything, I soon recovered my usual boisterous spirits and much later read, with pleasure, both the spy novel and Blatty's hilarious memoir. But as I sat there then, pulse pounding, staring out at an empty parking lot that seemed to symbolize my pitiful future life behind bars, I decided to look at the third of my ill-gotten goods, the volume I had acquired mainly through happenstance.

I still have the book, or rather its loose pages, now held together by a rubber band. These days Clifton Fadiman practically epitomizes American middle-brow culture. But for a young boy, *The Lifetime Reading Plan,* a guide to 100 great books, did precisely what it was intended: it made classics sound as exciting as Tarzan or Fu Manchu. In short essays of 500 or 600 words, Fadiman inspired, exhorted, enticed; sometimes he talked about an author's life; sometimes about a book's particular pleasures; often about its difficulties. But always he made clear that reading a serious book—like *The Magic Mountain* or the *Poetics* or *Lost Illusions* or the novels of Jane Austen or the plays of Aeschylus—was more than intellectually enriching or spiritually uplifting: it could be an adventure. For me, that serendipitously acquired paperback might well have been emblazoned with Kipling's quietly thrilling words from his classic spy novel, *Kim:* "Here begins the Great Game."

The Quest for Scrivener

A dozen or so years ago, I was sleepily turning the pages of E. F. Bleiler's stupendous *Guide to Supernatural Fiction*—no home is complete without a copy—when the entry for Claude Houghton (1889–1961) caught my attention: "British author of psychological romances, often embodying personal mysticism and a remote allegory. . . . Best-known work the fine psychological-mystical-mystery story *I Am Jonathan Scrivener.*" At that time I had never heard of Houghton, but this brief description made *Scrivener* sound intriguing. I read on. While discussing one of Houghton's out-and-out fantasies, Bleiler commented that "like other of Houghton's novels, notably *I Am Jonathan Scrivener, This Was Ivor Trent* is essentially a description of the hollow man of the 1930s—a person who is seemingly a successful, well-adjusted person, but is internally empty, shattered and abysmally lonely." Houghton sounded better and better. According to Bleiler, the writer had even won the praise of Graham Greene for his craftsmanship. I made a mental note to look out for *I Am Jonathan Scrivener* when browsing through the fiction shelves of secondhand bookstores.

Several years then passed without my ever seeing a copy of *Scrivener.* Not that I made any strenuous effort to track down the novel. People who frequent used bookshops know that sooner or later a wanted title will magically appear: One need only bide one's time. *Ivor Trent* did turn up occasionally—for $10 or $15, often in a handsome jacket—but I wanted Houghton's alleged masterpiece. Why start with the second-best?

Sometime in the late '80s, I traveled to Philadelphia on business but naturally allocated Saturday afternoon for a little booking. I duly visited antiquarian dealers, used-book emporiums, and even one or two dingy paperback exchanges. In the rattiest of these last I paused, just before leaving, to spin a revolving wire rack next to the front door. And there it was, right at the top: *I Am Jonathan Scrivener.* Begrudgingly, I plunked down $2.95, convinced that in a just world the price should have been 50 cents.

Back home in Silver Spring, I studied my newly acquired treasure more carefully. Beneath the title was a woodcut of a Millet-like sower, backed by a rising sun. At the base of the front cover appeared the words "The Inner Sanctum Novels: New Fiction at $1." Though printed in 1930, the 382 thickish pages weren't brown or brittle in the least; the binding was actually sown, though loose between a couple of the gatherings. Typically, the back cover outlined the action of the novel and listed other Inner Sanctum offerings. I recognized almost none of the authors or titles, many of which struck me as endearingly dated, even campy: *The Earth Told Me,* by Thames Williamson; *Beloved, O Mon Goye,* by Sarah Levy; *Denny and the Dumb Cluck,* by J. P. McEvoy; *Fifteen Rabbits,* by Felix Salten. Could this last, by the author of *Bambi,* be another children's classic? Perhaps a history of Thumper's offspring?

When I finally opened *Scrivener,* I discovered an unexpected notice, headed "To the Buyer of this Book": "The Inner Sanctum Novels are an experiment in book publishing. It is the thought of the publishers that the buying of new fiction has been seriously handicapped in recent years by two chief causes:

"1) The Price. Whereas many non-fiction books are bought not only to read but to reread and refer to, most fiction is bought for one reading only." (Such refreshing honesty, I thought.) "The price of fiction has remained relatively high because it has not been bought in quantities sufficient to enable a publisher to make use of the savings concomitant with large production." (Concomitant! You couldn't get away with that today.) "Meanwhile, unless the reader were certain he wanted to retain a book in his library, he has been content to borrow the book from a library or from a friend (whenever the occasion might arise) or else he has decided not to read the book at all."

"2) Library Space. This has in recent years become a serious problem." (Hoo, boy!) "More and more people live in relatively small apartments in which the area of library shelves is limited." (In the '90s that last word would be "nonexistent.") "Where to put the books once they are read has become a real question. The book has been bought, but who wants to throw away a bound book? To meet these two factors, the publishers of this series of books have brought the price of all fiction . . . down to a dollar. You have now bought this book. If you do not wish to keep it, lend it to a friend, or send it to a hospital. Or, if you are clearing your shelves, throw it out with magazines." (!!!) "If, on the other hand, this is a book that you wish to keep bound in permanent form, take it to any bookbinder or send it back to the publisher with a remittance of one dollar, and it will be bound in cloth and returned to you postpaid." The notice ends by assuring the reader that this is "a first edition copy."

Needless to say, I found this announcement extremely ingratiating, from the unsentimental method of book disposal to the pleasing tentativeness and lack of hype. I also wondered if Simon and Schuster would still honor their contract and bind the book for a dollar. And then return it postpaid.

Inaugural Pleasures

Despite these winsome enticements, I didn't immediately find a sofa and settle back with *I Am Jonathan Scrivener*. I did read the first few sentences: "This book is an invitation to share an adventure. It is necessary for me to introduce myself as I am the only person in the world who can tell this story, but you will be wise to regard me simply as a mechanism for the narration of certain events. It is not necessary to know much about me, but it is essential to know something, since the adventure I am inviting you to share was the result of a dramatic and mysterious change which totally transformed the whole manner of my life." All this sounded cozily sinister and the invitation to share an adventure was . . . inviting. Nevertheless, I laid the book aside. I was pleased finally to own a copy, but there were other claims on my reading time.

For several more years *I Am Jonathan Scrivener* sat on a shelf in a little storage room for books, papers, and office supplies. Every so often I would pick it up and turn the pages. Once I had occasion to telephone E. F. Bleiler and mentioned Houghton's novel: He assured me it was a book that merited rediscovery. More and more I thought about actually reading it, but somehow the moment never seemed quite right. Then, a few years ago, I began to pack the book along with the mysteries and classics I usually take on vacation. *Scrivener* traveled to a house on Ocracoke Island, even visited Ohio a time or two. I moved the Inner Sanctum paperback to a mound of must-read books piled near my bedside. And finally, on the Saturday before Inauguration Day, I casually picked up the novel, leaned back against the pillows on my bed, and read for three hours. Being a slow reader, I later finished the book on Inauguration night, just about the time the Clintons went toddling off to bed.

I Am Jonathan Scrivener proved to have been worth the twelve-year wait. In some ways it resembles a novel by Paul Auster, *City of Glass* perhaps, or *Moon Palace,* a blend of the spooky and the philosophical, with a twisty, slightly artificial structure. There are also flashes of Chesterton's *The Man Who Was Thursday,* early Evelyn Waugh, and the religious supernatural tales of Charles Williams. I liked it a lot.

Here's the plot: James Wrexham, 39 years old, has been living a life of demoralizing loneliness. Orphaned at 19, he has passed two decades working for a vulgarian entrepreneur, and gradually come to regard himself as one of life's spectators. Sitting in a barber shop one afternoon, he suddenly feels the overwhelming wretchedness of his existence—just as his eye notices an advertisement in the *Times:* "A gentleman of independent means who is leaving England requires a secretary to attend to his correspondence during his absence and to catalogue his library. The individuality of the applicant is of greater importance than his technical qualifications for the position." Wrexham immediately determines to apply for the job and sends in a rambling autobiographical epistle.

Rather to his surprise, he is invited to visit a prominent lawyer, who explains that Mr. Jonathan Scrivener desires him to begin employment at once. Mr. Scrivener himself has recently left for parts unknown. In due course Wrexham discovers that he has the run of spacious rooms in Pall Mall, a servant who cooks the best meals he has ever eaten, an exceptionally generous salary, and a written request from Scrivener to make himself comfortable, take a box at the theater, and in general follow his own inclinations. Not surprisingly, Wrexham tries to puzzle out the personality of his unseen employer. The books in Scrivener's library have obviously been read, but they reveal an improbable range of tastes and interests, from philosophy to pornography. Then one night, as Wrexham sits daydreaming among the books, he turns around to discover that a beautiful young woman has quietly let herself into the apartment with a latchkey.

The ethereal Pauline Mandeville claims to be a "friend" of Scrivener's, but then so does the vampirically glamorous Francesca Bellamy, whose millionaire husband committed suicide in Paris under dubious circumstances. As the novel proceeds, Wrexham encounters other friends of his elusive employer—the disillusioned, alcoholic Middleton, the playboy Rivers, the apelike Denvers. Each appears to have known a distinctly different Scrivener, and each is oddly obsessed with the man. Weeks go by. Wrexham grows increasingly convinced that Scrivener has embarked on some kind of bizarre experiment, using himself and this motley collection of humanity as guinea pigs. But to what end?

Throughout his story Houghton creates a sense of foreboding and psychological unease, even in his wittiest turns of phrase. "I've met a number of people who had endured agonies in their determination not to suffer." The soup in a Japanese restaurant "was neither hot nor cold, clean nor dirty, thick nor clear, and it had long weeds in it which looked rather like serpents who had died in youth." Says the desperate pleasure-seeker Rivers, "All people who are decent want to give. You have only to ask in the right way. . . . Here's an example. I met a marvellous girl at supper three nights ago. I drove her home. Naturally, I suggested that we should become lovers. That is, I gave her the opportunity of collaborating with me in the creation of beautiful memories. She's thinking it over. She's intelligent. She'll see that I'm right." "Most of us," says another character, "commit suicide, but the fact is only recognized if we blow our brains out." When Wrexham encounters the seductive Mrs. Bellamy for the second time, she appears to him "in evening dress and her beauty suggested a sword half drawn from its scabbard."

A biographical note at the end of my copy of *Scrivener* indicates that by 1930 Claude Houghton had already written a couple of volumes of poetry, a book of essays, two plays, and four novels. He'd been praised by Arnold Bennett for his dialogue and been called a genius. To little avail: Houghton is almost completely forgotten. *I Am Jonathan Scrivener* may not be a lost masterpiece, but it is a highly diverting, philosophical novel of considerable merit. Its disappearance invites mild despair: For the most part, we all read the same authors, the same old novels and stories, the same approved masterworks taught in school. Yet how many other really good books lie moribund, awaiting a reader to restore them to life? Take up this New Year challenge. This spring or summer go to the library or used bookstore and pick up a novel at least fifty years old by an author you have never read, perhaps never even heard of. Then do your bit to enlarge the canon. Read at least one of the forgotten books of the past. You may be astonished by what you discover.

Talismans

Even now I own four typewriters: a green Hermes portable, an IBM Selectric, a Royal manual from the 1940s, and a little laptop made in Switzerland. Recently it was all I could do to prevent myself from buying an office-sized Olympia for $20, in perfect working condition. Fortunately, it had elite type, which I dislike. In fact, I never use a typewriter anymore; I simply love the machines for themselves, as works of art from the age of mechanical reproduction.

I sometimes do use a fountain pen—blue, an Esterbrook—that once belonged to Glenway Wescott, author of *The Pilgrim Hawk,* which I first read in Mr. Wright's eighth-grade English class at Hawthorne Junior High School in a 50-cent Dell paperback entitled *Six Great Short Modern Novels.*

When reviewing relatively simple novels, I record quotations and any ideas I might have—poor things but mine own—into one of those sixteen-page college blue-books (preferably from my alma mater, Oberlin); for more complicated texts I prefer a black-and-white-speckled composition book. Each fall I buy a dozen at back-to-school sales; sometimes you can find them on special at three for $2. When I feel like splurging, I pick up one of those European-style notebooks of quadrille paper. Writing across those little squares, sometimes with my Esterbrook fountain pen, always makes me feel like a continental intellectual.

The most continental of all intellectuals is surely Paul Valéry (for whom we await a decent biography). I'm especially fond of his little symbolist masterpiece, "An Evening with M. Teste." It opens unforgettably: "La betise n'est pas mon fort," "Stupidity is not my strong point." Such serene chutzpah.

The books I read the most are Martin Seymour-Smith's *New Guide to Modern World Literature;* E. F. Bleiler's *Guide to Supernatural Fiction;* David Thomson's *Biographical Dictionary of Film;* John Clute and Peter Nicholson's *Encyclopedia of Science Fiction;* Jacques Barzun and Wendell Taylor's *Catalogue of Crime;* the *Annals of English Literature;* the *Penguin Guide to Classical Music; Brewer's Dictionary of Phrase and Fable;* Benet's *Reader's Encyclopedia;* Allen and Pat Ahearn's *Collected Books;* an old *Roget's Thesaurus;* and the *American Heritage Dictionary.* All reference books, of course. And just maybe the dozen titles I'd take to a desert island, perfect for daydreaming the rest of one's life away.

Wonders and Epiphanies

My Pleiade edition of Gérard de Nerval's works is inscribed "en toute sympathie" from its French editor to Enid Starkie, the noted Oxford eccentric and biographer of Baudelaire and Flaubert. I found the slightly worn volume in a secondhand bookshop in Arlington for $6, and have often wondered how it got there.

The most restful place in the world is the periodicals reading room of any public library.

In eleventh grade we studied *Oedipus the King* in a translation for students by Bernard M. W. Knox. Fifteen years later I became friends with Knox, then director of Harvard's Center for Hellenic Studies here in Washington. It was almost like meeting Sophocles.

"The order to abandon ship was given at 5 P.M." So opens the greatest true-life adventure classic, Alfred Lansing's *Endurance,* the incredible story of Sir Ernest Shackleton's epic—and ultimately triumphant—struggle to save his men after disaster strikes the Imperial Trans-Antarctic Expedition of 1915. Before the last page, a year and a half later, three open boats will have been dragged 350 miles across shifting ice; five men, including Shackleton, will sail one of those boats over 870 miles of polar water, ultimately crossing the Drake Passage, once described as "the most dreaded waters in the world"; and finally three exhausted men, again including Shackleton, will slowly make their way across the treacherous mountains of South Georgia, with only a rope and a carpenter's adze. The most amazing part? Not a man died: Shackleton returned and saved them all.

In a burst of understandable enthusiasm, the critic Steven Moore once wrote that he wished to be buried with his copy of Alexander Theroux's novel *Darconville's Cat.* It was, he said, his kind of book. What is mine? I would probably choose *The Count of Monte Cristo,* a novel that has haunted me since childhood. As it did Stephen Dedalus. My favorite passage in *Portrait of the Artist as a Young Man* begins "The figure of that dark avenger . . . " and ends with the mock-romantic words "Madame, I never eat muscatel grapes."

Nabokov's "American" works have recently been published in three thin-paper volumes. Am I alone in liking the idea of the Library of America, but finding many of the actual volumes uninviting, when not positively dispiriting? To think of those bright butterflies, Lolita and Ada, trapped in those gray, official pages!

Some titles are so good one hardly needs the book: e.g., H. P. Lovecraft's long poem "Fungi from Yuggoth"; Ronald Firbank's camp classic *Concerning the Eccentricities of Cardinal Pirelli.* However, a few great novels have terrible titles: To me *The Great Gatsby* and *Les Misérables,* for instance, seem more than a little vulgar and overblown. The most purely perfect book title is that for Jane Austen's last completed masterpiece: *Persuasion.*

The lost books one would most like to read: Sappho's complete poems and Byron's memoirs, the latter burned by his publisher after the poet's death, apparently because of their licentiousness. Which may also be the reason why so little of Sappho has survived.

The noted writer on food and France, M. F. K. Fisher, and I were once tenants of the same landlady in Aix en Provence—two decades apart. Fisher knew Madame Wytenhove's son as a little boy; to me he was a sophisticated twentysomething. After I reviewed Fisher's book on Marseille, where I lived for a year, she wrote me a letter, saying that my words about *A Considerable Town* were so enthusiastic that she almost wanted to read the book herself. Note the charming "almost."

Sorrows of a book reviewer: when otherwise charming and obviously well-to-do Washington lawyers and bureaucrats admit that they don't take time to read books. Even worse: when they ask what you think of the latest John

Grisham or Stephen King, as if the bestseller list were actually a guide to the best in contemporary fiction. Worse yet: when the same people haven't heard of any of the titles or authors you've actually reviewed recently. The pits: when you realize that nearly everything you care about is irrelevant or utterly unimportant to most of the people who open the *Washington Post.*

Collecting the novels of Ford Madox Ford, I picked up a secondhand copy of *The Rash Act,* for a few dollars, and noticed writing on the flyleaf. The owner, Paul M. A. Linebarger, had signed the book twice, once in 1935, then again in 1945. An explanatory note followed, in the same hand: Apparently Linebarger had lost his copy of the novel, then five years later found it again in a used bookshop. Interesting, yes, but exciting only when you realize that Linebarger wrote, under the pen name Cordwainer Smith, some of the greatest science fiction stories of all time. Look for "Scanners Live in Vain," "The Game of Rat and Dragon," and "The Ballad of Lost C'Mell."

I once thought it would be fun to construct a horror story about what happens when Miskatonic University, in an effort to save money, decides to deaccession the *Necronomicon,* that handbook to all things foul and eldritch by the mad Arab Abdul Alhazred. Perhaps some agent of Cthulhu could acquire the original, turn it into a mass-market paperback, and thus wreak wide-ranging havoc on a naive and uncomprehending world.

Among the best novels of the past twenty years is Russell Hoban's *Riddley Walker.* Hoban's latest novel, *Fremder,* has been recently published in England. No U.S. company appears to be interested in acquiring it. One of the funniest, most well-written books of the '80s is John Sladek's satire about robots and modern life, *Tik-Tok.* Sladek's last novel, *Bugs,* came out in England several years back; it never found an American publisher either, and Sladek has since, to all appearances, given up writing fiction. The best collection of children's short fiction in recent memory is Richard Kennedy's *Collected Stories.* So far as I can tell, Richard Kennedy has also pretty much stopped writing. Disheartening, altogether disheartening.

Never having enjoyed the standard children's classics as a child, what pleasure to discover *Charlotte's Web, The Phantom Tollbooth,* the *Just So Stories,* and numerous fairy tales for the first time when I finally read them aloud to my children. Some nights I could hardly wait to hurry the older boys into bed so we could continue with the next chapter of *The Hobbit.* Now, of course, the guys would rather listen to CDs from Metallica and the Butthole Surfers. These days I often read Winnie-the-Pooh silently to myself.

The first real poem I ever memorized was A. E. Housman's "When I Was One-and-Twenty." Including the second stanza: "When I was one-and-twenty / I heard him say again, / The heart out of the bosom / Was never given in vain; / 'Tis paid with sighs a plenty / And sold for endless rue. / And I am two-and-twenty / And oh, 'tis true, 'tis true." I was only three-and-ten when I learned this by heart, but figured that it was never too soon to become world-weary.

People talk about the canon, but many of the best works of the past have never been part of our educational system's generally unambitious literary curriculum: Are there any better—more exciting, more artful—books than *Njal's Saga, Sir Gawain and the Green Knight, The Arabian Nights,* Pushkin's *Tales of Belkin, The Pillow Book of Sei Shonagon,* Kleist's stories, or Jules Renard's journal? Each is a masterpiece.

In a headline meeting we once had to come up with a short, catchy hed for a book about terrorist activities by the Jewish Defense League. I suggested "Torah! Torah! Torah!"—which wasn't used, of course. In fact, most headline suggestions are utterly unsuitable for a family newspaper, since they tend to be obscene, politically incorrect, or, in *Book World*'s case, too literary. A few we did go with? "Cheever by the Dozen"; "Odets, Where Is Thy Sting?"; "Wild Irish Prose"; "The Mark of Zora."

Pleasures of a book reviewer: to open a new book tentatively, with indifference even, and to find oneself yet again in thrall—to a writer's prose, to a thriller's plot, to a thinker's mind. Let the whole wide world crumble, so long as I can read another page. And then another after that. And then a hundred more.

Maxims, Etc.

While reading the latest issue of *Conjunctions* magazine—titled "Radical Shadows" and devoted to "previously untranslated and unpublished works of 19th and 20th-century masters"—I realized that my favorite kind of book has always been the journal, the collection of letters, the slim volume of maxims or brief observations. Much as I admire huge, panoptic works— literature, after all, thrives best when a writer's reach just slightly exceeds his grasp—my heart goes out to scraps and remnants, to work done on the fly, to thoughts scribbled quickly in pocket notebooks. Truths, I suspect, come unbidden at odd moments: We tend to learn more from the sudden epiphany than from an elaborate summa.

E. M. Cioran ranks high as a master of such philosophical jotting, and the highlight of this bumper issue of *Conjunctions* is the selection from his *Cahiers*—though a half-dozen translations from C. P. Cavafy's unfinished poems run it a close second. In fact, "Radical Shadows" displays perfect modernist taste, offering appealing poetry by Djuna Barnes, a ten-minute "dramalette" by Thomas Bernhard, stories by Mikhail Bulgakov, drawings with captions by Eugene Ionesco, a war memoir from Michel Leiris (author of the unsparing autobiographical classic *Manhood*), and some short pieces by Robert Musil, not to mention work by even better-known figures like Nabokov, Akhmatova, Kawabata, and Proust. Even Chekhov is here, represented by a handful of early pieces, including a dozen or so "Questions Posed by a Mad Mathematician":

"Ptolemy was born in the year 223 A.D. and died after reaching the age of eighty-four. Half his life he spent traveling and a third, having fun. What is the price of a pound of nails, and was Ptolemy married?" That pretty much sums up most people's memories of high school math. Cavafy, famously described by E. M. Forster as standing "at a slight angle to the universe," was little-known in his lifetime, but to many readers now seems the greatest poet of modern Greek ('twas ever thus), chiefly for his moon-in-the-gutter lyrics about handsome young men and his wistful reflections on classical themes: "The God Abandons Antony," "Waiting for the Barbarians," "Ithaka." Cavafy's work has long been available in superb translations by Edmund Keeley and Philip Sherard (buy the collected poems now, don't wait), but one is grateful for even fragments by such a haunting rhapsode of profane love. "The News in the Paper" opens with a killer first line:

> There was also something about blackmail.
> On this point, again, the paper stressed
> Its utter contempt for such depraved,
> Shameless and corrupt morals . . .

"Radical Shadows"—edited by Bradford Morrow and Peter Constantine—also reprints a tale by Proust once intended for *Les Plaisirs et les Jours* (his first book: over-ripe, luxuriant stories of snobbery and lust), a school fiction-writing assignment by Truman Capote (composed at age 10 or so), and unexpurgated extracts from the dancer Nijinksy's diary. Printing such work—the lost, the oddball, and the marginalized—has long been among the important functions of a literary magazine, in part because young writers always need to discover new models. Metaphorically, a literary generation learns from raffish uncles and free-spirited aunts, not from canonical fathers and mothers. That said, these Cioran selections remind us, if we need such reminding, of how deeply this Romanian essayist has journeyed into the modern self:

"'Sadness will last forever.' These seem to have been Van Gogh's last words. I could have spoken them at any moment of my life."

"It is when you feel ill that you discover something new, health being a state of absence, since you are not conscious of it. . . ."

"Colette is supposed to have said of Bach: 'A sublime sewing machine.' There is nothing worse than Parisian wit."

"For some, the prospect of dying (Proust, Hitler . . .) impels them to a frenzy of activity: they want to conclude everything, complete their work, and thereby become eternal; not a moment to lose, they are stimulated by the notion of their end—for others, the same prospect paralyzes them, leads them to a sterile sagesse, and keeps them from working: what's the use? The idea of their end flatters their apathy, instead of disturbing it; whereas among the first group, it rouses every energy, good as well as bad."

"My strength: to have found no answer to anything."

Readers attracted by these reflections should look for Cioran's major works: *A Short History of Decay; Drawn and Quartered; The Trouble with Being Born;* and *Anathemas and Admirations.* His astringent nihilism is astonishingly tonic: "One can imagine everything, predict everything, save how low one can sink." And—a lesson for some of us who shall remain nameless—"Beware of thinkers whose minds function only when they are fueled by a quotation."

Pith and Vinegar

Inspired by Cioran's *Cahiers,* here is a list of ten favorite books of fragments, aphorisms, and original thinking *in petto,* with sample quotations:

1. *7 Greeks,* translated by Guy Davenport. The surviving works of the philosopher Herakleitos, the poets Sappho and Archilochos, and others. From Herakleitos: "A bow is alive only when it kills." "The river stepped into is not the river in which we stand." "Life is bitter and fatal, yet men cherish it and beget children to suffer the same fate."

2. Pascal, *Pensées.* Has there ever been such a sadly profound mind as Pascal's? "The condition of humanity: inconstancy, weariness, and disquiet." "When we see a natural style we are quite surprised and delighted, for we expected to see an author and we find a man." "However beautiful the rest of the play, the last act is bloody. At the end a little earth is thrown on our heads, and all is over for ever." If you can, read him in French.

3. La Rochefoucauld, *Maxims.* "The mind is always the dupe of the heart." "One is nearly always bored by the people with whom one is not allowed to be bored." "There are few virtuous women who are not tired of their vocation." Wisdom doesn't come more worldly than this.

4. *Selected Letters of Sydney Smith.* The most charming clergyman in English history. In one celebrated letter, Smith lists twenty means to assuage melancholy, advising his correspondent to adopt "short views of human life—not further than dinner or tea" and to "keep good blazing fires." Don't miss Hesketh Pearson's sprightly biography *The Smith of Smiths.*

5. Emerson, *A Modern Anthology,* edited by Alfred Kazin and Daniel Aaron. There are plenty of anthologies of the great transcendentalist, but this one is arranged by topic as a kind of secular breviary. "Scholars should not carry their memories to balls." "The loves of flint and iron are naturally a little rougher than those of the nightingale and the rose." "Every writer is a skater, and must go partly where he would, and partly where the skates carry him." Forget tenth-grade English—Emerson is funny, shrewd, and deeply iconoclastic.

6. Nietzsche, *The Gay Science.* Everything by this notoriously attractive philosopher is aphoristic and provocative, but this may be his most appealing single book. "The Christian resolve to find the world ugly and bad has made the world ugly and bad." "No victor believes in chance." "Those who are slow to know suppose that slowness is of the essence of knowledge." "Thoughts are the shadows of our feelings—always darker, emptier, and simpler."

7. Samuel Butler, *Notebooks.* Does anyone still read *The Way of All Flesh? Erewhon,* I know, is studied as an example of Utopian literature. Still, Butler saves some of his most engaging thinking for his private moments. "Man is a jelly which quivers so much as to run about." "The one serious conviction that a man should have is that nothing is to be taken too seriously." "Books are like imprisoned souls till someone takes them down from a shelf and frees them."

8. *The Maxims of Marcel Proust,* compiled by Justin O'Brien. This little volume—hard to find—gathers up observations on time, love, memory, society, and art—all the great themes of *In Search of Lost Time.* "An absence, the decline of an invitation, an unintentional coldness, can accomplish more than all the cosmetics and beautiful dresses in the world." "Every reader reads himself. The writer's work is merely a kind of optical instrument that makes it possible for the reader to discern what, without this book, he would perhaps never have seen in himself." "Let us leave pretty women to men without imagination."

9. *The Unquiet Grave,* by Cyril Connolly. I know, I know, Dirda's old favorite, but there's nothing quite like this "word-cycle," with its reflections on the passing of love, the consolations of memory, the refuge of art. "Life is a maze in which we take the wrong turning before we have learnt to walk." "There is no fury like an ex-wife searching for a new lover." "Our memories are card-indexes consulted and then returned in disorder by authorities whom we do not control."

10. *Wodehouse Nuggets,* compiled by Richard Usborne. The master of the simile—and a guaranteed medicine for melancholy. "Like so many substantial citizens of America, he had married young and kept on marrying, springing from blonde to blonde like the chamois of the Alps leaping from crag to crag." "He drank coffee with the air of a man who regretted it was not hemlock." "I attribute my whole success in life to a rigid observance of the fundamental rule—Never have yourself tattooed with any woman's name, not even her initials." Ah, time to reread *Leave It to Psmith* and *The Mating Season.*

Heart of the Matter

Somerset Maugham, whose outlook on life was never what you'd call jolly, used to recommend a careful reading of Benjamin Constant's *Adolphe* to any young couple thinking about marriage. That novel, a short course on sexual disillusionment, relates how Adolphe falls for the settled Ellenore and eventually woos the somewhat older woman away from her longtime lover. In fact, Ellenore sacrifices everything—children, stability, social position—for Adolphe and compensates by making him the be-all and end-all of her life. At first the young man is delighted by the constant shower of affection, then annoyed, finally bored and resentful. Too weak to rid himself of a now-burdensome connection, he allows the liaison to drag on, in mutual torment and increasing recrimination. Finally, Ellenore, like many a frail Romantic heroine before her, conveniently dies of a broken heart. At which point Adolphe comes to realize—too late—that without this woman his life is absolutely meaningless.

According to La Rochefoucauld, that genial cynic, there may be good marriages, but there are no delicious ones. In fiction it is certainly hard to find a happy one—Nick and Nora Charles, perhaps, in Hammett's witty mystery *The Thin Man*. Passionate love, it has been suggested, requires obstacles, barriers, taboos; so the great love stories naturally dwell on frustrated yearning or clandestine embraces rather than contented fulfillment.

Why read about Darby and Joan when you can suffer so deliciously with Tristan and Isolde?

As usual, books also cause a lot of trouble in marriages, mainly by raising expectations. Emma Bovary might have stayed a faithful doctor's wife if she hadn't devoured all those romantic novels; they simply put ideas into the poor woman's head. Inexorably there followed the horseback rides into the countryside, the closed carriages, the torrid afternoons in one-night cheap hotels. Certainly had Paolo and Francesca skipped that fateful reading of the tale of Lancelot and Guinevere, they might have simply gone their separate ways and never ended yoked together through eternity in Hell.

One of the most harrowing accounts of the "woe that is in marriage," Ford Madox Ford's *The Good Soldier* stands among those few novels that everyone really should read, if only to be shaken to the very toes. "Trust no one"—such is the key to its intricate unfolding. While Ford's novel remains fairly well known (i.e., it is sometimes taught in colleges), George Meredith's scenes from a marriage breaking up, the "sonnet" sequence entitled *Modern Love,* is certainly underappreciated.

The last poem sums up the story:

> Lovers beneath the singing sky of May,
> They wandered once; clear as the dew on flowers:
> But they fed not on the advancing hours:
> Their hearts held cravings for the buried day.
> Then each applied to each that fatal knife,
> Deep questioning, which probes to endless dole.
> Ah, what a dusty answer gets the soul
> When hot for certainties in this our life . . .

Meredith's understanding of the human heart predates Freud, who tended to feel rather differently about "deep questioning." Still, the good doctor of Vienna gave credit to writers and artists for many of his own "discoveries." In *The Symposium,* for instance, Plato explained love's restlessness by a tall tale—that primordial human beings were cut in two by the gods, and that each of us yearns to be whole again by uniting with his or her other half. As with many of Plato's myths, there are psychological, as well as philosophical, truths here. Still, to my mind, the best account of how love works is Stendhal's book-length ramble *De L'Amour* (On Love). The author of *The Red and the Black* explains, amid entertaining digressions, that falling in love is basically a process of self-delusion, what he calls crystallization, by which the lover inexorably enhances the beloved with every perfection. Naturally, familiarity shatters this crystal state, and it is little wonder that Stendhal's couples awake on the morning after and exclaim, with some bewilderment, "Is that all there is?"

Well, yes and no. In Tolstoy's shocker "The Kreutzer Sonata," the narrator reduces love to sex and sex to depravity, eventually going mad and murdering his wife because of her suspected infidelity with a violinist. "The minute their eyes met I saw that the animal crouching inside each of them, in defiance of all the rules of their social position, posed the question, 'May I?' and answered, 'Indeed you may.'" But is the glandular tug in truth all there is? One hopes not, especially in June. Maybe Donne's great poem "The Extasie" suggests as compactly as any the truth about these very human matters: "Love's mysteries in souls do grow / But yet the body is its book."

Suggestive Language

While thinking over these amatory perplexities, I realized that many of the best sex scenes in literature never quite take place. In *Sir Gawain and the Green Knight,* the Arthurian hero must face certain death in three days' time. He is awaiting his sad destiny in a mysterious castle, the home of a strangely gregarious nobleman and his appropriately drop-dead-gorgeous wife. Each morning this courtly beauty, with a becoming simplicity and directness, steals into Gawain's bedroom and says, in Middle English, "You are welcome to my body." To take up this kind offer would, of course, violate all the laws of hospitality, as well as the chivalric code, not to speak of endangering the knight's immortal soul. But in a few hours Gawain knows he will be dead, and never has a woman or life looked more beautiful. The sexual electricity of these bedside meetings can send jolts across six centuries.

Then there is the hero of Flaubert's *The Temptation of St. Anthony,* an anchorite in the desert, beset by the devil's lures and his own sinful visions. In one of these appears the Queen of Sheba, more languorous than the serpent and as voluptuous as ripe fruit, who proceeds to detail the sensual pleasures that will be Anthony's, if only, if only. She whispers that she will become all women for him, from the little streetwalker at the crossroads to the high-born lady amid her roses. All he need do is ask, merely reach out his hand and touch her. This verbal seduction—a masterpiece of decorated prose—builds to the believable assertion "I am not a woman, I am a world."

In *Salammbo,* Flaubert's other novel about antiquity, his Carthaginian princess wears earrings made of hollowed-out pearls filled with perfume.

A small hole allows a drop of the scent to fall, periodically, on Salammbo's naked shoulder. Because the virgin princess is an acolyte of the snake-goddess Tanit, her ankles are always linked by a slender gold chain. After barbarians surround Carthage, Salammbo goes to the tent of their leader Matho to sue for peace, knowing that she must offer herself as part of the deal. Nothing overtly physical is described. Instead Flaubert focuses on the warrior Matho mesmerized by the droplets of perfume from Salammbo's earrings, waiting for each one to collect slowly on the pearl's surface and then fall onto smooth, delicate skin. With each drop the sexual tension grows increasingly unbearable. The couple's actual lovemaking appears between the lines: All Flaubert writes is that Salammbo leaves Matho's arms and notices that her ankle chain is broken. But what more need be said?

In an even more famous scene in *Portrait of the Artist as a Young Man*, Joyce also builds up to the sexual moment, and then cuts away just as his adolescent hero Stephen yields to the disordering of his senses. "His lips would not bend to kiss her," writes Joyce; but then "With a sudden movement she bowed his head and joined her lips to his and he read the meaning of her movements in her frank uplifted eyes. It was too much for him. He closed his eyes, surrendering himself to her, body and mind, conscious of nothing in the world but the dark pressure of her softly parting lips. They pressed upon his brain as upon his lips as though they were the vehicle of a vague speech; and between them he felt an unknown and timid pressure, darker than the swoon of sin, softer than sound or odour." End of chapter.

In contrast to the tender Joyce, Proust views jealousy, with its never-ending suspicion and uncertainty, as the catalyst for sexual love; the account of Swann enamored of the demimondaine Odette is consequently a tale of obsession, illness, and unsolvable mystery. Is Odette betraying Swann? Is she a lesbian? So long as this golden-haired beauty eludes her besotted lover, she remains irresistible. Swann eventually sacrifices almost everything for Odette; only years later does he emerge from his fever-dream to discover that he has wasted his life on a woman who isn't really his type at all.

To these classics—and there are, of course, many others—I would add at least one modern novel in which graphic sexual content is, in fact, artistically necessary to create a heartbreaking story: James Salter's *A Sport and a Pastime*. For its understanding of love, this is a book that belongs on the same shelf as, say, Turgenev's *Torrents of Spring*, Svevo's *As a Man Grows Older*, and Colette's *Julie de Carneilhan*.

Bookman's Saturday

8 A.M.: Awakened by 4-year-old, who wishes to discuss some of the more abstruse points raised by a picture book about snakes. Which is better—a python or a king cobra? Is a cottonmouth more poisonous than a diamondback rattler? Wouldn't it be great to own a snake for a pet? No.

9 A.M.: Drive 4-year-old to soccer practice. While sitting on bleachers, try to read the opening pages of Umberto Eco's new novel, *The Island of the Day Before.* Lost cause: How can any book, no matter how good, compare with watching fifteen or so pre-schoolers, aquiver with glad animal spirits, as they tear across the dewy grass in noisy pursuit of a black-and-white ball?

10 A.M.: Housekeeping. Having finished a piece on Stanley Elkin's *Mrs. Ted Bliss*—a tour de force, by the way, in case you missed the review—I gather up my Elkin books and return them to the appropriate steel industrial shelf in the basement. Empty the all-important dehumidifier. Later, urge 8-year-old middle son, in vain, to reshelve some half-dozen of his own books: Richard Kennedy's *Collected Stories;* an album of Far Side cartoons; a book of palindromes; the latest issue of *GamePro,* a magazine for video-game addicts and other lost souls. Remind number-one son, age 11, that he needs to read a book every two weeks for his English class, and that he'd

better get cracking on Lloyd Alexander's *The Black Cauldron.* Like talking to the wall, as my father used to say.

10:30 A.M.: All three male offspring improve their minds with violent Saturday morning cartoons.

11 A.M.: Double-check the hours of the nearby "antiquarian book fair" to which I have a complimentary ticket: 10–5. Wonder how to broach subject to Beloved Spouse. Energetically demonstrate husbandly worthiness (a matter of occasional doubt) by making beds, washing dishes, vacuuming.

Noon: Make lunch of soup and sandwiches. One child eats sandwich but no soup; another only soup; middle son refuses everything, preferring to toast a couple of frozen waffles. All demand dessert, the true goal of any meal. During "lunch," attempt to discuss school activities, homework, reading. Oldest son rolls eyes at ceiling. Beloved Spouse says the latest Dick Francis is pretty good.

1 P.M.: Donate several boxes of no-longer-wanted fiction to local branch library, much of it originally acquired at . . . library book sales. Buy two paperbacks from the 25-cent shelf near the door, including John Dunning's *Booked to Die,* a mystery about the murder of a book scout. Am clearly a sick man.

1:30 P.M.: How can I escape to the book fair? Miraculously, Beloved Spouse announces that the three sons will be occupied during the remainder of afternoon: one visiting some hapless friend, another at a birthday party, the third clothes-shopping with Mom. Visions of sugar plums dance in head. On to the book fair!

2–5 P.M.: The display area provides space for twenty or thirty dealers from around the East Coast. Talk only briefly with fellow bibliomanes; mustn't waste precious minutes on idle chitchat.

How wise I was to come! During my first quick tour of the booths, I notice several possible buys. My first actual purchase is of Iris Murdoch's *The Black Prince,* in a nearly fine dust jacket for $8. Over the past two years I've been trying to gather the most admired Murdoch titles: *The Bell; A Severed Head; A Word Child; The Sea, the Sea;* and now *The Black Prince.* A. S. Byatt once wrote a short pamphlet on this novel, a favorite of many Murdochians; for some reason, I've been having trouble locating an American first at an acceptable price, i.e., under $10. Someday soon I will go on a Murdoch binge, having already whetted my appetite with the anthropological black comedy *A Severed Head.*

At another booth I notice a dust-jacketed copy of Joyce's *Finnegans Wake*. By the size of the volume, I recognize that it must be an early American edition, and it turns out to be the third, priced at $30. Normally, I wouldn't even think about the book, except for two facts: (1) I own the 1939 American first—but without a jacket; (2) my memory tells me that the jacket on this 1943 printing looks identical to that on the first. The only possible difference is the printed price. Did the book sell for $5 in 1939? I talk with a dealer friend, who can't remember. Of course, he adds, one could always snip off the price. Decide to trust my hunch and buy the book. There is, moreover, the added attraction of a sixteen-page booklet of corrections, apparently inserted with later printings. Vaguely wonder if this could be a Joyce A item.

At the same booth I cannot help admiring a nearly perfect copy of Mervyn Peake's first novel, *Titus Groan* (1946), an intensely visual fantasy, written with Jacobean brilliance, about power-plays inside a crumbling Gothic stronghold. I already own several editions of the complete Titus trilogy (the other volumes are *Gormenghast* and *Titus Alone*): paperbacks from Ballantine and Penguin, revised hardcovers from Overlook Press, and two copies of this very same American edition, the better wrapped in the tattered remnants of its dj. As I study the brooding cover painting—by Peake himself, one of the century's great illustrators—I yearn to possess this darkly beautiful copy. For a second I flash on a frequent daydream: to build some kind of frame into which one could slide a book, or books, for wall display. Like fine art. Would my Beloved Spouse permit such a thing? Hmmmmm. The Peake is priced at $35. That's serious money, but by God this is a classic of modern English literature, as well as a Burgess 99 (one of the 99 best novels since World War II, according to novelist Anthony Burgess). But I really shouldn't. Then I notice that the scout also has a near-perfect copy of Christina Hole's *Witchcraft in England* at $25. The subject interests me, but above all I know that the book is illustrated, on virtually every other page, by Peake. Obviously, a sign. In a burst of enthusiasm—either a peak experience or a fit of pique, as I pun to myself—I offer him $50 for the pair. He takes it.

At this point I am feeling a familiar mixture of elation, tempered with guilt, having spent more than my self-allotted allowance. Yet again. But I'm sure I've bought well, not frivolously. With luck, I've even wedded a jacket to my orphaned *Wake*. Not that I'm going to sell the precious baby. Wed, wake, orphan, baby: Shem the Penman would have approved such linguistic play with the rites—writings?—of passage.

When I return to my dealer friend to show him the Joyce, I naturally scan his wares as we talk. Booksellers are accustomed to this kind of impoliteness. Long ago, I made a rule always to pull out any book when I couldn't read the title on the spine. Such a good rule. Nevertheless it is a surprise to find myself grasping a slender volume that would have been easy to overlook: *Poems,* by William Empson. The price is $40, even without a jacket, but what is money in such a case? Earlier in the day I had been sorely tempted by a copy of Randall Jarrell's academic comedy *Pictures from an Institution,* inscribed to Karl from Randall—almost certainly poet Karl Shapiro's copy, but at $400 too dear even for my hot blood. Now, Jarrell and Empson have long been my two favorite poet-critics, the great discoveries of my freshman year in college. I eventually wrote an honors thesis on Empson's poetry, nearly all of which can be found in two volumes: *Poems* (1935) and *The Gathering Storm* (1940, which I already own). How I used to pore over this dense, image-packed verse some twenty-five years ago! And how much I still love it! "Imagine, then, by miracle, with me, / (Ambiguous gifts, as what gods give must be) / What could not possibly be there, / And learn a style from a despair."

By this point, I know the booking gods are smiling. My sacrifices have been accepted. I have been found worthy. With the sale about to close, there is even time for one last booth. Who knows? Perhaps one more little trinket . . .

And then I saw it, not quite believing that I saw it: *Jorkens Remembers Africa,* a book for which I have been searching ever since I first read a copy in ninth grade. Lord Dunsany's several Jorkens collections offer wonderfully told "club stories," tall tales related by either the world's greatest adventurer or its most consummate liar, Mr. Joseph Jorkens. Even now I remember picking up this very book, misshelved in the travel section of my high school library, and starting to read its winey, ingratiating prose. The stories were about ancient curses, monsters, interplanetary travel, and trees that walked. May we, just this once, speak of shivers of delight? Such I then felt. Poorer by another $40—though what is money compared to a living fragment of one's past?—I trudge home from the fair like a man who has done an honest day's work.

6 P.M.: Sneak books in house. Sip at a small whiskey, while daydreaming about becoming a member of Jorkens's club. Five minutes later, children and Beloved Spouse arrive. Usual supper-time brouhaha. Dinner of leftovers. Afterwards, wash dishes, while listening to oldies on radio. Weep over lost youth.

7 P.M.: Escape to attic, where I slip my first of *Finnegans Wake* into its new jacket. Perfect fit. Consult a bibliographical guide to Joyce, but it doesn't mention the jacket price. However, I notice—to my intense pleasure—

that the little pamphlet of corrections is an A item and goes for around $125. He who dares, wins.

8 P.M.: Begin urging children to take baths and ready themselves for the realm of Morpheus. Explain that Morpheus is god of sleep. Wash up 4-year-old and curl up with same on the "big bed," where we peruse an album about sea creatures. Would you rather be shocked by an electric eel or bitten by a barracuda? Don't know. Is a leatherback sea turtle bigger than a Galapagos land tortoise? Don't know. Could we have a seal for a pet? No, and it's time for a sleepy-time song: "If you miss the train I'm on, you will know that I am gone . . . "

9:30 P.M.: Older boys finally in bed, plead for nightly reading. Continue with Robert Heinlein's *Citizen of the Galaxy,* the adventures of an orphan who starts life as a slave, becomes a beggar, and is now working on an interplanetary trading ship. I've read the novel before—long, long ago—and know that Thorby will next become a soldier and eventually end up the most powerful man in the galaxy. The dreams of boyhood.

10 P.M.: Sit down in living room chair to start Umberto Eco. As usual, almost immediately fall asleep. Book falls on floor, where it is nibbled by pet rabbit Skippy.

12:15 A.M.: Rouse self from slumber. Scold rabbit and lock in cage. Stumble upstairs. And so to bed.

Supplementary Materials

Book collecting is often a form of hero worship—or heroine worship (no one bows lower than I before the genius of Angela Carter, Colette, and Agatha Christie, to mention only three high Cs). After a while, though, one yearns for more than first editions and scholarly sets of an author's complete works. Enthusiasm spreads, insidiously, into what one may call supplementary areas.

Take author photos. For a long time I gathered pictures of writers, cutting out illustrations from magazines, saving dust jacket and publicity photographs, buying volumes of David Levine caricatures. Even now in the recesses of my desk linger scores of authorial postcards. Like Madame Sosostris, I can whisper "And here is your card," choosing among a handsome William Gaddis in a checked sport jacket, Rilke staring soulfully, Nabokov about to snag some helpless species of lepidoptera with a gigantic net, the creator of Cheri writing in bed, or even the young Evelyn Waugh looking as handsome as a film star (oh what a falling off was there!).

For many years I used to keep an old *Saturday Review* cover of Edmund Wilson tacked above my desk at home. Inspiration, I suppose. Yet much as I admire Bunny, who looks rather dyspeptic and annoyed in this picture, what I really liked to look up at were his bookshelves. They not only filled his workroom, but appeared to run down a hallway and on into infinity. Just the kind of library Borges, or should I say Borges y Yo, would have liked.

Once upon a time I had a chance to acquire a pair of large woodcuts of James Joyce and William Faulkner. The local artist Leonard Maurer actually designed some of Faulkner's dust jackets, and appears to have been a man of exceptionally cultivated taste: Wonderful leftovers from his library still occasionally surface in secondhand and antiquarian bookstores. Alas, I hesitated, and the two woodcuts went elsewhere. Some time afterward, I discovered that *Book World* actually owned a copy of the Joyce; the print currently hangs above our art director's computer, and almost every day I think about stealing it.

There is, after all, a fine line between the collector and the fetishist. I sometimes cut grass with my will-to-power mower while wearing a shirt displaying the heavily mustachioed visage of Friedrich Nietzsche; I don my Gustave Flaubert T—the author of *Madame Bovary* sports a tattoo that says "Emma"—when I go to the Y for some halfhearted exercise; and my son the Hobbit fan wears J. R. R. Tolkien to bed instead of pajamas. The noted critic Hugh Kenner once told me that he actually unscrewed the nameplate from the mailbox of novelist and painter Wyndham Lewis; I would have done the same, and might not have waited for Lewis to be dead. As it is, I don't have any Lewis material, but am pleased to possess a copy of Marshall McLuhan's *Understanding Media* inscribed to . . . Hugh Kenner.

In the wake of a visit to the Library of Congress, nearly two decades ago, to peer into a glass case at the index cards upon which Nabokov composed *Pale Fire,* I took to buying only Ticonderoga No. 2 pencils, the great novelist's graphite of choice. A smart marketer should have labeled the twelve-count packages with the phrase "As used by the author of *Lolita.*" Or perhaps not.

Even now I treasure a letter from William Empson inviting me to lunch at his Hampstead home, and a brief note from V. S. Pritchett refusing to write a book review. Years ago I shoved half a week's pay into library photocopiers to acquire then-uncollected magazine articles by Randall Jarrell and Anthony Burgess. (Somebody said that the true test of one's devotion to a writer is a willingness to collect his journalism. Perhaps this accounts, too, for my ownership of long runs of *Kenyon Review, Horizon,* and *Partisan Review.*) I have shelled out some really serious cash for signed copies of books by Cyril Connolly and Evelyn Waugh, the two great twentieth-century masters of classic English prose. When a friend of mine told me that his mother had, astonishingly, bought Edmund Wilson's old stone house in upstate New York, I asked him to look around for a pencil, an old envelope, a washcloth, anything that the Great One might have touched or used. Like Frederick Exley in *Pages from a Cold Island,* I secretly aspire to own one of the writer's walking sticks, or maybe a fragment of one of those special windows etched with some lines by Auden or Dawn Powell.

Do not imagine that I regard my taste for such artifacts as anything but shameless and vulgar. I have sunk so low as to covet Edward Gorey coffee mugs. I yearn for a bust of Dante to place on a bookcase. Recently, I've even been thinking that it would be neat to make color photocopies of favorite dust jackets—say, of *The Maltese Falcon* or *The Great Gatsby*—and frame them like posters. I own a real dictionary stand and would like to add a library cart and a revolving bookcase. Most of all, I daydream about possessing enormous wealth so that I could employ a personal librarian, someone to catalogue my books properly, answer my correspondence, delicately bring to my attention one or two choice items coming up for auction at Sotheby's. I would, of course, wear a velvet smoking jacket at my desk, take breakfast in the conservatory, and in the late afternoon go for long walks on graveled paths.

How utterly pathetic! How jejune! How unAmerican! A real man would daydream about a VIP box at the new Redskins stadium or even about being the Redskins' new quarterback. Who, after all, would care to be Robertson Davies when he might be a Sonny Jurgensen?

Hear! Hear!

Happily, much of this youthful ardor for the artifacts of literary culture has cooled with age—though I still lie awake at night trying to imagine the look and feel of those special custom-made notebooks used by Bruce Chatwin. But the flames of desire, even when banked, may always be rekindled. Since adolescence I have occasionally purchased LPs of modern poets reading their work (hearing "Still falls the rain" chanted by Edith Sitwell marks a man for life), as well as boxed sets of the Marlowe Society's recordings of Shakespeare. More recently I have rented cassettes from the library—Dick Francis, P. G. Wodehouse—for long car trips. But only in the past few years have I become consumed with a passion for audio books.

Not that I am unfaithful to what I persist in thinking of as Real Books. Reading means turning pages; it occurs when you pause and look up, think a moment, admire a couplet or a paragraph, mark a passage, check a detail, sip your tea, and then plunge back into the text. No, I have come to think of tapes not so much as substitutes for books as supplements to them.

Once I would listen only to unabridged recordings. But I've changed my mind. A shortened text, expertly performed, brings its own illuminations and insights. To hear John Gielgud read passages from the Authorized Version of the Old Testament can convey the beauty and power of Scripture better than a week at theological school.

Or consider Jeremy Irons's mesmerizing recording of *Lolita* (Random House). As it happens, I couldn't imagine the 1997 film of the novel, starring Irons, as much more than a travesty: Any movie would make visually over-explicit everything that Nabokov—a butterfly darting among blossoms—merely touches upon in his subtle and beautiful prose. But in his unabridged reading, Irons re-creates the clarity, precision, and lilt of every glorious sentence. Walter Pater talked about writing aspiring to the condition of music: Irons's performance of *Lolita* does more than aspire; it becomes music. Being unable to listen to the eight cassettes around my children, in part because of the subject matter and in part because my offspring are would-be Visigoths, I found myself actually looking forward to driving in Washington, even to sitting in rush-hour traffic, a painted car upon a painted Beltway.

Just as much a tour de force is Jim Norton's performance (Naxos) of highlights from James Joyce's *Ulysses*. This text is, famously, a sea of many voices and one easy to drown in. But Norton is riveting, dazzling as Bloom, Stephen, and the fulminating Citizen; he is hilariously loud-mouthed in the noisy pub chapters and as sentimental as a Hallmark card in the seaside idyll of lame Gerty MacDowell. For an American it is particularly useful to hear the Irish pronunciations, and the occasional musical highlighting—a bit of "Love's Old Sweet Song" played on a piano, an aria from *Don Giovanni*—is exactly appropriate. Marcella Riordan melodiously and sexily murmurs her way through Molly Bloom's soliloquy down to that final "Yes." If you've ever stalled in *Ulysses,* or if you simply want to augment your appreciation of this aural masterpiece, this set of four cassettes (or two CDs) is a real bargain.

Many unabridged recordings can be daunting. I have listened to the opening of Robert Fagles's translation of *The Odyssey* (Penguin) read by Ian McKellen: wonderful stuff, and intended to be heard. Yet I'm not sure I can stick with it for thirteen hours. On the other hand, Philip Madoc reads sections of Gibbon's *Decline and Fall of the Roman Empire,* and the result is utterly thrilling. Gibbon's rolling periodic sentences, that telling choice of adjectives, those wasp-stings of irony—all these demand recitation. Madoc's voice is rich and plummy; he keeps to a brisk march-time pace with a slight hovering on the last word of a sentence, and his tone sounds an appropriately sardonic gravitas, with just a soupçon of patrician sniff and an occasional Iago-like unctuousness. I've taken to listening in the dark at bedtime: Nothing beats a good account of moral degeneration as one drifts off to sleep. So soothing.

In the summer, when travel is frequent, I really stockpile the spoken arts: For instance, a twelve-tape edition of English poetry, issued by Penguin, is probably the equivalent of a lit survey at one of our better state universities. The last volume is stuffed with tasty English chestnuts like Masefield's "Sea-Fever" and "Cargoes" ("Quinquireme of Nineveh . . . "), the war poems of Wilfred Owen, Rupert Brooke's deliciously funny memories of Grantchester ("And is there honey still for tea?"), Kipling's harrowing "Danny Deever," the stoic and wistful lyrics of A. E. Housman.

In the American vein, Highbridge Audio offers Garrison Keillor reading his favorite sections from *Huckleberry Finn*—surely the next best thing to having them declaimed by Mark Twain himself. I've already finished a brilliant abridgment of Erskine Childers's classic spy thriller *The Riddle of the Sands,* read by Dermot Kerrigan (Naxos), with highlights from Schumann's Fourth Symphony to add to the feeling of mounting danger. Come the long drive to visit relatives in Ohio, I look forward with considerable eagerness to David Suchet—TV's Poirot—reading the full text of Agatha Christie's *The Mysterious Affair at Styles* (Audio Editions), one of this year's winners of an Audie Award. My children have listened again and again, night after night, to Benjamin Soames relate *Tales from the Greek Legends* (Naxos), including an unDisneyfied account of the adventures of Heracles. When I finish Neville Jason's *Swann's Way* (Naxos again: what can I say, they do good work), I plan to enjoy it once more from the beginning and then proceed to his subsequent Proust recordings. With paternal enterprise, I have offered my two older sons monetary incentives to listen to *Don Quixote,* read by Edward de Souza (Naxos), and to a couple of different sets of highlights from the Old Testament, including Gielgud's (Modern Library). For my youngest son, I have saved another Audie winner: *Snow White and the Seven Dwarfs,* read by Sharon Stone. For a fairy tale, it sounds deliciously wicked.

Listening to My Father

My father, a soul ravaged by discontent, always prey to righteous indignation and of a brooding temperament, daydreamed that his children, especially his only son, would accomplish great things in the world. He yearned to see my name—his name, too—metaphorically or even actually in lights, and was constantly urging me from an early age to better myself. I should learn to handle tools. I should sell newspapers door to door. I should invest my pocket money in stocks. I should jog each night around the block and build up my muscles by lifting weights. We are talking here about a pudgy, shy little boy, with thick glasses, bowed legs, and an incomprehensible passion for reading.

I never saw my dad read a book in his life. When he arrived home from National Tube, he would open the screen door without a word, and merely grimace or grunt as my mother gave him a quick peck on the cheek and a cheery "Hi, hon." As soon as my sisters and I heard his footsteps, we would immediately switch off the television—even if Zorro was just about to be unmasked or the Lone Ranger blown up in the abandoned silver mine. Dad would drop his big grocery bag, filled with dirty work clothes, by the back door and then sit down, without a word, at his place at the head of the dining-room table. The newspaper would be there waiting, next to his plate, and my mother would instantly bring him a fifth of Seagram's and a cold Stroh's beer, along with a bottle opener. Dad would glance at the front page, unscrew the cap from the whiskey bottle, and measure one shot. After knocking that back, he would open the beer and carefully pour half the bottle into a glass, then take a sip. Meanwhile, my mother would produce some breaded Lake Erie perch, a mound of scalloped potatoes, a serving of canned corn, maybe a couple of rolls, a little salad of lettuce, cucumber, and tomato. My father would spend at least half an hour at the table, slowly eating his dinner, sipping his beer, reading his paper.

In the summer he would often take the *Lorain Journal* outside and relax under the oak trees in one of the big Adirondack-style lawn chairs he had built. Sometimes he would chew on a toothpick as he folded and unfolded the paper. My dad could make a couple dozen pages of newsprint last half an afternoon or most of an evening. He particularly loved to read about the discomfiture of the rich, whom he passionately hated and envied. He was convinced that politics was simply a means for the upper classes to protect their wealth and to get more of it. What could be more obvious? In particular, he came to loathe John Kennedy and could never quite understand why his death received such extravagant attention. "The man was only doing his job. He knew the risks. On the same day Kennedy was shot, three autoworkers in Detroit were killed when a crane collapsed on them. Why don't they get a fancy funeral? They were killed doing their job. What's the difference?" And he would wave his hand with disgust, dismissing an invisible crowd of political hypocrites and toadies. For a long time he kept a news clipping that appeared a week or so after Kennedy had been buried. A group of Catholic school kids had come to pay their respects to the dead president. As a priest or nun started to bless the grave, the container of holy water broke open, snuffing out the eternal flame. "God has spoken," intoned my father.

Sometimes, while my mother put my three sisters to bed, Dad would invite me to scrunch down next to him in the cream-colored recliner (with special Magic Fingers vibrating action) and look through the pages of an old illustrated encyclopedia or a Sears catalogue. One evening when I was perhaps 7 or 8, I sat next to him while he slowly read aloud a highly abbreviated kids' version, with smudgy watercolors, of *Don Quixote*. Now, forty years later, I remember how close I felt that night to my father, strong and handsome with his aquiline nose and curly black hair, as he described the misadventures of the deluded knight. Perhaps even then I suspected that this quick-witted, unhappy man, troubled by a fierce but unfocused desire for material success, had much of Don Quixote in him: He never ceased wanting the world, his children, his own life, to be better than they were or were ever likely to be.

Long before I could read, my father introduced me to the beauty and evocative power of words. When I'd ask him for a story, he would tell me about Ulysses and the Cyclops, chuckling at the Greek hero's ingenuity and applauding the comeuppance of an oppressor. Sometimes he would chant the tall-tale ballad of Abdul Abulbul Amir and Ivan Skavinsky Skavar: The two great warriors embark on an epic duel after Ivan treads on Abdul's toe. "They fought all that night 'neath the pale yellow moon / The din it was heard of afar / Great multitudes came so great was the fame / Of Abdul and Ivan Skavar." In the end both die, leaving comrades to mourn and a Circassian maiden heartbroken. Often as we rode down the highway in our old green Chevy, Dad would break out in song. "Old Dan and I our throats are dry / for the taste of water / cool water." At other times he would recite the lyrics to a then-current hit about Mary Ann "down by the seashore sifting sand." "Even little children love Mary Ann," he would repeat to himself, "down by the seashore sifting sand." Once, I remember, I was sick with the flu when Dad suddenly arrived home and, hearing of my illness, rushed to the blue davenport where I had been shivering under mounds of covers. He stroked my fevered brow and then began to recite: "'Twas many and many a year ago / In a kingdom by the sea / That a maiden there lived / Whom you may know / By the name of Annabel Lee." I was enchanted by the music of the sounds, a sing-song melodiousness that my father took pains to emphasize. "She was a child and I was a child / In this kingdom by the sea," he went on but soon stalled, not knowing much more of the poem than this. I've sometimes wondered how he knew it at all.

My dad had dropped out of school at 16 when his own father died, leaving him the support of a mother, two sisters, and a brother. Naturally, he went to work in the same steel mill that had killed my Russian-immigrant grandfather, and where he himself proceeded to labor for the next forty-odd years, despising every minute. There were many such stories in the Depression: My mother's mother was a widow with ten children; my mother-in-law raised her younger siblings. These people were tough customers. Though their own lives might be desperate, they were nevertheless convinced that their sons and daughters would dance in the sunshine, live in big houses on hilltops. "Get rich," my dad used to tell me, "and vote Republican."

🐌

Believing in education mainly as a way up in the world, my father built two substantial bookcases in our dining room. At meals he could glance up from his newspaper and see them, loaded with the books he never opened. To stock the shelves, he scavenged castoff boxes of tattered nonfiction, picked up remainders at department stores. My mother acquired the Funk and Wagnalls Standard Encyclopedia from the local A&P—and the first volume of half-a-dozen other reference sets. Back then, an encyclopedia might offer its initial volume for a come-on price of 59 cents; Mom would purchase that volume and then cancel her order. Who would pay $9.99 for each of the subsequent twenty-five volumes? Ridiculous. And so we kids wrote our school reports on artichokes, asteroids, and aardvarks, Alaska and Antarctica.

As I grew older, I would take down the books from these family shelves. There was Guy Endore's *Werewolf of Paris;* a faded blue volume of Cellini's cloak-and-rapier *Memoirs;* numerous titles on how to make more money, one with the unforgettable advice: Find a need and fill it. There was George Sisler on baseball; a volume of Keats's poetry; Ivy Compton-Burnett's *A Father and His Fate* (my dad would sometimes moodily murmur its title aloud); a little green-backed collection of five Shakespeare tragedies; several novels by F. Van Wyck Mason and Thomas B. Costain; an omnibus of Captain Horatio Hornblower adventures; a big anthology of short stories titled *The Golden Argosy* (in which I read "The Lady or the Tiger?" and "The Damned Thing" and "A.V. Laider" and "The Monkey's Paw"), and, not least, a first American edition, mint in dust jacket, of William Golding's *Lord of the Flies.* "Could have picked up a couple dozen of them," Dad said years later, when I told him the book was then worth two or three hundred bucks; "they were on a table at O'Neill's department store, 29 cents each."

When I became a teenager, my father would kick books out of my hands because he feared I had become a bookworm—all too true, alas— and then send me down to the basement to build something. Nevertheless, for most of my childhood, he faithfully ferried my sisters and me to the library every two weeks. I can remember vividly my first glimpse of a room completely filled with books. For some reason, Dad decided to take me across town to a small, dark branch library on Pearl Road in South Lorain, the depressed area of town where my parents had grown up. Could this have been the library of his own childhood? The single big room was narrow, cramped with desks, tables, and shelves, more like a used bookstore than a fluorescent-bright modern info-learning media center. I looked around and eventually selected some adventurous-sounding titles, only to be informed by a well-intentioned librarian that these particular works were far too difficult for a beginning reader of 5 or 6. The old biddy made me put everything back and then steered me to Curious George albums and comparably simple stuff. I remember feeling angry, frustrated, and helpless. Meanwhile, my father spent his time nervously browsing the adult shelves, looking distinctly ill at ease, going so far as to study with feigned casualness an illustrated version of *Moby-Dick*. I resentfully checked out my kiddie books, while he went home completely empty-handed.

He was a difficult man, and there was no pleasing him: He never had a kind word for anyone. For years I handed him tools while he tinkered with carburetors, fixed plumbing, built a new bedroom onto the house, sweated vigorously, and cursed his fate. Why couldn't his useless son learn how to do something useful? Why won't this pipe budge? Why was I such a good-for-nothing, completely worthless . . . ? But then his anger would subside, and we'd go for long walks in the woods, or down to Hot Waters to cast for white bass, and I never, ever doubted how much he loved me. Of course, he'd never let me forget my good fortune either. "You're lucky you have a father. . . . You're only able to go to college because your father's alive and working. . . ." If I reminded him that I had received a scholarship and that my education wasn't costing him a penny, he would explode, "You could be down in Four-Seamless, or in the rolling mill. You could be bringing in a good week's pay every Friday. You could be contributing a little after all these years of leeching off of your mother and me." When I graduated in 1970 from Oberlin College with highest honors in English, he wasn't there: Jesse Jackson's commencement remarks had so enraged him that he walked out of the ceremony.

Six years ago this spring, as my father lay dying from cancer, unable to speak or eat or move, I would read aloud at his bedside bits of poetry, sections of the Bible. I don't think it meant much to him. If I was so smart, why wasn't I rich? I should have been driving a new Cadillac, been a bigshot lawyer or stockbroker, or at the very least, for God's sake, have won the Pulitzer Prize.

Two years later, when he was dead at 74 and it was too late, I did just that. Naturally, I could hear his voice strong and clear, half-disgusted, half-amused: "That just goes to show you, kid. You never could do anything right, and you never could do anything when you were supposed to."

No, I never could, Dad. But today of all days I'd sure give a lot to hear you yell at me just one more time, "Get your nose out of that book and go do something useful."

Romantic Scholarship

Almost everyone who likes to read looks back fondly on early adolescence as the Golden Age, when books really were magic casements opening on faery lands forlorn. Back then entire afternoons might slip by unnoticed as we journeyed to the center of the earth and around the world in eighty days, shivered at the immortal words "Mr. Holmes, they were the footprints of a gigantic hound!," and dreamed our way through Africa and Mars and Pellucidar with Edgar Rice Burroughs. But those days are past, and all their dizzying raptures. Now we snatch a few minutes on the subway to peer at computer manuals, law texts, self-help guides, book-club main selections. The old enchantment is harder and harder to rediscover. Sure, most bestsellers offer cheap thrills, but reading about serial killers or high-tech whizbangery or complicated sex is hardly the same as surrendering to the perfect bliss of Sir Arthur Conan Doyle's *The Lost World*.

Wonder, it seems to me, is what's missing from most adult reading. Too many of our books feel middle-aged—stale, desperate, flat, tricked out in gaudy colors but tired and jaded inside. Is there any escape from such humdrummery?

One way out may be found in what I call Romantic Scholarship. Now, most academic writing these days is, to be kind, uninviting. Frequently unreadable. Often downright unforgivable. Recently, a book about Byron—Byron!—appeared with a dust-jacket blurb, ostensibly intended to make the volume irresistible to the impulse buyer, that announced the study as "a fully historicized account built not upon the materialism of a sociohistorical analysis but upon the materialism of the signifier in a discursive field," then added that it "effectively rewrites our entire conception of Romanticism."

Well, maybe it does. But how many of us are going to bother to find out?

Needless to say, this is not what I mean by Romantic Scholarship. The works I am thinking about present research as an Indiana Jones adventure, an expedition into the outback where science, history, and literature touch the marvelous.

🖎

Examples? Toward the end of the nineteenth century, a mild-mannered Cambridge academic decided "to explain the remarkable rule which regulated the succession to the priesthood of Diana at Aricia." To do so took thirty years and a dozen volumes, but the result was *The Golden Bough*, a virtual encyclopedia of strange lore, myths, and rituals—and a key influence on T. S. Eliot's *Waste Land* and other works of early modernism. Anthropologists now pooh-pooh much of Frazer, but he remains thrilling to read. The faint of heart should look for the single-volume abridgment (1922), which opens with the once-famous question: "Who does not know Turner's picture of the Golden Bough?" Nowadays, sad to say, most people don't.

At roughly the same time as Frazer's early volumes, W. P. Ker was composing his own masterwork, that swashbuckling survey of ancient heroic literature, *Epic and Romance* (1897): "No kind of adventure is so common or better told in the earlier heroic manner than the defence of a narrow place against odds." G. K. Chesterton's ever-rereadable *The Victorian Age in Literature* (1913) makes literary criticism even more aphoristic: "While Emily Bronte was as unsociable as a storm at midnight . . . Charlotte Bronte was at best like that warmer and more domestic thing, a house on fire." In *The Road to Xanadu* (1927), John Livingston Lowes wended his astonishing way through a poet's mind by studying the travel books, histories, and forgotten potboilers upon which Coleridge drew, often unconsciously, to create "The Rime of the Ancient Mariner" and "Kubla Khan." Nearly as monumental, and perhaps more appropriate to these troubled times, is George Saintsbury's soothing *The Peace of the Augustans: A Survey of Eighteenth Century Literature as a Place of Rest and Refreshment* (1916). The title alone should give today's academics a coronary.

Of course, the nineteenth century has its charms too, albeit rather perverse ones in Mario Praz's *The Romantic Agony* (1933), an almost voyeuristic account of decadent literature from Sade to Swinburne. Even the chapter titles sound right out of Krafft-Ebing: "The Beauty of the Medusa," "La Belle Dame Sans Merci," and my favorite, "The Shadow of the Divine Marquis." While indulging in such dubious textual pleasures, one might also pick up Montague Summers's *The Gothic Quest* (1938), which lays out the plots and publishing background of scores of Gothic stories, as well as providing an introduction to this mysterious scholar. It was said of Summers, reputedly a defrocked priest, that he could be seen around Oxford in the company of either a small black dog or a fair young man, but never with both at the same time. Incidentally or not, Summers also wrote unusually knowledgeable books about witchcraft, vampires, and—I suppose for a change of pace—Restoration drama.

Readers fond of folklore and legend should certainly turn to the prolific Sabine Baring-Gould's *Curious Myths of the Middle Ages* (1872), wherein are retold the stories, among others, of Pope Joan, the Seven Sleepers of Ephesus, Prester John, and The Wandering Jew. Baring-Gould reminds us that this last, a favored anti-hero of the Romantics, probably got his unhappy start from these haunting words of Christ: "Verily I say unto you, There be some standing here, which shall not taste death till they see the Son of Man coming in His kingdom." Clark B. Firestone's *The Coasts of Illusion: A Study of Travel Tales* (1924) chronicles all "the realms and races of prodigy," and is more wide-ranging than such better known collections as T. H. White's *Book of Beasts* (1954) and Borges's *Book of Imaginary Beings* (1967). In all three one can read of rocs and hippogriffs and mermaids and manticores and of the strange places that lie beyond the sunset, those unknown realms that old maps emblazoned with the words "Here Be Dragons." The tales of such strange shores and monstrous beasts, writes Firestone, "are the stories wanderers told in hall when the world was young; and in out-of-the-way places still they tell them, and men believe." A similar, albeit more factual book of "romantic zoology" is Willy Ley's *The Lungfish, the Dodo, and the Unicorn,* in which, for instance, Ley describes how the legend of the unicorn began, apparently through a mistranslation of an Old Testament reference to the reem. Assyrian bas-reliefs later revealed that the reem was no unicorn but rather an animal nearly as exotic, that largest of wild oxen, the now-extinct auroch. (Remember the beautiful closing sentences of *Lolita,* those that begin "I am thinking of aurochs and angels . . . ") The most complete treatment of this particular legend, however, remains Odell Shepard's *Lore of the Unicorn* (1930). Herodotus's *Histories,* Pliny's *Natural History,* the voyages of John Mandeville and Marco Polo—all these are chockablock with marvels and wonders. But you don't have to go back to the ancients for such Arabian Nights scholarship. Robert Graves's dazzling and obsessive *The White Goddess* (1948) aims to unriddle the mysteries of poetic inspiration. "The reason why the hairs stand on end, the skin crawls and a shiver runs down the spine when one writes or reads a true poem is that a true poem is necessarily an invocation of the White Goddess," and hardly a lady to mess around with. For she is also "the female spider or the queen-bee whose embrace is death." In the course of his research, Graves not only deciphers an ancient Celtic tree alphabet but also addresses those two "impossible" questions, made famous by Sir Thomas Browne: What song did the Sirens sing? And what name did Achilles assume when he hid himself among the women?

In Washington, the heaven of poli-sci majors, Robert K. Merton is best known as the author of several classics of sociology. But Merton also composed one inimitable example of romantic scholarship: *On the Shoulders of Giants* (1965), a "Shandean Postscript" that traces the history of Newton's famous remark "If I have seen farther, it is by standing on the shoulders of giants." In his meandering investigations, Merton discovers so many earlier forms of what he calls The Aphorism that he even coins the useful term "anticipatory plagiarism." The works of Frances Yates, especially *Giordano Bruno and the Hermetic Tradition* (1964) and *The Art of Memory* (1966), explore some of the more esoteric byways of Renaissance intellectual history. To read them is to feel as though you were looking through the secret notebooks of the Elizabethan magus John Dee or the doomed philosopher Bruno. *The Art of Memory,* for instance, describes how scholars in an age before printed books were able to retain seemingly incredible amounts of information: One prodigy could recite all of Vergil's *Aeneid* backwards. By using a "theater of memory," derived from some actual building, a student would place images of what he wanted to remember at selected locations. Then he need only stroll mentally through this imaginary building and glance at his memory-sites to have the images reappear to him in their proper order. Yates uses this intriguing system to explain aspects of Renaissance thought, even the very design of Shakespeare's Globe Theatre.

A few of these books are out of print, but try good libraries or used bookstores, where you might also ask for Morton W. Bloomfield's *The*

Seven Deadly Sins, Jean Seznec's *The Survival of the Pagan Gods,* Marjorie Hope Nicolson's *Voyages to the Moon,* and Don Cameron Allen's *Mysteriously Meant.* One could almost certainly find at least a couple of these titles in that dusty run-down shop we all sometimes hurry by on the way to work, the one crowded with curios, odd volumes, a bit of wild ass's skin, and that old lamp in need of a good rubbing. The place always looks closed. But perhaps if we were to ring the bell a little after dusk, someone just might open the door.

Avram Davidson

A postscript: More than a few readers may recall that novelist Evan S. Connell made two excursions into romantic scholarship: *A Long Desire* (1979) and *The White Lantern* (1980). There Connell discussed such matters as ancient astronomy, Latin America's lost cities of gold, and the career of the alchemist Paracelsus. Good as those books are, I prefer the marvelous, meandering, funny "adventures in unhistory" of Avram Davidson. These antiquarian investigations appeared over the past twenty years in various science fiction magazines—Davidson was an inimitable writer of short fantasy, the heir to Dunsany and John Collier—and have been collected in *Adventures in Unhistory: Conjectures on the Factual Foundations of Several Ancient Legends.*

In these pieces Davidson takes up such matters as where Sindbad sailed, how the phoenix legend got started, the truth about dragons and werewolves, the mysteries surrounding Aleister Crowley, the practice of preserving human heads, the location of Hyperborea, and much, much else. The result is an utterly enchanting book, even if one may occasionally question some of its scholarly conclusions. Davidson's digressive style— half Robert "Anatomy of Melancholy" Burton, half S. J. Perelman—delights me, but may madden more stolid readers who want just the facts. But for anyone desperately seeking to renew his sense of wonder, *Adventures in Unhistory* is a good place to start. Or end.

Weekend with Wodehouse

Friday, 9 A.M.: As the plane lifts off from National Airport, I immediately open *Young Men in Spats*. It's not, as the old joke has it, that I'm afraid of flying; it's crashing that worries me. Sudden lurches, unexpected grating noises, changes in the cabin pressure, the gremlin out there on the wing, fiendishly grinning as it claws away at the bolts around the engine casings—how else can these be explained except as signs of imminent doom? Especially the gremlin. Still, if this flight does end up on the front page of the A section—"Fireball over Indiana Cornfield": "It was like a meteor a-shootin' down out of the sky, ain't never seen nothin' like it"—I plan to go as I've lived: with a book in my hands. And not just any book by anybody. No, if there's one writer who can ease aeronautical timor mortis, it's Dr. Pelham Grenville Wodehouse, Plum to his friends, and the creator of Jeeves, Psmith, Madeline Bassett, Uncle Fred, and a body of fiction that has brought more joy to readers than even the *Kama Sutra* of Vatsayana. When angels in heaven want a book to read, they buy a paperback of *The Code of the Woosters*, then lean back into a cloudbank and sigh with pleasure over sentences like these:

"He, too, seemed disinclined for chit-chat. We stood for some moments like a couple of Trappist monks who have run into each other by chance at the dog races."

"Into the face of the young man who sat on the terrace of the Hotel Magnifique at Cannes there had crept a look of furtive shame, the shifty hangdog look which announces that an Englishman is about to talk French."

"Years before, and romantic as most boys are, his lordship had sometimes regretted that the Emsworths, though an ancient clan, did not possess a Family Curse. How little he had suspected that he was shortly to become the father of it."

Noon: Having unexpectedly landed in Chicago, instead of on the banks of the River Styx, I make my way to the Hotel Intercontinental, site of the biannual convention of the P. G. Wodehouse Society. As a member of Capital! Capital!, the D.C. chapter of this least objectionable of all organizations, I've foolishly agreed to talk about "Wodehouse and the Critics." Doubtless some post-hypnotic command accounts for my inability to recollect exactly how I was brainwashed into this. While entering the hotel lobby, I bump into a dark-complected young man, perhaps of Pakistani or Indian descent, sporting a top hat, gray cutaway, soft gloves, and, it goes without saying, spats. He murmurs "Sorry, old chap" and strolls off down Michigan Avenue, apparently unconscious of the stares from numerous passersby.

1 P.M.: At the registration table—next to a life-size cardboard cutout of an English bobby—I receive a totebag overflowing with goodies, courtesy of the Chicago Accident Syndicate. This ominous-sounding group is not, by the way, an insurance company, but the Wodehouse gang sponsoring the weekend's browsing and sluicing; their shifty-looking capo, Dan Garrison, claims to be head of the classics department at Northwestern University. Who's he kidding? Next this raffish character will be telling me he's not only the author of *Who's Who in Wodehouse* but also the editor of a standard Latin text of Horace. Obviously a fiendishly clever con artist—or quite possibly deluded.

In such circs, a bland smile is the stratagem called for. Transported to a quiet corner, the navy blue tote disburses a plastic license plate frame— "Ask Me About P. G. Wodehouse"—and various items embossed or engraved with PGW insignia: a coffee mug, a tie tack, a key chain, a notepad, and, not least, a refrigerator magnet in the image of that prize-winning example of porcine magnificence, the Empress of Blandings.

2 P.M.: Check out the huckster room, where paperbacks, reprints, audiotapes, and expensive firsts of the Master's work are for sale. Should I buy the jacketless copy of *Full Moon* for $35? A kindly friend from Capital!

Capital! tells me, with the becoming modesty for which book collectors are famous, that he purchased a lovely first of *Leave It to Psmith* for $20 not more than five minutes before I ambled into the dealers' area. He beams with satisfaction, happy in the knowledge that he's ruined my afternoon and quite possibly the rest of my life.

8 P.M.: After the opening ceremonies, the convention hosts a spirited reading of two Wodehouse stories, "Jeeves Takes Charge" and "Bertie Changes His Mind," performed by members of the City Lit theater company. During the question period following, a member of the audience lauds their full-dress performance of *Right Ho, Jeeves,* but adds somberly: "I was in the audience in the first row, and I have one nit to pick: Both Jeeves' and Bertie's shoes needed shining." Doubtless a recent grad of valet school.

10 P.M.: In the hotel bar, sipping a beer, I lounge with an elite circle of Wodehouse fans, serious men with fresh, modern ideas about *Love among the Chickens,* when a quartet of drunken maenads, all with slurred Southern accents, swarm down from out of nowhere. "How come you boys all wearin' the same ties?" The creatures flounce and undulate among us. "That's a helluva tie," says one, eyeing the official neckwear of the Wodehouse Society, a masterpiece of black, gold, and plum-colored silk that somehow manages to impart a subtle, if unmistakable, feeling of vertigo in all who behold it. Before long, the conversation has lost its elevated tone. "I just couldn't get a date back in Kentucky, so I had to marry a guy from Chicago." Theirs was not, one felt, a marriage destined to last.

Saturday, 9 A.M.: Before my talk, the latest round of questions in the Wodehouse Scripture contest. Sporting a striped jacket and a tie emblazoned with pink pigs, the quizmaster, Tony Ring, looks like a particularly untrustworthy racing tout, but is in fact one of the world's supreme experts on the Wodehouse canon. In the competition, three-person teams from the Drone Rangers, Capital! Capital!, Blandings Castle, Chapter One, and the Newts display a knowledge of Wodehouse minutiae that inspires nothing less than holy awe: They on honeydew hath fed and drunk the milk of paradise. By the bucketful. Over the weekend the battle of wits attains an intellectual intensity not matched since Kasparov played Deep Blue: "In *Uncle Fred Flits By,* how many people did Uncle Fred and Pongo impersonate?" (Seven.) "Which Mulliner invented Buck-U-Uppo?" (Wilfred.) "Who wrote *My Chums, the Pixies*?" (Mrs. Lavender Botts.) "What kind of animal was Sam Goldwyn in *The Mating Season*?" (Answer: "A dog." Pause. "What kind of dog?") Some competitors, in particular Helen Murphy, the daughter of Wodehouse historian N. T. P. Murphy, can actually quote passages verbatim when answering Ring's increasingly arcane stumpers. "For whom did Spink buttle in *Spring Fever?*" "Who was Lady Constance Keeble's second husband?" It should be noted that chairman Ring, for many years a prominent English tax adviser, has built a special annex at home just for his Wodehouse books and archives, is the author of *You Simply Hit Them with An Axe* (the definitive study—accept no substitutes—of Plum's entanglement with the IRS), and is currently completing the multivolume Wodehouse Millennium Concordance, compared to which the reconstitution of the Dead Sea Scrolls is so much child's play.

9:30 A.M.: Fearing the possibility of a hangover, or even delirium tremens, I have presciently prepared a written talk, instead of relying on my native woodnotes wild to charm some 150 auditors. The burden of my discourse, of a silver-tongued eloquence that St. John Chrysostom might have envied had he been there, is quite simple: In the opinion of various critics, fellow writers, and professional editors, which of Wodehouse's more than 90 books can be called his best? Rather than doggedly reproduce my speech in toto, let me skip straight to the peroration, if that's the word I want.

The plums of Plum's oeuvre, his funniest and most dazzling verbal confections are, starting from the top, *The Code of the Woosters; Right Ho, Jeeves; Leave It to Psmith; Joy in the Morning; The Mating Season;* and *Uncle Fred in the Springtime.* Of the non-series books, the most generally admired is *The Small Bachelor.* Among the stories, two classics stand out— "Uncle Fred Flits By" and "Lord Emsworth and the Girl Friend"—followed by such old reliables as "Strychnine in the Soup," "Ukridge's Accident Syndicate," "Honeysuckle Cottage," and virtually all the misadventures in *The Inimitable Jeeves* and *Very Good, Jeeves,* especially "The Great Sermon Handicap." If you don't know and revere these masterpieces, your life is little more than a hollow shell.

Saturday afternoon: The convention tootles on. Soprano Lara Cazalet, Wodehouse's granddaughter, sings "Bill," the most famous of the Wodehouse–Jerome Kern collaborations. Helen Murphy discusses the popular Edwardian fiction behind the Rosie M. Banks "masterpieces," *Mervyn Keene, Clubman,* and *Only a Factory Girl.* Wodehouse's editor at Simon and Schuster, Peter Schwed, reminisces about Wodehouse and the musical. Funniest of all, businessman Peter Sinclair relates, with slides, the saga of J. Fillken Wilberfloss (inspired by a character of that name in *Psmith Journalist*). As a lark, Sinclair began telling unwanted callers to his D.C. company that they needed to speak with Mr. Wilberfloss, who had, unfortunately, just stepped out. In fact, Wilberfloss, like Sam Walton, spent nearly all his time out in the field. Nevertheless, this obviously tireless executive—

who never returned a call or answered a letter—was soon receiving huge quantities of mail from banks, job applicants, and even a reference book publisher that hoped to honor him in a forthcoming volume devoted to titans of industry.

Saturday evening: A banquet of the Wodehouse Society makes even the most unbridled saturnalia resemble a lenten tea taken with some elderly archbishop of very strict views. The wine naturally flows like water, and rather fast-moving water at that. Many guests gambol about in Wodehouse-inspired costumes—silk bathrobes, Red Devil outfits, tuxedos, shimmery flapper dresses, velvet smoking jackets, green beards, schoolboy uniforms. One conventioneer from Capital! Capital! snuffles by as the Empress of Blandings, and a particularly distinguished-looking toff claims to be the British consul general, which, it turns out, he is.

Midway through dinner the bread rolls begin to fly, as table turns against table and every man's hand is raised against his brother. Or sister. Reverting to the primitive, the veneer of civilization a distant memory, even this reporter lobs crusty missiles at Jon Lellenberg, kingpin of Capital! Capital!, and Daniel Cohen, prolific children's author extraordinaire, and Margaret Slythe, former librarian of PGW's alma mater Dulwich College. A constant rain of bread—a martial antitype to manna from heaven?— falls upon the costumed assembly, which soon begins to resemble a Halloween party of gigantic children, boisterous, drunk, and very happy.

Sunday morning: Woozy and headachey, I wake for the convention brunch; first toast, then toasts. "It doesn't matter what you do in real life, here you love Wodehouse!" Soon back in room, packing bags with loot. It's only 11:30, and my plane doesn't leave until 5:30. One doesn't need a Jeeves, the most gigantic brain this side of Spinoza, to calculate that this means six hours before takeoff. Which gives me—and my old college roommate Clint Vose, who's waiting outside in a maroon roadster—most of an afternoon to hit a few of Chicago's finest secondhand bookshops. What ho! What ho! What ho!

An Abecedary

A—*Anti-Intellectualism in American Life,* by Richard Hofstadter. Anyone hoping to understand the current debates about multiculturalism, artistic freedom, and religious and ethnic fundamentalism should read this exhilarating book, one of the true classics of intellectual history. "Life adjustment educators would do anything in the name of science except encourage children to study it."

B—Roland Barthes, Georges Bataille, Walter Benjamin, Kenneth Burke, Maurice Blanchot, Mikhail Bakhtin, Harold Bloom. If you wish to become a famous literary critic—not precisely a crowded field—pick a last name that starts with B.

C—Commonplace book. An old-fashioned name for a notebook into which are copied favorite passages from one's reading. Two samples:
"Overambitious projects may be objectionable in many fields, but not in literature. Literature remains alive only if we set ourselves immeasurable goals, far beyond all hope of achievement" (Italo Calvino). "There was a young fellow called Price, / Who dabbled in all sorts of vice; / He had virgins and boys / And mechanical toys, / And on Mondays he meddled with mice" (Anon, of course).

D—Dantes, Edmond, aka the Count of Monte Cristo. The hero of the supreme masterpiece of pedagogical fiction, an account of the metamorphosis of an ignorant young seaman into an urbane, educated and self-confident man of the world. "Wait and hope" may be the Count's motto, but study and hard work are the virtues that he really teaches.

E—Ecclesiastes. Long ago my parents would permit an antsy, bored me to read the Bible in church, and I soon discovered Coholeth's appealingly cynical, angst-ridden observations: "I returned, and saw under the sun, that the race is not to the swift, nor the battle to the strong, neither yet bread to the wise, nor yet riches to men of understanding, nor yet favour to men of skill; but time and chance happeneth to them all."

F—First editions. Many are the times when I've wished I'd never so much as heard these two words.

G—Green Lantern. The best of all superheroes. When Hal Jordan charged his power ring, intoning something along the lines of "In brightest day, / in blackest night, / no evil shall escape my sight! / Let those who worship evil's might / beware my power . . . Green Lantern's light," a generation of 10-year-olds recited the words with him. If a certain beloved mother hadn't given away a certain collection of several hundred comic books, a certain literary journalist could now afford to send his kids to college.

H—Anthony Hecht, Geoffrey Hill, Donald Hall, Seamus Heaney, Robert Hass, Ted Hughes. What is it about the letter H and our best contemporary poets? Could the Muse have a taste for alliteration?

I—"Intellect, each day I set less store on," or in the original French, "Chaque jour j'attache moins de prix à l'intelligence." This is my favorite Proust quotation.

J—Jeffrey, George. When this legendary bookseller died a few years back, all literary London mourned. Dressed in his blue storekeeper's coat, apple-cheeked George Jeffrey held the last remaining license to sell books from barrows on the streets of London. On Saturday mornings book runners and dealers from all over the city would converge on Farringdon Road. George—a consciously Dickensian character—would keep the new treasures under tarps until the tension had mounted to a fever pitch, at which point he would suddenly pull away the canvas and let the feeding frenzy begin. One blustery morning I acquired, for a pound apiece and a couple of hard pokes in the ribs, two bound volumes of the *Strand* magazine featuring the first six adventures of Sherlock Holmes.

K—*Kim.* For years my late colleague Reid Beddow would say, "Dirda, you've got to read *Kim;* it's soooooo good." Reid was right as usual: "She liked men and women, and she spoke of them—of kinglets she had known in the past, of her own youth and beauty, of the depredations of leopards and the eccentricities of Asiatic love. . . ."

L—Locked-room mysteries. The highest form of the classic detective story. The supreme examples are all by John Dickson Carr, in particular *The Three Coffins* and *The Judas Window*. One sterling example easily overlooked: Randall Garrett's science fictional *Too Many Magicians*. Garrett posits an alternate Earth on which magic works, and he locates his supernaturally sealed chamber at a convention of master wizards. Who done it, and how was it done? Fans of magic and mystery should also look for Clayton Rawson's novels about the Great Merlini, especially *Death from a Top Hat* and *The Footprints on the Ceiling*. Wonderful 1930ish period flavor.

M—MacArthur grant. In the old television show *The Millionaire,* a front doorbell would ring, and some lucky—or occasionally unlucky—person would open to a resonant voice saying, "My name is Michael Anthony, and I have here a check for a million dollars." How we kids would daydream about what we would do with such a well-deserved fortune! Some of us still daydream.

N—Neal Obstat, D. O. Volente, Perry Bathhouse, Mrs. Dulcie S. DeCrumb. For some obscure reason, I once wrote a story in which all the characters' names were taken from Latin tags and foreign-language phrases. Thomas Pynchon does this sort of thing all the time, and it works for him; think of Mucho Maas, husband to Oedipa in *The Crying of Lot 49.*

O—Oulipo. The acronym for the French Workshop for Potential Literature, devoted to showing how constraints, limitations, and mathematical formulas can liberate the creative imagination. Among its members are several distinctive contemporary writers, including Italo Calvino, who once used the Tarot to construct a novel; Raymond Queneau, who created a sonnet-producing machine; Harry Mathews, whose hilarious "Country Cooking" is based on a recipe; and Georges Perec, who fused the ingenuity of a crossword puzzle creator with the novelistic energy of a Victorian storyteller. Along with the Drones Club, Oulipo is the only organization I have ever really wanted to belong to.

P—"Pfui." Consulting detective Nero Wolfe's signature expression of disgust. Just two syllables, and one instantly sees the brownstone, the leather chairs, wisecracking Archie Goodwin, the fat, self-satisfied Wolfe, a complete and long-vanished world of wit, decorum, and cocktails.

Q—Quietus, Clare Quilty, Quintilian, "three quarks for muster mark," Quilp, Peter Quince, Quiller, Quincunx.

R—R is the spymaster in Somerset Maugham's *Ashenden,* that brilliant collection of World War I secret-agent stories. M, of course, is 007's boss in Ian Fleming's James Bond novels. C denotes the hero of a novel, of the same title, by Maurice Baring (Nancy Mitford's favorite novelist). *Z* is the title of a political thriller made into a classic '60s movie. Q became the nom de plume of literary scholar Sir Arthur Quiller-Couch, once a name to conjure with. *S.* is a novel by John Updike; Nicholson Baker named his playful homage to that literary all-rounder *U and I.* Louis Zukofsky composed the long poem *A,* quite literally the work of a lifetime. Agatha Christie titled a mystery *N or M?,* and John Berger wrote a Booker Prize-winning novel about Don Juan called *G.* Pauline Reage set down *The Story of O,* and J penned *The Sensuous Woman. V.* is Thomas Pynchon's first novel, and Joseph K was arrested without having done anything wrong. Anthony Burgess constructed the rhyme-scheme titled short novel *ABBA, ABBA;* L. P. Hartley wrote a ghostly chiller titled *"W.S.";* and Ellery Queen imagined *The Tragedy of X.*

S—Sagas. Why don't more people read the Icelandic sagas? Imagine spaghetti westerns with swords, set in a bleakly beautiful Northern landscape. In *The Saga of Grettir the Strong,* the protagonist is the most formidable warrior in Iceland, but he is pitiably afraid of the dark. The hero of another story dies when he breaks his bowstring and his icy-hearted wife refuses to cut some strands of her long golden hair as a replacement. In *Njal Saga,* old Njal and his many sons are burned to death by some forty enemies, the only survivor being the adopted Kari: Like some driven gunslinger, the young man spends half his life relentlessly tracking—and killing or bringing to justice—the men who murdered his family. Finally, only their leader is left, and on his way to fulfilling his vengeful quest our hero is shipwrecked. Nearly drowned, half-frozen, Kari has no choice but to crawl to the house of his deadliest enemy and ask for the ancient right of hospitality. . . .

T—Time paradoxes. What locked rooms are to mysteries, time-travel stories are to science fiction. In Robert Heinlein's tour de force "All You Zombies," there is only a single character, who ultimately becomes both his own mother and father. In *Time and Again,* Jack Finney's hero goes back to the 1880s and prevents the parents of the inventor of time travel from ever meeting. In Ray Bradbury's classic "A Sound of Thunder," the death of a small butterfly-like creature in the age of the dinosaurs causes drastic consequences when extrapolated over the millennia. Other timely tales: Robert Silverberg's twisty *Up the Line;* John Crowley's somberly beautiful novella "Great Work of Time"; John D. MacDonald's light-hearted romp *The Girl, the Gold Watch, and Everything;* and, not least, C. L. Moore's evocative "Vintage Season," about the arrival—and ultimate vampiric purpose—of decadent tourists from the future.

U—*The Unquiet Grave,* by Cyril Connolly. There are books to which we lose our hearts, and this is mine: a collection of melancholy aphorisms, quotations, and reflections on the consolations of art and love. Connolly is often self-pitying but nearly always with a knowing wink: "When very bored say to yourself: 'It was during the next twenty minutes that there occurred one of those tiny incidents which revolutionize the whole course of our life and alter the face of history. Truly we are the playthings of enormous fates.'"

V—Vance, Jack. The grandmaster of living science fiction and fantasy writers. Ironic, elaborately descriptive, consistently humorous (especially in the adventures of Cugel the Clever), capable of Grand Guignol adventures (*The Star King*) or highly wrought puzzles ("The Moon Moth"), Vance possesses the most distinctive style in sf. You can hear his world-weary voice in just ten words: "Ixax at the best of times was a dreary planet."

W—Wee Willie Winkie. Someday I will prove my theory that this nursery rhyme ultimately derives from Caesar's famous phrase "Veni, Vidi, Vici" ("I came, I saw, I conquered")—and an awestruck scholarly community will entreat me to accept the Boylston Chair of Rhetoric at Harvard.

X—*The X-Files.* I watched one episode and was so scared I've never dared to look at the show again.

Y—G. M. Young. Here is the opening from this historical essayist's masterpiece, *Victorian England: Portrait of an Age:* "A boy born in 1810, in time to have seen the rejoicings after Waterloo and the canal boats carrying the wounded to hospital, to remember the crowds cheering for Queen Caroline, and to have felt that the light had gone out of the world when Byron died, entered manhood with the ground rocking under his feet as it had rocked in 1789."

Z—"Zénon, cruel Zénon, Zénon d'Elée"—"Zeno, cruel Zeno, Zeno of Elea." Why have these few words, from a poem by Paul Valéry, obsessed me ever since I first read them? Why should this particular pre-Socratic philosopher, the source for several celebrated logical paradoxes (Achilles' footrace against a tortoise), be termed "cruel"? I don't know, yet that single adjective grants the line a strange and haunting beauty.

Mr. Wright

In eighth grade I was lucky enough to have a brilliant young teacher named Delmar Wright for honors English. Mr. Wright sported tortoise-shell glasses, wore neatly checkered sport jackets, drove an MG, and had three young children: Sean O'Casey Wright, Thomas Carlyle Wright, and Emily Dickinson Wright. To my 13-year-old self he seemed as wonderfully exotic as his Waspy first name, for my hometown was a classic Ohio rust-belt city, home to Slavs and Italians, Puerto Ricans and blacks, a place of washed-out wooden houses, with grit and sulphur in the air and the kind of desolation we associate with Edward Hopper paintings. I had long loved to read—the Hardy Boys, Tarzan, *The Hound of the Baskervilles*—but Mr. Wright was the first person I'd ever met who seemed deeply, personally excited about novels and poems and stories and plays. He was probably the most influential teacher in my life. I don't suppose he was then more than 30. But he possessed dash, the kind of suavity and ease that I instinctively admired, perhaps knowing that such nonchalant grace would never be mine. His tenor voice was precise, his sentences grammatical, his diction crisp yet lilting, even musical. When he spoke, I listened closely to the way he carefully chose each word and shaped his phrases; later in the day, on the long walk home from school, I would practice repeating his sentences while trying to mimic his pronunciation. The classicist William Arrowsmith used to insist that a good teacher should embody his subject—literally—and it was obvious to everyone that Mr. Wright loved the English language and its literature.

He was, naturally enough, unconventional, as the best teachers always are. In his late afternoon classes we would often spend the entire hour just reading aloud. We would go round the desks, each student speaking as distinctly, as dramatically as possible a paragraph or two from some mysterious, richly ambiguous story—Shirley Jackson's "The Lottery," perhaps, or E. M. Forster's allegory of time and brotherhood, "The Other Side of the Hedge." Once we devoted most of a week to arguing about the meanings in E. B. White's little classic, "The Door." I see now that Mr. Wright must have chosen such modern parables just because they are so deliberately, even heavy-handedly, symbolical, and thus ideal for heated classroom discussion. To this day I recollect my dazzled first reading of the White story—in which human life is compared to that of a rat trapped in a maze: "I remember the door with the picture of the girl on it (only it was spring), her arms outstretched in loveliness, her dress (it was the one with the circle on it) uncaught, beginning the slow, blinding cascade—and I guess we would all like to try that door again, for it seemed like the way and for a while it was the way. . . ."

Some periods Mr. Wright would saunter in with a portable record player under his arm, set it up, and then pull the blinds shut to block out the afternoon sun. In the resulting half-light he would carefully place an LP on the turntable, while we would all hush with expectation. Once the needle picked up the vinyl clamor of a great battle, fought apparently during a thunderstorm and followed by a short, spooky silence. Then frightening, otherworldly voices suddenly half-whispered, half-cackled: "When shall we three meet again? In thunder, lightning or in rain? When the hurly burly's done / When the battle's lost and won. / That will be ere the sun of sun. / Where the place? Upon the heath / There to meet with Macbeth." Martial music sounded forth at this point, and the voices chanted in hideous unison: "Fair is foul, and foul is fair. . . . By the pricking of my thumbs / Something wicked this way comes." I shivered with excitement. This was even better than reading "The Wendigo" from *Tales to Be Told in the Dark*. It was also my introduction to Shakespeare, and made me a fan for life—despite having to sit through some terrible high school productions of *A Midsummer Night's Dream* and *Twelfth Night*.

But Mr. Wright was nothing if not up to date. In his class we also listened to the then-recent Broadway recording of Samuel Beckett's *Waiting for Godot*, which we were crazy about because it was both funny and very peculiar; we especially marveled when the slave Lucky was told to speak and he spewed forth a nonstop torrent of naughty and subversive verbiage. In particular, I marveled at the play's final stoically comic lines: Vladimir and Estragon say to each other, "Let's go," while the stage directions read: "They do not move." How could I not love Beckett? Who could resist him? On another day we listened to Basil Rathbone intone, in his most lugubrious voice, "The Tell-Tale Heart," by Edgar Allan Poe. At its hysterical climax, the actor's voice rose to a shriek that echoed down the halls of Hawthorne Junior High, and brought teachers running. I would give much to hear those records again, ideally on a snowy Friday afternoon, while sitting just right of my old friend Tom Mikus and only a few seats away from my beloved Paula Shagovac.

In those days my hometown of Lorain had no bookshops. Department stores all carried a few recent bestsellers next to the children's classics and Bibles, but that was about it—excepting, of course, the thrift shops and Goodwills, in which as a teenager I would pick up Agatha Christie's *Murder of Roger Ackroyd,* Robert Heinlein science fiction stories, Cornell Woolrich's *Deadline at Dawn,* and even the second printing of the first American edition of *Ulysses.* Fortunately for me, though, Mr. Wright used to drive to Cleveland one night a week to take a course at Western Reserve University; on his way, he told us, he always stopped at a big bookstore near Terminal Tower and would be delighted to buy any paperbacks we might need. I still own the first three books I asked him to pick up for me: Dale Carnegie's *How to Stop Worrying and Start Living* (even as a boy I tended to excessive introspection), Thoreau's *Walden,* and Wilkie Collins's *The Moonstone.* Carnegie quoted a lot of inspirational verse in his earnest pages, including Kipling's "If," which I duly memorized, vowing always to "fill the unforgiving minute / with sixty seconds' worth of distance run." The glad-handing author also recommended that people study the Bible, Shakespeare, and the Gettysburg Address to improve their diction. So I studied them. In his turn, Thoreau stirred me with his philosophy of life ("Simplify, simplify"; "We do not ride on the railroad; it rides upon us"), while providing a model of limpid, no-nonsense Yankee prose. I learned by heart favorite sentences and paragraphs: "Beware of all enterprises that require new clothes." "While men believe in the infinite, some ponds will be thought to be bottomless." "If one advances confidently in the direction of his dreams and endeavors to live the life which he has imagined, he will meet with a success unexpected in common hours." I still have my copies of these books, as well as my paperback of *The Moonstone.* After thirty-five years, it's probably time to reread that great Victorian mystery-shocker.

I presume we must have studied a little grammar that year (1962), maybe diagrammed a few sentences, but mainly I recall our required reading list: the fourteen very eclectic titles Mr. Wright insisted we all know in addition to those we might choose for book reports. Over the course of the year, we swept through Faulkner's *The Unvanquished,* Vance Packard's *The Status Seekers,* Harry Golden's *Only in America,* James Joyce's "The Dead," Gogol's "The Overcoat," Orwell's *Nineteen Eighty-Four,* James Hilton's *Goodbye, Mr. Chips,* Glenway Wescott's "The Pilgrim Hawk," Katherine Anne Porter's "Noon Wine," and a half-dozen others, all wonderful. The Orwell was particularly cherished by my classmates, chiefly for the sex scenes between Winston Smith and Julia starting on, I believe, page 113 of the Signet paperback. (It's the sort of detail that sticks in the mind.) Though it's been decades since I read the novel—another book due for revisiting—even now I shudder at the dispiriting final sentences of that grim parable: "He had won the victory over himself. He loved Big Brother." Back then, those simple words came as a revelation: I had never realized that irony could be so brutal.

At the end of the school year, Mr. Wright asked each of us to write a short story. Mine, called "Faster and Faster," was scribbled one Sunday afternoon in my backyard at a picnic table, its author having fled some all too common domestic uproar. Alas, the story never quite worked. In it the unlikable protagonist—a touch of verismo that I particularly relished— finds himself obsessed with speed, with the desire to go "faster and faster." At its end, our hero, now an experimental jet pilot, simply disappears, presumably into another dimension. It earned me a B. I suppose I had hoped to create a richly allegorical tale about man's hunger for the infinite or something. It didn't really matter. There would be lots of time to improve, since by then it was clear to me that I wanted to spend my life reading and talking about books. To be, insofar as I was able, just like Mr. Wright.

But the following year, having started high school, I saw my favorite teacher only a few times before he moved his family to another state and another job. I remember riding my bike over to his house once, and sitting on his porch to tell him I'd won a scholarship to Oberlin College. He was pleased for me yet then somehow started talking, with obvious wistfulness, about the passage of time. He spoke about the inherent tragedy of having children, of how they had to be willing to abandon you at 18 and go off on their own, else you'd failed in your duty as a parent. Mr. Wright himself looked older, his face already lined. But then he brightened and told me about a Shakespeare course he was looking forward to taking at Ohio State during the summer. As I left, he even gave me a graduation present: a copy of Edwin Arlington Robinson's poems, inscribed with the command "To Mike, keep reading!" Whenever I turn to "Miniver Cheevy" or "Eros Turannos," I think of that afternoon.

"Keep reading." Seldom, I suspect, has a teacher's injunction been followed so . . . diligently. I have kept reading, yes, and to a large degree because of the example, instruction, and character of Mr. Wright. Thank you, sir, wherever you are. I have not forgotten what you taught me.

Heian Holiday

Washington's cherry blossoms have already faded, and once again I failed to see them during the short period of their fleeting beauty. Perhaps it's just as well. I would have wandered among the branches heavy with flowers and thought somber thoughts about the passage of the years and the transitoriness of life, surrendering to that sweet sorrow which the Japanese call *mono no aware:*

"As he wandered from one familiar spot to another it affected him strangely to find those whom he had recently thought of as mere children playing the part of dignified masters and possessors amid the scenes where he himself had once submitted to his elders' rule."

"For days it had rained unceasingly. But now, just at the moment when the heavy rain stopped and only a few scattered drops were falling, the moon rose; and soon it was one of those exquisite late spring nights through whose stillness he had in earlier years so often ridden out on errands of adventure."

"Again and again Murasaki told herself that life was very short. Soon this and all else would be over; what sense could there be in minding things so much?"

"A mist lay over the hills and outlined against it was the figure of a heron stiffly poised on a bare ledge of rock. The bridge lay shimmering in the mist, looking a long way off. Now and again a boat would pass under it, laden with timber. A strange, a haunting place—this Uji."

A strange, a haunting book this *Genji Monogatari—The Tale of Genji* —from which all these quotations come. Written during the Heian renaissance of the early eleventh century, Murasaki Shikubu's classic—twice the length of *War and Peace*—has often been called the first psychological novel; it is certainly the supreme Japanese work of art, the model and inspiration for much later drama, poetry, and fiction, the subject, it is said, of more than 10,000 book-length works of criticism. For some time a scholarly friend, John Auchard, had been urging me to read this masterpiece, and over the years I had gradually acquired, in various used bookshops, the six volumes of Arthur Waley's famous translation (1926–33). Somewhere I'd also picked up a hefty trade paperback of Edward Seidensticker's more accurate and scholarly English version (1973), as well as a hardback copy of Ivan Morris's magnificent background study, *The World of the Shining Prince* (1964). These were central texts. To further prepare myself, I eagerly read Donald Keene's incisive paperback *Japanese Literature,* studied the chapter on *Genji* in Keene's monumental history of early Japanese literature, *Seeds in the Heart,* and paid hard cash for a copy of *The Princeton Companion to Classical Japanese Literature.* I was ready for a great reading adventure—if only I could find the time. Quite a lot of time.

Was it Napoleon or Lincoln who said, "I will prepare myself and my chance will come"? Years passed, and I was beginning to think that I might end up like one of the minor characters in *Genji:* "But while he was still impatiently counting the months and days that must elapse before his schemes could be fulfilled, death suddenly carried him off, and the dream of his life, which was that one at least of his daughters should be accepted at the Palace, had now no prospect of being fulfilled." But I was to be luckier than Higekuro. In January 1996 the *Post* awarded me a four-week fellowship to study at Duke University, and, blithely abandoning work, family, adult responsibilities, and the Washington winter, I took a slow train down to Durham and soon lost myself in Heian Japan.

As the Buddhist priest Kenko wrote in his *Essays in Idleness,* "the pleasantest of all diversions is to sit alone under the lamp, a book spread out before you, and to make friends with people of a distant past you have never known." Most days at Duke I would get up around 8 A.M., shower, dress, and browse around in Keene's history while munching my cornflakes and sipping coffee. Then I would trudge across the West campus to the Sanford Center, where I passed most of the daylight hours working on My Secret Writing Project, with interruptions for lunch, occasional classes, and an hour at the gym. Come 6 P.M. I would meander back to my little apartment, prepare a bachelor supper (bagel and scrambled eggs or store-bought barbecued chicken or a big salad), followed by a glass of wine and a little channel surfing. (Rather to my surprise, I discovered that there is virtually nothing worth watching on television even if you do get cable.) Then from 8 o'clock until 11 or so, I would read *Genji,* usually pausing midway to have a cup of instant coffee. Around midnight I would crawl into bed, insert a cassette into a tape player (borrowed from my number one son), and drift off to sleep to the strains of *H.M.S. Pinafore* or Dvořák's "American" quartet. The next day I would get up at 8 and do it all over again.

It was obviously wonderful, though after the first week just slightly pervaded with the melancholy of the temporary and evanescent: In nine more days, eight more days, seven more days, I must return to the real world. Still, for nearly a month I deeply enjoyed myself—in my fashion. I used *Genji* as my intellectual base, but before long I was branching out, reading J. Thomas Rimer's *Guide to Japanese Literature* and Earl Miner's *The Japanese Tradition in British and American Literature,* William Puette's (rather unsatisfying) *Reader's Guide to "The Tale of Genji"* and Richard Bowring's fine Cambridge Landmarks of World Literature monograph on Murasaki. I checked out a score of books from the Duke library (including a delightful collection of memoirs and appreciations of Arthur Waley), skimmed studies of Japanese diaries and Japanese court poetry, consulted the notes in scholarly tomes, photocopied essays from journals. I even listened to early koto music. Soon I also began to dip into the witty Sei Shonagon, whose *Pillow Book* revealed a soulmate's liking for lists ("Unsuitable Things," "Poetic Subjects," "Things That Should Be Short"), and who was, in some ways, Murasaki's rival (the two served competing empresses). On one memorable night, while paging though Keene's *Anthology of Japanese Literature,* I fell hard for the amorous Ono no Komachi, one of whose poems I memorized in Japanese:

> The flowers withered,
> Their color faded away,
> While meaninglessly
> I spent my days in the world
> And the long rains were falling.

Most of all I became entranced by the aesthetic sensibility embodied in so many Japanese words, and I was soon copying out definitions into a notebook. *Yugen*—"a kind of ethereal and profound beauty, one that lurks beneath the surface of things, unamenable to direct expression." *Eiga*— "the love of colour and grandeur, of pomp and circumstance." *Mujokan*— the Buddhist sense of the transitoriness of worldly things. *Miyabi*—courtly beauty, elegance. *Sabi*—"the desolation and beauty of loneliness; solitude, quiet." *Aware*—a sensitivity to "the tears in things." *Utsutsu*—reality; *Yume*—dream. *Yume no Ukihashi*—The Floating Bridge of Dreams. This last serves as the title for the final chapter of *Genji;* it is, of course, life itself that is the bridge of dreams.

What I came to enjoy most deeply about *The Tale of Genji* is the very fact that nothing much really happens in it. As Murasaki herself writes, "it was indeed a moment in the history of our country when the whole energy of the nation seemed to be concentrated upon the search for the prettiest method of mounting paper-scrolls."

The novel's action is almost entirely given over to Genji's disruptive love affairs, filled out with court intrigues (mostly involving marriage), beautiful descriptions of landscape and weather, Proustian depictions of jealousy, elaborate set pieces detailing religious dances and rituals, and accounts of artistic competitions. The book is unfailingly interesting without being in the least exciting or suspenseful: One watches Prince Genji—the Shining One—as time after time he discovers a beautiful young woman in some out-of-the-way spot, falls for her, and then slowly resolves the various complications that this entanglement leads to.

On occasion, Genji discovers that he has overstepped the bounds: His very brief affair with the Empress Fujitsubo (his stepmother) serves as the template for several other characters' later, equally forbidden passions. There are two or three Gothic moments—for instance, when the evil spirit of Lady Rokujo destroys the fragile beauty Yugao—and even bits of comedy, such as the portrait of a countrified nobleman who pushes his daughter at the prince and a scene in which monks mistake a beautiful young girl for a spectral were-fox.

Perhaps the single most dramatic, and utterly unexpected, sentence in the whole book occurs at the very beginning of Volume V: "Genji was dead, and there was no one to take his place." The final third of the novel chronicles the rivalry in love between the self-centered, neurotic Kaoru (thought to be Genji's son) and the self-confident womanizer Niou (Genji's grandson). In these chapters, both darker and more artfully organized than the Genji sections, Murasaki relates a series of almost Hardy-like love tragedies, all set against the ominous background of the swirling waters of the river at Uji.

"How swiftly the locks rust, the hinges grow stiff on doors that close behind us!" The month at Duke flew by, but I still vividly remember the morning when it was raining so hard that I decided to stay home in my apartment and read all day. The thunderstorm raged outside, but I sat snug in my chair, hour after happy hour. I remember thinking how strange it was that already in the eleventh century, in the middle of the world's first novel, Genji was saying that his adventures sounded "like something out of an old romance." I remember thinking too that modern feminist critics should be studying Heian literature, since virtually all its greatest authors were women.

Most of all, reading Waley's beautiful translation, I marveled at the sentences: "'Were you now to die, I think I should soon follow you . . . ' He paused, but there was no reply; for she had died suddenly like a candle blown out by the wind, and he was left in bewilderment and misery." I enjoyed Murasaki's occasional addresses to the reader—a human voice speaking directly across a thousand years: "I would indeed have been glad to carry my story a little further, but at this moment my head is aching and I am feeling very tired and depressed."

Above all, I admired the subtle ways Murasaki evokes the destructive power of eros, without ever being sexually explicit: "She was only a singularly handsome girl, looking up at him with a shy, questioning yet almost trustful air. His good resolutions suddenly broke down. Soon the world and its inhabitants seemed nothing to him, nor would he have stretched out a hand to save them from instant destruction."

Discovering *The Tale of Genji* has been one of the great literary revelations of my life. If I could, I'd like nothing better than to start rereading it immediately, this time in Seidensticker's translation. But I doubt that I will ever again be able to re-create the nearly ideal conditions of my mini-sabbatical at Duke. For four weeks I lost myself in a book in a way that normal adult life rarely allows. And such a book, so filled with *eiga* and *yugen* and *aware*! Even now, two months later, I feel deeply grateful simply to have had the chance to experience such a great masterpiece. "At last the moon rose and it was time for the music to begin."

Childhood's End

"Too many books," said my Beloved Spouse. Not for the first time, of course, but now she turned her baleful gaze upon piles of Dr. Seuss and Gail Gibbons and James Stevenson, five or six Commander Toads and Magic School Buses, several dozen paperbacks about shy forest creatures, dinosaurs, and outer space.

"You," said my gentle dove, "I have given up on. You're hopeless. But our children, my children, will not have their rooms overrun by old books they no longer need. Isn't it enough that I have to put up with these rodents?" added my sweetest one, pointing to the gerbil and the frog. "And there must be enough loose Legos around here to build an addition to this house—which we sorely need, by the way." Naturally, I expostulated. "Boopsie-woopsie, you're just not used to boys. They need a certain amount of clutter, just to feel relaxed. Probably something to do with the X chromosome," I added, with a thoughtful, scientific air. Wrong approach. Terribly wrong. "That's the Y chromosome, you nitwit! I want these shelves reorganized, and I want it done now."

"But, light of my life, there are a lot of treasures here." "Don't give me that. They're all treasures to you. Nobody in this household is still reading *Hop on Pop* or *The Berenstain Bears*. We're beyond primers."

"But I like to look at them every so often. Reminds me of those peaceful evenings, the ones we'll think back upon when we're old and gray, when we'd read aloud to the guys about the wheels on the bus or Angus and the ducks or the tetherball that bounces all over town." I started to grow teary-eyed. "The best years of our lives. And now you want to throw it all on the trash heap."

"Not the trash heap," barked my angel. "The Goodwill. The Salvation Army. That used-book place at the library you spend hours at." I looked stricken. "Don't give me that look." For a moment I thought she was going to add, "young man." I had never before quite realized how schoolmarmish my princess could be. "You take your sons, and sort these shelves."

An hour later, glazed with sweat and dust, I had reduced the overflow by six books in my youngest offspring's personal Jurassic Park and Beanie Baby refuge. By contrast, my oldest son, now a teenager's teenager, had declared that I could cart away all the books in his room, including his English, math, social studies, and Spanish textbooks. Ha, ha. "No kidding, Dad. Just leave my collection of Mad paperbacks." Didn't he at least want to keep this underlined copy of *The Giver* that he'd studied in sixth grade? A look of exasperated astonishment preceded one of despair and resignation. "Dad, you just don't get it, do you?" Calling upon rhetorical skills honed by a lifelong study of Quintilian, I eventually persuaded the ninth-grade sophisticate to retain a few childhood favorites, for auld lang syne, if nothing else. Happily, my middle son declared that he wanted to keep all his books. Stout lad.

Alas, at this moment, my life's partner reappeared in the upstairs hallway. She peered in a bedroom, expecting to see, like some traveler from an antique land, floor space as boundless and bare as the level sands. "This is it? Six books? You spent two hours and got rid of six books?" She repeated this like a mantra. Then something snapped, and her tone softened. "All right, all right. It's not your fault. You can't help yourself. It's the way you are. I've just got to accept this. This is my burden, my cross." Following a tremor of self-control, stoic resolution nobly asserted itself. "I'll just have to do the job myself. You go sort the laundry and put in a load of whites."

Happy to have gotten off so lightly, I skipped downstairs, and in the cool dark of the basement, surrounded by cartons of my books, I poked listlessly through the dirty clothes. I turned on the radio and listened to "My Word" and "My Music." Then I poured in the laundry detergent and bleach, added socks, underwear, and T-shirts, decided to let everything soak a while. Naturally, I peeked—as who would not—into a few of my boxes, including one precariously perched on the dehumidifier. "Well, what do you know?" I said to myself, discovering a copy of Panofsky's *Studies in Iconology.* "Just what I was looking for." An hour later, I turned on the washer and picked up a small stack of books that I obviously needed to move up to the pile by my bedside: Marjorie Hope Nicolson's *Mountain Gloom and Mountain Glory,* a study of "the aesthetics of the infinite" in European literature; a beat-up paperback of Bulwer Lytton's first novel, *Pelham,* one that reprinted the original first edition before he toned down some of his more cutting observations; William Bolitho's famous *Murder for Profit;* a bound volume of the classical journal *Arion;* some old issues of the *Book Collector,* and several other things by Brigid Brophy, Harry Mathews, and Elizabeth Smart. Good stuff.

Whistling "La ci darem la mano" noiselessly to myself, I trudged slowly upstairs with my arms full. And came to a halt. While I had labored in the dank basement, overhead a barbarian queen had loosed her legions upon the bastions of civilization. Children's picture books were piled high in the second-story hallway, like fagots for a martyr's burning. The belle dame of my youth was showing no mercy. "What, what," I spluttered, incredulous. My blonde Valkyrie shot me a glance, her blue eyes cold as steel. "Somebody had to do it. The kids need more room. Of course, you can look through them before they go out, just in case there is something we really do need—which," she growled sweetly, "is not going to be the case, is it?" At this point, my darling noticed the stack I was carrying. "Tell me that those aren't books in your hands."

In the end, I saved some of the treasures. How could anyone in her right mind consider discarding a big retrospective album of Uncle Scrooge comics? Or the two Cat in the Hat classics? Or . . . or . . . or . . . Fortunately, I was able to hide a few dozen pearls beyond price in the garage, where my rosebud won't think to look until spring. Admittedly, the boys' rooms do seem airier and more inviting without books scattered everywhere. But we'll soon change that, don't you worry.

Phaidon's Chariot

Not long before the bloodbath chronicled above, I was blithely lying in bed reading an essay by Clive James titled "On the Library Coffee-Table"; it's in a book called *Snakecharmers in Texas.* James is best known, I suppose, as a British television personality, but he's more than a tube boob, and his literary and cultural essays are always intelligent as well as witty. This particular essay starts off by reviewing a volume by Mario Praz (the great Italian literary scholar) called *An Illustrated History of Interior Decoration,* but quickly settles down to a paean to the art books produced by the Phaidon publishing house during the late 1930s and '40s. "The now lavish use of full colour in art books, a change partly made possible by Phaidon itself, has led to a lot of people, or more likely their grown-up children, releasing an avalanche of old, largely black-and-white illustrated art books on to the second-hand market, where the bookshop owners tend to price them low for resale, on the assumption, no doubt correct, that the casual collector is unlikely to want a book which has been rendered technically obsolete. If the emphasis is on paintings rather than drawings, then any volume whose plates are mostly in monochrome is sure to look like a back number. So for a few pounds you can take your pick between multiple copies of those crown folio albums which often had the double function of introducing a major artist to the general public while allowing a qualified scholar to get his thoughts down, albeit in compressed form." James goes on to describe his acquisition of albums devoted to Vermeer, Raphael, Velazquez, Van Gogh, and Leonardo, of works of Egyptian history and studies of self-portraiture, of the smaller crown octavo volumes by various learned notables, including the Dutch medievalist Johan Huizinga (writing about Erasmus). He praises Phaidon's printing, the paper, and the quality of the gravure reproductions. "Books about art, they were works of art in themselves. Collecting them now, I feel like a buyer for the Pierpont Morgan Library commissioned to make a hoard of all the best illuminated hours, except that the cost is negligible and they belong to me instead of Morgan."

Even before I finished reading James's essay, I could feel the book-longing rising fast within me. Hadn't I seen an old Phaidon edition of Tiepolo at a Silver Spring bookshop? Certainly there must be a lot of these older art books around Washington. Happily, like many liberal arts majors, I already owned a few: Burckhardt's *Civilization of the Renaissance,* Berenson on the Italian painters. But I yearned to turn up a copy of Max J. Friedlander's *On Art and Connoisseurship,* which James calls "one of the best books of criticism in any field that I have ever read," or of the Phaidon edition of the *Journal of Delacroix,* "which ideally should be owned in no other way."

Ah, connoisseurship, 'tis thou hast ravished me! Seeing the names of these old European scholars and their works, I soon found myself thinking about Harper Torchbooks, that amazing 1960s trade paperback series devoted to serious historical scholarship: the art essays of Erwin Panofsky; Jean Seznec's *Survival of the Pagan Gods;* E. R. Curtius on the Latin Middle Ages; a dazzling Festschrift for Ernst Cassirer, *Philosophy and History;* Paul Kristeller on Renaissance thought . . . Just to hold such books in your hands was a liberal education. These men (and comparable women—Frances Yates, Marjorie Nicolson, Margaret Schlauch, Rosamond Tuve) were so smart, so formidably educated. That their scholarship is nowadays half-forgotten seems to me a pity, if not a disgrace.

Ah, well. Still, this winter I can look at the pictures in my newly acquired Phaidon editions, then slowly linger over their editors' leisurely introductions. The prose will be stately, thick with recondite allusions to classical motifs and Christian symbolism; I will feel as though I were back in college, listening to a lecture on early Netherlandish painting or southern Baroque art. . . . But before long, I will doubtless hear the throbbing whine of an electric guitar, or a mincing high-pitched voice chanting "I'm a Barbie girl, in a Barbie world." Then my children and their friends will swarm into the room, the phone will ring, the dog bark, the TV go on, the computer games start blasting, and my lovely Phaidon editions will be returned, tenderly, to a bookshelf. Or possibly to a box. In the basement. Sigh.

The One and the Many

Among the tenderest scenes in literature are those in which a benevolent, often elderly scholar shuffles off to a snug little study to reread for the nth time some favorite book. There he or she, with a sigh of anticipatory pleasure, takes down from the shelf a much-loved copy of *Pride and Prejudice* or *The Decline and Fall of the Roman Empire* or Boswell's *Life of Johnson*. In years past such people might be referred to as the man—or more rarely, the woman—"of one book," and were frequently the occasion for a dire warning: Make any single volume a personal scripture and some kind of gleaming fanaticism was sure to result. The model here, of course, was the hellfire preacher who could quote his Bible by chapter and verse as he thunderously delivered sinful unbelievers into the hands of a God even angrier than he was. But there are other examples too: the young Maoist with his *Little Red Book,* the pale Joycean with his marked-up copy of *Finnegans Wake.*

Being one who has read thousands of books—a statement that sounds more than a little grotesque even to me—I have always secretly wished to be a one-title guy. E. B. White, for instance, toted *Walden* around in his pocket for years; he could quote Thoreau, aptly, humorously, on just about any subject. Just so, the grandmother in Proust's *In Search of Lost Time* could cite the letters of Madame de Sevigné, and the house steward in *The*

Moonstone the wisdom of Robinson Crusoe. Samuel Johnson famously recommended that would-be writers devote their days and nights solely to
Addison's essays. Even Alexander the Great, who admittedly didn't have
quite as much reading material to choose from as we do, never left for
Central Asia without his bejeweled copy of Homer's *Iliad.* And, of course,
a World War I soldier always went over the top with a compact edition of
Palgrave's *Golden Treasury of English Verse* snug in his breast pocket, ideally
situated for stopping the odd bullet or piece of shrapnel.

There have been occasions when I've daydreamed about reducing my
library to just one small bookcase of essential volumes, maybe even a single
shelf. Surely this would make one feel light and clean, like a bather in a
Whitman poem. In a sense, of course, the books that reside permanently
on my bedside night table represent just such a selection—the Bible, the
Concise Oxford English Dictionary, the five-volume Auden and Pearson *Poets of the English Language,* Montaigne's essays, *The Oxford Book of Aphorisms,* Jules Renard's journal, F. W. Bateson's *Guide to English Literature,*
Brewer's Dictionary of Phrase and Fable, Lempriere's *Classical Dictionary,*
and a dozen or so others. (I have a crowded night-table.) But these are all,
for the most part, browsing books, classic references more suitable for in-
somniac diversion than for passionate devotion.

No, what I'd like is to possess a really well-thumbed edition of, say,
Robert Burton's *Anatomy of Melancholy* or Saint-Simon's memoirs or Plato's
dialogues, books that would stand up to repeated readings and provide
every kind of mental nourishment, as well as a fund of apt quotation and
an oasis of spiritual consolation. I would turn daily to this chosen volume,
marking favorite passages, scribbling on the endpapers, dog-earing pages,
eventually binding together the loosened signatures with a thick blue rubber band. I might even keep a notebook, one of those large ledger-like
tomes associated with Bob Cratchit, in which I would record at length the
noble sentiments and philosophical divagations inspired by my favored
title. When I had occasion to address audiences, my speeches would be
thoroughly salted, peppered, and leavened throughout with anecdotes and
bons mots taken from my unrivaled knowledge of, say, *Tristram Shandy* or
Macaulay's *History of England.* Eventually I would come to be regarded as
the leading authority on My Book, periodically refusing attractive offers
from university presses to compile variorum editions or annotate paperbacks for college survey courses. Naturally, sometime in the far, far distant
future, full of years and the kind of serene wisdom one acquires from the
diligent perusal of a classic, I would be buried with my now-tattered life's
companion, as thousands mourn.

Such is the fantasy. Unfortunately, like most readers, I lack the single-mindedness needed to make it a reality. To begin with, I'm not precisely what you would call a rereader, except of poetry. I try to go through novels and nonfiction slowly, with great attention to detail, flipping back and forth to check points, aiming to "see" the book as a whole. Since I mark favorite passages, I can and sometimes do pick up a book to refresh my memory of its contents. Still, I don't suppose there are more than a score of titles I have ever reread from cover to cover.

Not that I don't want to reread more. Oscar Wilde used to say that "if one cannot enjoy reading a book over and over again, there is no use in reading it at all." Who would doubt him? I'd love to be an anchorite of literature, a St. Jerome devoted to a single particular scripture. But in truth I'm a flighty creature, always darting from one bright blossom to the next; I contemplate my groaning bookshelves and see only fresh fields and pastures new. How is it, I ask myself, that I have managed to live so long without any firsthand knowledge of *The Story of the Stone* or *I promessi sposi* or the longer poems of Arthur Hugh Clough? With such treats still before me, how can I turn away and go back to works I have already read, no matter how deeply enjoyed?

❧

Of course, it is utterly ludicrous of me to say that I already know, say, Thomas Mann's *Magic Mountain*. I haven't looked at the novel since devouring it one long-ago summer when I was 15. I can see myself slumped in one of our heavy wooden yard chairs during a week of sweltering evenings. I remember that I had checked the book out of the library because of Clifton Fadiman's enthusiastic essay about it in *The Lifetime Reading Plan*—"one of the most magnificent works of art produced by our unhappy century." I recall the X-ray taken of the heroine's tubercular chest. I can dredge up the names of some of the main characters—Hans Castorp, Peeperkorn, Settembrini, Naphta. There were, I recollect, a good many discussions of art, politics, love, and similar high-minded matters. And I am certain that the novel concludes with Hans Castorp leaving the sanitarium to fight in World War I. Unfortunately, these few altogether paltry sentences sum up virtually everything I know about *The Magic Mountain*. How can I say that I've read it?

Here is when I begin to grow depressed and start daydreaming about knowing at least one book inside out. Think of any novel you've ever read, and what do you really possess? Perhaps a few vague memories of its plot, characters, and tone; more likely than not, you remember, in the most general way, only how much or how little you liked the book. In truth, next to nothing. Just so, detective-story fans regularly grumble about being halfway through some Agatha Christie whodunit before realizing that they've already pored over its clues and suspects before. I know professional book reviewers who cannot call to mind the titles of novels they once acclaimed as masterpieces.

Alas, one carries away so little from even the greatest works of art. Of the longer classics I have read more than once and, in some instances, actually taught to students—*Hamlet; The Divine Comedy; Walden; Huckleberry Finn; Crime and Punishment;* a few others—I am shocked at how little I retain, especially for one often credited with a good memory: only a handful of quotations, a spotty sense of plot. Obviously, were I to open these books again, my understanding of them would prove—I hope—deeper than this: Familiarity with the action allows one, at the very least, to focus on the artistry. But stay away for a few years and even the most analyzed text utterly vanishes from the conscious mind. For example, I read Stendhal's autobiographical *Vie de Henry Brulard* ten or eleven times during 1974–76; I literally studied my Gallimard edition to pieces. Yet what remains of that beloved, much-lived-with book now, twenty years later? Only the memory of Stendhal's autumnal sensibility—passionate, disappointed, and forgiving.

The memory of a tone, the rhythm of an author's sentences, the sorrow we felt on a novel's last page—perhaps that is all that we can expect to keep from books. As we turn their pages, they amuse/shock/inspire/console/instruct us; but after we return them to our shelves or the public library, they linger in our souls only like the distant images of childhood. Years ago our elementary school was the burning center of the universe, a place of anxiety, triumph, and heartbreak. Now it's just a building whose windows we peer into on an idle Saturday afternoon. Once upon a time this playground may have helped shape our lives, but today it's simply the place we walk our dogs.

So is it with the novels and nonfiction we read long ago and now only vaguely recall. But while we can never, barring the occasional Proustian *intermittence du coeur,* go back to elementary school again, we can still reopen *Great Expectations* or *Invisible Man* and plunge once more into the lived experience itself. Perhaps poems and stories, like paintings and music, truly exist only when we are actively engaged with them. Afterwards they lose their substance, grow wispy and vague, or find themselves diminished to little more than a few cold facts. The actual art, all that makes a great work funny, sorrowful, and real, fades away like a dream at morning.

So when I think back over the books I have loved, I seldom feel any unalloyed pleasure. This copy of *The Good Soldier* made me weep, and now

I merely remember its opening sentence and Ford Madox Ford's twisty narrative technique. I can only hope that deep within me, in my soul or subconscious, more of the novel lingers on. Only by rereading it could I reexperience its quite overwhelming artistic and emotive power. Should I therefore put aside my current book? Or should I instead rush to, oh, *The Good Soldier Schweik*? It does seem a pity never to have opened one of the great comic masterpieces of the world. Or maybe instead of *Schweik* I ought to reread Shaw? It would be lovely to listen once more to the banter of "Man and Superman." On second—or is that third—thought, I definitely should look into Carol Shields's award-winning *Stone Diaries*. Only a fool would miss out on the literature of his own time.

Amid such an internal tohubohu, is it any wonder that I think fondly of the man of one book, the hedgehog who—in the phrase made famous by Isaiah Berlin—knows one big thing and doesn't need to know any other? In very low moments I sometimes think that a passion for omnivorous reading has seduced me into a lifetime of one-night stands, while the less promiscuous have managed to find a single true and more fulfilling love. But it's too late for me and my kind to change now, no matter how much we may yearn for those carpet slippers and one or two well-worn volumes. How, after all, can I resist that flashy new thriller or sloe-eyed biography, let alone the new novel that promises hitherto unimagined pleasures? Sirens all. Of the reading of many books there is no end.

❧

Holding with Coleridge that the reading of
novels entails over a period of time the
complete destruction of the powers of the
mind.
                              —Anthony Burgess

Commencement Advice

Anyone who's ever gone to school is likely to feel a certain jauntiness come the end of June. Summer is here. No more classes, no more books, no more teacher's dirty looks. Swimming pools and parks beckon; trips to the mountains, beaches, or grandparents loom. The world, once more, seems, as Matthew Arnold said, "a land of dreams, so various, so beautiful, so new."

For a 17- or 18-year-old graduate, that elation is multiplied a hundredfold. School is not only out for the summer; it's over with for good. Oh, for many there's college in the offing, but that's somehow different: an Eden of parties and romance, broken hearts that rapidly heal, kegs of foaming beer, lazy Saturday afternoons at the stadium watching football, and—after four years of mind-numbing, dizzying bliss—a degree, rapidly followed by a high-paying job, a Porsche 911, and that first million. So goes the pastoral daydream. Alas, our barefoot boy or girl will discover soon enough that the world is actually, as Arnold also reminded us, a "darkling plain / Swept with confused alarms of struggle and flight, / Where ignorant armies clash by night."

Literature offers various aesthetic pleasures, but it has also traditionally provided instruction and counsel on how to live, confront adversity, and find solace. The moral essay—from Marcus Aurelius to Montaigne to Matthew Arnold—has a long tradition, and one that still lingers on in bestselling manuals about the lessons we learn from kindergarten and the soul's need for chicken soup. Over the years I have been an occasional skimmer of such guides but have found that most of my own ground rules for better living—or at least for getting through life—derive from some of the less obvious byways of my reading. Since commencement speakers traditionally offer advice to the young in June, here, in no particular order, are a dozen of the quotations that one reader calls to mind in moments of confusion, stress, and sorrow.

1. "Life is trouble." So proclaims the hero of Nikos Kazantzakis's novel *Zorba the Greek.* Struggle, conflict, tension, disappointment, failure—these are all signs that one is alive. If you try new things, some of them simply aren't going to work out. But one ought to shine in use, and the all too common desire for a Lotos-land existence of endless summer is really an unacknowledged death wish. Expect the worst, says Carl Sandburg in his forgotten poem "The People, Yes," and you won't be disappointed. Life is trouble. Only death is no trouble at all.

2. Keep an "interior citadel." The philosopher-emperor Marcus Aurelius passed much of his reign on battlefields. But even on the fraying edges of the Roman Empire he always strove to maintain a stoic's inner tranquility, amounting almost to indifference to the world outside. He accomplished this by retreating regularly to an "interior citadel," a place in the mind where he could fortify himself against what Hamlet, that failed Danish stoic, called the "slings and arrows of outrageous fortune." From there, atop the crenelated ramparts, one can metaphorically look down on troubles from a great height, serene and detached. As Satan once observed, the mind is its own place, and in itself can make a Heaven of Hell, a Hell of Heaven.

3. "Constant work is the law of art as it is of life." Balzac followed every word of this sentence to the letter, burning many candles at both ends so that he could write all night the magnificent, melodramatic novels of *La Comédie humaine.* If you hope to accomplish something worthwhile during your time on earth, you will have to work. As a young man or woman, your goal should be to find the kind of job, craft, profession, or useful activity that you are willing to marry, till death do you part. After all, to miss out on one's proper work may be the greatest mistake of a lifetime. If you are born to be an artist, don't settle for being a mere lawyer or stockbroker. Compared to satisfying work, even pleasure pales to insignificance.

4. "Do what you are doing." This, I believe, is both a Jesuit motto and a

Zen imperative. That is, if you are making dinner or playing soccer or writing a memo, really focus your whole being on just that. Do it well. Thereby, you invest even the most trivial activities with significance, turning the mundane into the spiritual, perhaps even the ecstatic. A monk tending a garden at dawn is praying. By concerted acts of attention, you can make everything you do a kind of poetry.

5. "The most effective weapon of any man is to have reduced his share of histrionics to a minimum." This was the watchword of André Malraux, the larger-than-life novelist, adventurer, art historian, politician. Malraux believed in maturity, in being a grown-up. Our natural tendency is to exaggerate our sorrows, anger, and desires. But deep within we know that we are overreacting, indeed overacting. We get caught up in the situation, carried away by our own pleasure in personal melodrama. So we perform for the audience, sometimes an audience of only one. Instead of such staginess, we should remind ourselves that clarity is as much a mental and emotional virtue as it is a stylistic one. Do we really feel this riot of emotion? Is there any point to all this brouhaha? Should a grown-up behave like this?

6. "Cover your tracks." Bertolt Brecht made this the refrain to one of his political poems. When you go into the big city, he says, know that you are never safe; people will be watching every move you make. Your only hope of getting out alive is to "cover your tracks." "Whatever you say, don't say it twice / If you find your ideas in anyone else, disown them. / The man who hasn't signed anything, who has left no picture / Who was not there, who said nothing: / How can they catch him? / Cover your tracks." For me, this phrase stands as the rough equivalent to the more famous "Trust no one" formula of *The X-Files*. In fact, one should trust everyone but give away nothing that really matters—except to those who love you. "Cover your tracks" means to be careful, destroy your rough drafts, and never let them see you sweat.

7. "A thing is only worth so much time." Parents tend to specialize in certain slogans, and this was my father's favorite. It is a doctrine that needs to be applied with caution, because some things—painting a picture, writing a poem—require that we spend whatever time is needed to do them right. But many activities can needlessly absorb immense chunks of our lives. You can spend every Saturday afternoon for a year test-driving new cars before you pick the wrong one anyway. You can agonize for weeks whether to go for a physical or not. You can work fourteen-hour days downtown. But should you? Aren't there more important matters to attend to? "The cost of a thing," wrote Thoreau, "is the amount of what I will call life

which is required to be exchanged for it immediately or in the long run."
This leads on to the following, associated motto:

8. "Get on with your work." At moments of emotional crisis, people sometimes just want to plop down and cry. You can do this for a minute or two,
and probably should, but also remember that, as Disraeli said, "Grief is the
agony of an instant: the indulgence of grief the blunder of a life." When I
grow melancholy—the occupational disease of writers—I start doing
household chores: I wash dishes and clothes, dust and vacuum, reorganize
my bureau, box up books. While performing such activities, I'm allowed to
be as depressed as I want, provided I keep on working. That's the key.
Usually, within a few hours I feel better. At the very least I end up with a
clean house.

9. "We must laugh before we are happy, for fear of dying without having
laughed at all." A corollary to this insightful observation from La Bruyere
is William James's dictum that if you act as though you were happy, even
when you're not, your mind will eventually trick itself into a cheerier mood.
What better gift, though, could the gods bestow than a sense of humor?
"One can pretend to be serious," said the French playwright Sacha Guitry,
"but one can't pretend to be witty." If you don't naturally possess a light-
hearted spirit, at least try to acquire a sense of irony and compassion, and
learn to smile at your own foolishness—and the world's. As a dear friend
used to remind me, self-pity is most unattractive.

10. "Live all you can. It's a mistake not to," announces Lambert Strether in
a climactic moment of Henry James's late masterpiece *The Ambassadors*. As
the years roll by, it is tempting to settle for a half-life of routine, order, and
accommodation. But all of us ought to strive to be overreachers, ever restless, ever adventurous. T. S. Eliot said, "Old men should be explorers," but
so should young men and women and 50-year-olds. Henry James also provides excellent advice for cultivating one's spirit: "Be one on whom nothing is lost." That is, pay attention, observe, learn, be as sensitive and re-
sponsive as your nature permits.

11. Choose some heroes and imitate them. To me, Montaigne, Samuel
Johnson, Stendhal, Jane Austen, Chekhov, and Colette are not merely great
writers; they are also wonderfully humane and sympathetic human beings.
Shrewd, self-aware, free of cant, urbane, kindly—they are my secular saints.
Once you have imbibed the personalities of such master spirits, you can
turn to them as guides through life's moral thickets and ethical swamps.
What would Samuel Johnson say in this situation? What counsel would
Colette give? How would Stendhal react?

12. "Memento mori." We must all die, and doubtless it will be on a sunny day when the whole world seems young and fresh. No one likes to think about that last bad quarter-hour, but it will come round eventually. Theologians in earlier centuries insisted that we meditate on death, so that we might review our lives, amending them where needed. That same practice can help even the most profane among us. If I were to die now, would I be wracked with regrets? Are there matters I should have attended to? Be prepared. In one of Tolstoy's parables, a peasant is plowing a field. The narrator asks the old man what he would do if he knew that Death was coming to take him away within the hour. The peasant answers, "Keep plowing." How many of us could offer a comparably serene reply?

So there's my advice to this year's graduates. Easy enough to give, I realize, and hard to follow—as I know, too. But let me conclude with one strongly personal plea, making a baker's dozen: Read the classics. The world is awash in bestsellers and frivolous nonfiction, but just as our bodies need physical exercise, so our brains need demanding books. Set aside some part of the day for real reading. Work your way through Plato; be touched by Cather's *A Lost Lady* and shocked by Rousseau's *Confessions;* feel the burning fever of *Death in Venice;* listen in on Samuel Johnson's repartee, and marvel before *One Hundred Years of Solitude.* Books, like great art and music and love, make us feel passionately alive. And isn't that what we all want?

Four Novels and a Memoir

People often complain that modern bestsellers are too long. After all, who really has time for even a 300-page book? Happily, in the case of the four popular novels and one uplifting memoir "excerpted" below, you don't need to read anything except the opening paragraphs to savor the entire work.

The Michelangeli Cadenza

(Thriller)

When the girl came out of the consulate, Richter immediately picked up the Beretta. The rain was sheeting down harder now and it would be a difficult shot. Should he risk moving in closer? His cloudy blue eyes squinted down the deserted, cobblestone streets. Nobody in sight. Why not?

Hunched inside his trenchcoat, Richter stepped out of the doorway and limped toward the white Peugeot. He couldn't help shivering a little. Marseille was supposed to be sunny, filled with laughing whores and drunken sailors. Instead he might be in Vienna or even Stockholm. Just his luck. Maybe it would be warmer in Athens. "Mademoiselle," he rasped. "You dropped this." Rampal's secretary was only a few feet from the car. As her eyes went instinctively to the portfolio under her arm, Richter hurried closer, lifted the gun to the back of her head and fired. The storm drowned out most of the sound. Every cloud, thought the old assassin, has its silver lining. After a moment, he removed the keys from the once pretty blonde's grip and picked up the portfolio. If there wasn't much traffic he might have time for a brandy before the meeting with Signor Pollini.

Just as the Peugeot disappeared around the corner, a light went on in the consulate and a well-dressed man with a salt-and-pepper mustache appeared at a second-floor window. M. Grumiaux looked down at the little *putain* dead on the rain-swept sidewalk and smiled thinly, then sighed. One more gone, and only six left. Pity it had had to be Anne-Sophie though. The memory of her silken underclothes rustled briefly through his mind. Ah, well, it really couldn't be helped. The Plan must go forward.

Brighton Belle

(Regency Romance)

"Never," sobbed Miss Jane Ravenel as she flung herself onto the chaise longue and buried her tear-streaked face in a Wedgwood-blue pillow embroidered with scenes from the Rape of Proserpina. Surely her heart would burst. To think that her own father would consent to such an absolutely monstrous arrangement. Marry Lord Randolph! Never. Not if he were the Prince Regent himself.

"I'm sorry, my dear, but you must try to see matters from my perspective. Everything in this house is entailed. At my death, which surely cannot be far distant, Lord Randolph would assume ownership of the entire estate—not only the house and its chattels, but the pasture lands, the London apartments, even the village. You, the prettiest girl in all Devonshire, would be left with nothing. I've always wanted the best for you, Jane, so don't pout and carry on so. Lord Randolph may be mature in years, but even at 60 he is one of the best catches in England. Show a little spirit, child. Marriage to so grand and vigorous a nobleman will surely be a great adventure."

Adventure! If Papa wanted her to lead a life of adventure, so be it. But let him marry Lord Randolph, not her! With a shake of Titian-hued curls, Jane scurried to her bedchamber, slipped off her day frock, and pulled out a small parcel secreted in the back of the old armoire. Last month she'd had Billy Blake the stable lad buy some simple, coarse apparel at one of the village shops. By this time tomorrow the family would be mourning the tragic drowning of 15-year-old Jane Ravenel. So sad! And she so young and beautiful, milord. Meanwhile, young "Jack Robinson" would be flying along the highways, sitting up top with the driver on the mail coach to Brighton. Brighton! With any luck at all there'd be a ball—with ices!—at the Pavilion this very Saturday night.

Understanding Poetry

(Academic Comedy)

"And so, in conclusion, we may point to the absolute privileging of the male gaze as the unexpressed purpose of the 18th-century connoisseur. Behind the locked doors of country house libraries or safely ensconced in cabinets of curiosities, these self-proclaimed virtuosi would unrestrainedly indulge in the basest of solitary pleasures. In the end, the so-called *objet de virtu* was nothing less than the stimulus for private vice."

With this flourish, Angelica folded her printout and sat down, as the other members of the seminar politely applauded. After a moment's silence, they all turned toward Dr. Allworthy—"Just call me Jeff"—and waited for his critique.

"Well, Angelica, I want to thank you for that very interesting paper. Very interesting indeed. At the very least, you open up some, uh, suggestive lines of thought." The young professor smiled at his little joke. "And yet there are a few points I'd like to raise with you and the class."

The course was an introductory one, "Modalities of the Corporeal in 18th-century Literature," and it wasn't going well. The semester was more than half over and most of the presentations had struck Allworthy as tired, unoriginal stuff. "Cultivating (Secret) Gardens: Masturbatory Candor in *Candide*," "Gulliver Unravels: Breaking the Fetters of Swiftian Discourse," and "Ho, Ho, Ho: Earthy Humor in *The Rake's Progress*"—not to mention "What the Doctor Ordered: Samuel Johnson and Sado-Masochism." There'd even been a particularly sad effort: "Is A. Pope Catholic? Penitential Imagery in the *Epistle to Dr. Arbuthnot*." He'd had hopes that the sexy Angelica—his prize student—might really show some spark of originality. Last fall in Cultural Studies 101, she'd delivered an astonishing paper on the communist element in Hurston's *Mules and Men:* "The Marx of Zora." But now this, this pitiful, conventional effort! At least he had next year off for a sabbatical at Bellaggio, where he hoped to finish his masterwork: "Displacement, Diaspora and Dismemberment in Dryden's *Absalom and Achitophel*." That was one book he knew would shake up the profession. He could almost see Morris Zapp's glowing review in *Diacritics*. "Not since Lacan's seminar on "The Purloined Letter." . . . The gnomic brilliance of a Canetti . . . Perspicuous . . . Merits the Christian Gauss award and even the

Foucault Prize." With a start Allworthy pulled himself away from his happy daydream just as the letter arrived from the Swedish Academy. "Now, Angelica, how does your theory account for, say, the pervasive imagery of sexual acquiescence in *The Rape of the Lock,* or even the crude Shakespearean punning in Gray's title, *Elegy in a Country Churchyard*? Do we not in both cases discern a surreptitious profanation of the textual that cannot be ascribed solely to. . . ."

Tears on My Pillow

(Southern Memoir)

I was only 9 when the state police finally shot my Daddy. Mama-Jean and I hadn't seen him for a couple of weeks when all unexpected we got a knock at the front door one summer's night. Before answering, Mama-Jean wrapped herself in that old maroon bathrobe she used to wear all the time and started sucking away on a Wint-o-Green Lifesaver to hide her whiskey breath. It made me laugh. No bitty piece of candy would've done her much good. That woman had a sour, unwashed smell about her that always made me think of a coon dog that'd been rolling in its own filth after treeing a skunk.

Even though I called her Mama-Jean, she weren't what you'd call my real Ma. Seems that my actual birth Mama run off with a Fuller Brush salesman from up Raleigh way. That sounds like a joke, I know, but it's God's own truth. After a while the poor woman just couldn't take any more of Daddy's meanness. He'd stumble home to the trailer late at night, with his shirt tail out and pee stains on his pants, and before you'd rubbed the sand from your eyes he'd be cussin' away at me and Bobbie Ann or hittin' hard at Mama. He even bit her something bad a time or two. Course, he could be even worse when he'd been drinking.

Mama finally up and left when I was 3 or 4. Who could blame her? Years later, I tried to track her down, just to say hello like, but she must've changed her name because nobody in Raleigh ever seemed to have heard of any Dorothea Brooke. Sometimes late at night, when I used to shake and scream in the detox ward, I'd imagine I was just a little kid again and Mama was rocking me slowly and I could feel her warm soft breasts as she hummed a lullaby. It would calm me a little and for a while I'd forget about all the smoke-filled honky-tonks, roadhouses and bars. Two-bit chippy! I'd show them, I'd show them all. Someday Tracy Sue McAllister would be the biggest star in Nashville since Loretta Lynn.

Sanctum Sanctorum

(Classic Horror)

Of the numerous shining luminaries at St. Athanasius College the world had long counted James Pethel the very brightest. Professor of ancient Sumerian, holder of the much coveted Aickman Chair, corresponding member of learned societies throughout Europe, the Reverend Pethel had, at the time this story begins, devoted more than four decades to archaeological study of the ancient stone circles at Yog-Sothoth, deep in the valley of the Euphrates. Over the years patient labor had uncovered much, but the deeper secret of these ruins continued to elude the tireless, but rapidly aging researcher. Despite an increasingly frail constitution, Pethel steadfastly refused to abandon his field work. "I have devoted my life to Yog-Sothoth," the professor told newspapers on the occasion of his 62nd birthday, "and it would seem to have been just so much wasted effort. And yet. Last week we discovered a chamber of exceptional size just beneath the central altar stone. I cannot help but feel that the answer to many mysteries lies nearly within our grasp."

Oh, how innocent are the ways of scholars! Certainly Pethel and his team—the brilliant papyrologist Filboid Studge, the explorer Sir Hector Munro, and the noted Anglo-German philologist Karl-Dietrich Ward—should have foreseen the events of the night of October 11–12. At the very least they might have sent Lady Carmilla and her young daughter Sylvia away while there was still time. The fools, the stupid, stupid fools. The theosophist Sredni Vashtar had tried to warn them at the seance in Cairo, but they rudely disdained him as little better than a charlatan. Yet surely they might have remembered the fate of the French antiquaries Vautrin and Rastignac, those hapless discoverers of Yog-Sothoth back in the earthquake-wracked summer of '46. When the Italian expedition eventually stumbled across Vautrin in the desert he was gnawing hungrily at the stump of his own left arm, while Rastignac reverently intoned, again and again, a single word in an unknown tongue: "Niripsa, Niripsa." The pair spent the rest of their broken lives in Charenton. The least tinkle of music would send them into the most violent paroxysms, and neither could ever again bear the sight of an ordinary leather shoe.

The October Country

Here's how a story ought to begin:

"The talk had veered round to runes and curses and witches, one bleak December evening, where a few of us sat warm in easy chairs round the cheery fire of the Billiards Club. 'Do you believe in witches?' one of us said to Jorkens. 'It isn't what I believe in that matters so much,' said Jorkens; 'only what I have seen.'"

Would anyone, could anyone, willingly stop reading at this point? Not that there aren't other good ways to introduce a cozy tale of mystery and the supernatural. The mere titles of M. R. James's "ghost stories of an antiquary" set off ominous reverberations: "Casting the Runes," "A Warning to the Curious," "The Tractate Middoth." My favorite is the quietly haunting "Oh, Whistle and I'll Come to You, My Lad." In these tales of faded Latin manuscripts, revenants, and necromancers, a little learning can be a very dangerous thing indeed.

Or consider the rush of events that opens G. K. Chesterton's "Tremendous Adventures of Major Brown" (from *The Club of Queer Trades*). The genial Major Brown goes for his late-afternoon constitutional, admires some pansies, and is told that on the other side of a garden wall lies a wonderful display of the flowers. When he hoists himself up to take a look, he finds that the pansy bed spells out "Death to Major Brown." Shaken and puzzled, Brown enters the manor house, where he encounters a beautiful, rather "elfin" lady who tells him she must keep her face turned to the street until 6 P.M.—at which point a raspy voice cries out, "Major Brown, Major Brown, where does the jackal dwell?" All these riddles, I should add, merely set up a tremendously zestful entertainment, half *Through the Looking-Glass,* half *Thirty-Nine Steps.*

Lord Dunsany's "club" tales of Joseph Jorkens, ghost stories by writers like M. R. James, Sheridan Le Fanu, and Algernon Blackwood, Stevenson's *New Arabian Nights,* the adventures of Sherlock Holmes or Father Brown—these are the proper books for damp autumn evenings, when we yearn for a tale that, in Sir Philip Sidney's words, holdeth children from play, and old men from the chimney corner.

Thirty-five years ago on a Saturday in late October, my parents announced that they would be visiting relatives that evening with my sisters. Yes, I might stay home alone to read. The afternoon soon grew dull, gray, threatening rain. With a dollar clutched in my fist, I dashed to Whalen's drugstore, where I bought two or three candy bars, a box of Cracker Jack, a bottle of Orange Crush. Once my family had driven off, I dragged down a blanket from my bed, spread it on a reclining chair next to a bright floor lamp, carefully arranged my goodies near to hand, turned off all the other house lights, and crawled expectantly under the covers with an emergency flashlight and a paperback copy of *The Hound of the Baskervilles*—just as the heavens began to boom with thunder and the rain to thump against the curtained windows.

Under these near to ideal conditions, I read and read, more than a little scared, learning the origin of the terrible curse of the Baskervilles. At the end of chapter 2, the excitement escalated unbearably. Sherlock Holmes and Dr. Watson have just been told how the latest Baskerville has been found dead, apparently running away from the safety of his own house. Their informant pauses, then adds, hesitantly, that near the body he had spotted footprints on the ground. "What kind?" eagerly inquires the great detective; to which question he receives the immortal answer: "Mr. Holmes, they were the footprints of a gigantic hound." I shivered with fearful pleasure, scrunched further down under my blanket, and took another bite of my Baby Ruth.

Every year since, come October, I yearn to replicate that almost mythical evening. One year, for instance, the Oxford Sherlock Holmes—nine handsome, hand-sized volumes—encouraged me to reread *A Study in Scarlet,* in which the original dynamic duo first meet. There, you may recall, Holmes needs but a glance to deduce seemingly everything about Watson, while the good doctor must resort to listing Holmes's areas of expertise and ignorance (e.g., profound knowledge of poisons, none of the solar system) in a vain attempt to guess his profession.

No doubt a sign of age, I found almost as much pleasure in Owen Dudley Edwards's learned introduction and capacious notes as in the story itself. Edwards relates the genesis of Holmes, the influence of Johnson, Carlyle, and Scott on Conan Doyle, the possibility that the book's title might be an inventive translation of the French mystery writer Gaboriau's *L'affaire Lerouge,* and much else. Unlike most students of the "Canon," Edwards and his associate editors make no pretense of believing that Holmes, Prof. Moriarty, and Irene Adler actually lived. In his invaluable *Annotated Sherlock Holmes,* W. S. Baring-Gould actually rearranged the stories to follow the supposed chronology of Holmes's life. Baring-Gould's notes also drew heavily, and delightfully, on the researches of donnish Sherlockians (e.g., Ronald Knox's groundbreaking paper "Studies in the Literature of Sherlock Holmes") and the ingenious scholarship of the Baker Street Irregulars.

If you are already completely at home with Holmes, a condition worth aspiring to, or if you yearn for slightly stronger stimulants, turn to the English ghost story. I fondly remember the worn library copy of *Tales to Be Told in the Dark,* edited by Basil Davenport, in which I first shuddered before the sublime terror of Algernon Blackwood's campfire standard, "The Wendigo," listened to the calmly logical voice of growing madness in Charlotte Perkins Gilman's "The Yellow Wallpaper" (now a feminist classic), and marveled at the artistry of those perfectly mitered short shorts, W. F. Harvey's "August Heat" and W. W. Jacobs's "The Monkey's Paw." In recent years, though, I confess to preferring the neglected spooky tales of Vernon Lee (especially "Amour Dure") and Robert Aickman's uncanny allegories (e.g., "The Stains").

One contemporary writer who deserves to be better known among adults is the late Robert Westall, a celebrated children's author—*The Machine-Gunners; The Kingdom by the Sea. Demons and Shadows: The Ghostly Best Stories of Robert Westall* offers some superb chillers in the understated English mode. In "Rachel and the Angel," for instance, a winged being appears to a teenaged girl in an empty church. Zaphael announces that the girl's village will be utterly obliterated, like Sodom, for its iniquity; so like Abraham before her, Rachel challenges the angel, asking that the city be spared if she can find a righteous person among its residents. Alas, even the most exemplary citizens turn out to be all too human. Only at the last moment does the despondent Rachel discover a means to thwart this pitiless angel of doom. The result is a powerful, disturbing story.

Bookish Fantasies

The personal ads for almost any newspaper or magazine dangle before our widening eyes the most lurid and delicious fantasies. Sadly, however, few of these address the pulpy dream-life of the ordinary reader and writer. Yet the bookish fantasize about leather as much as the next man (or woman), though that leather is, of course, liable to be a full morocco binding, with blind-stamped decorations and a hubbed spine. Naturally, other tastes may be more earthy (a craving for trashy, cheap paperbacks from the 1940s), but then almost every book lover has a secret daydream, a favorite literary fantasy . . .

" . . . and you alone truly understand my work: Count me your greatest fan. Sincerely, J. D. Salinger. P.S. Why don't you come up for a visit? The foliage around here is glorious in the fall . . . "

"Dear Nathan Madrid, In 40 years as a senior editor at Knopf, I have never read an unsolicited manuscript with greater pleasure and excitement . . . "

"Speaking professionally, I'm sorry to say that your condition is somewhat worrying, though not serious. What you need is lots of fresh sea air, a long cruise perhaps through the Caribbean or Mediterranean. Basically, you should just lie in a first-class lounge chair and read mysteries and P. G.

Wodehouse for the next two months. I'm sure I can convince your insurance company to foot the bill . . . "

"Dad, I just want to thank you for staying on my case about reading. I really love books now and can't thank you enough, especially considering all the grief I used to give you and Mom . . . "

"Dear Miranda Pascal, on behalf of the Mont Blanc Corporation please accept, absolutely without charge, this limited edition Diplomat fountain pen. It is our small way of honoring you and your work for the public library . . . "

"Hello, Mr. Matson, this is Frontier Volumes and Discs: You're our winner! This Saturday, armed with a grocery cart, you will have one culture-packed quarter-hour to load up on as many books and CDs as you can push to the front of the store . . . "

"Wynton asked me to call: He just loves your poem—may I call you Melanie?—and he's already working on a setting for its wonderful, truly uplifting words. We all feel you speak for an entire generation of African Americans . . . "

"Hey, Chip, this is Sherry down at the library. We've just gotten the new *Oxford English Dictionary* on CD-ROM, and we were wondering whether you might like to take the old thirteen-volume set off our hands . . . "

"Dear Tony, this is Bill Clinton. I've had some tough times since I came to Washington, but I wanted you to know that your pieces on Sunday have been the one gleam of sunshine I could always count on in even my darkest hours."

"You're absolutely right. That was a rare use of the optative. Well, I suppose even a tenured Yale Greek professor can nod occasionally . . . "

"Jack, this is Sonny. Sorry I missed you. Just wanted to tell you that we've got the jacket blurbs lined up from George Steiner, Toni Morrison, John Grisham, Stephen King, and Gabriel García Márquez. I don't think there'll be room for the Byatt and Cornwell, let alone Oprah's . . . "

"Spielberg wants to do the memoir as a kind of intimate art-house film. Harrison Ford is not only hungry but downright ravenous to play you, though DiCaprio will be taking the scenes set in the '60s. How do you feel about Cameron Diaz as your lovely wife . . . "

"Those old books, you can have 'em all if you want. I just need to get rid of this junk from my late mother-in-law's place. What is the Limited Editions Club, anyhow? . . . "

"I'm really dreadfully sorry, Ms. Meyers, but I'm afraid we're going to have to move your poetry reading to a much bigger hall . . . "

"Dear Nathan Madrid, the Oxford symposium on your work in cultural studies will be chaired by Frank Kermode. We hope that that will prove acceptable and regret having suggested John Bayley . . . "

" . . . pay you $10 a word . . . "

"Well, Brian, I generally scribble my initial drafts with a No. 1 Ticonderoga pencil on a cream-colored Fabriano writing bond. My pocket notebooks I buy in Paris from a rather louche stationer near les Halles. Bruce Chatwin told me about the place . . . "

"We will, per your instructions, reserve the usual cabin near the pond. Everyone at Yaddo is looking forward to . . . "

"Hello, Nathan Madrid. This is Chet Hinkle. I'd like to grovel and apologize for calling you a four-eyed bookworm back in fifth grade . . . "

"Oooh! I just love nearsighted intellectuals. When you look at me through those thick tortoise-shell glasses, I just go all melty inside . . . "

"With your permission, the Library of America would be honored to gather your literary journalism of the past twenty years. We envision a volume of approximately 1,000 pages. Happily, Mr. Joseph Epstein has volunteered to compile and introduce the selection . . . "

"I've never seen so many people at a signing. Not even . . . "

"Yes, our experts do confirm that the volume in question is a first printing of Poe's *Tamerlane*. Where did you find it? You must be joking. A thrift store in Beltsville. And what's that you say? You paid a quarter for the better of the two copies . . . "

"Dear Ms. Paxton, as you know, the college has recently created an endowed chair of women's studies, with an annual stipend of $125,000. Some of the trustees and I were wondering whether you might consider taking it? You'd only have to be on campus for the fall semester . . . "

"Stephen Sondheim here, Jeanne. I'm stuck for a rhyme for hypotenuse. I've got the melody, but can't quite find . . . It's kind of a children's musical. Did you say Dr. Seuss? That's—that's perfect. I insist on giving you a percentage of the box office . . . "

"Dear Mr. Madrid, you don't know me, but you saved my life. In the spring of 1993 I hit bottom: I was smoking crack, my wife had left me, and I'd just been fired from my brokerage firm. Then I read your piece about. . . . And to make a long story short, I've decided to devote my new fortune to the cause of experimental literature and the promotion of world peace. God bless you."

"Anyway, Ashbery wants to reprint your review as the introduction to his collected poems. He just goes on and on about how you managed to make clear, even to him, the deep-seated purpose of his entire artistic enterprise . . . "

"Is this Nia Wa Mfune, the writer? My name is Michael Anthony. I currently represent the MacArthur Foundation . . . "

"Now that Bob Silvers is stepping down, we naturally thought of you as the logical successor. Could you see your way clear to flying up to New York for lunch with a few people . . . "

"Not only will we match what Clancy's getting, we'll . . . "

"Darling, it's a beautiful Saturday morning. The sky is blue, the birds are twittering. Why don't you take off and spend the day visiting dusty secondhand bookstores . . . "

"Did you see that Clifton Fadiman included your book in his revised edition of *The Lifetime Reading Plan*?"

"So here at St. E's we have a patient who has insisted for donkey's years that he was really you. Naturally we just humored him. No big deal. Then last month, a new inmate announced that he was the real Nathan Madrid. Arguments and fights broke out. Before long, almost everyone in the ward claimed to be the true Madrid . . . "

" . . . for your distinguished contributions to the cause of literary scholarship, arise Sir Francis . . . "

"My name, it is no matter. Let us just say that I am an elderly businessman who admires your prose style. No, my throat isn't hoarse; I always speak softly. I was—how to put it—somewhat disturbed by a recent journalistic attack on your writing. Your enemies are my enemies . . . No, only the kneecaps. Keep up the fine work."

Pages on Life's Way

I am sitting in my bedroom when my father appears at the door with a large paper sack. He has just come home from the 7-to-3 shift at the steel plant. "Here," he says, "a guy was cleaning out his locker and gave me these." He hands me the grocery bag, which contains perhaps two dozen Rex Stout mysteries about Nero Wolfe and Archie Goodwin. I can still remember the titles: *Fer-de-Lance; The Golden Spiders; The Final Deduction; The League of Frightened Men.* Because of those books, New York City has always been for me, current visual evidence to the contrary, a place of elegant brownstones and ritzy nightclubs, of wisecracks and funny expletives like "Pfui," of cocktails and orchids and beautiful heiresses in trouble . . .

As a boy I used to give my three younger sisters books as Christmas presents. I always chose a new Hardy Boys adventure, a jungle tale of Tarzan I hadn't read, or some science fiction title with a space cadet on the cover. Of course, in return I soon began to receive tea sets and Barbie doll accessories. Ours was not a subtle family . . .

Now and again, usually at twilight, I think back to the books that have changed my life, and the first that always comes to mind is Dale Carnegie's *How to Stop Worrying and Start Living.* I can still remember this supersalesman of self-improvement urging me, a lugubrious eighth-grader, to "live in day-tight compartments." What I loved about this once well-cared-for paperback, and about Carnegie's other guides to making friends and speaking effectively, was the inspirational quotations: Because of Carnegie I started to read Shakespeare and study the King James version of the Bible.

Familiarity with these monuments of English literature, I was assured, would build up my obviously puny vocabulary. Being then of a docile nature, like so many devotees of self-help books, I soon acquired a Dell paperback of *Four Great Tragedies of Shakespeare.* I started with *Macbeth* and found that lines about life being a walking shadow, full of sound and fury, told by an idiot and signifying nothing, agreed very well with my gloomy adolescent temperament. By the time I got to *Hamlet,* Mr. Melancholy himself, I was firmly hooked on classics. Those by Shakespeare, anyway. Unfortunately, I never did quite learn how to stop worrying and start living. But then life is full of trade-offs . . .

Turning point: It is Sunday morning, and I am lying on our faded living-room rug perusing, with Talmudic rigor, the Cleveland *Plain Dealer*'s comics page. For some reason, I start looking through the entertainment section of the paper, where I notice an article about an omnibus volume of Raymond Chandler mysteries. Soon I am reading the first book review of my life. Alas, I have quite forgotten its author (the unhappy destiny of so many who have hitched their wagon to the shooting star of literary journalism). All I can now recall is a long passage quoted from *The Long Goodbye* about blondes, their various qualities and quiddities. Being 14 or 15, I'm not sure if it's art but I certainly know what kind of girls I like.

Playback

Though I came to love Chandler more than thirty years ago, I have been somewhat leery about reopening his novels: Would they sound unpleasantly dated, a little cutesy even, with their relentless repartee, their steady rain of similes? I needn't have worried. A few years ago I was sick in bed with a cold, feeling slightly shivery and achey all over in the strangely pleasant way that makes the prospect of becoming a valetudinarian so immensely attractive. Propped up against a mound of pillows, warmed by half the blankets in the house, I lay back, sighed contentedly, and opened volume 1 in the new Library of America Raymond Chandler. I decided to start with *The High Window,* not generally esteemed among the author's best efforts.

Surely, I can remember thinking, one ought to read Chandler in a tattered 1950s paperback, with some brazen cookie posing leggily on the cover and Philip Marlowe looking rumpled with a cigarette dangling from his lower lip. The Library of America, however, represented officially sanctioned Literature, not scarcely licit pleasure. To learn about the stolen Brasher Doubloon and vicious blackmail and runaway wives in these two elegant, thin-paper volumes didn't seem quite jake. Besides, for the $35 or so each costs, you could have hired Marlowe for a day. Back in 1940, that is.

But the LOA people knew what they were up to. Two pages into *The High Window* I was convinced that Chandler, despite some stylistic excesses, belongs in the canon as well as the cigar store:

"A large black and gold butterfly fishtailed in and landed on a hydrangea bush almost at my elbow, moved its wings slowly up and down a few times, then took off heavily and staggered away through the motionless hot scented air."

Nabokov couldn't have described a butterfly more tellingly (though he probably would have noted its species and genus). "Staggered away" is perfect. Now consider this: "An old man sat inside it [an elevator] slack-jawed and watery-eyed on a piece of folded burlap on top of a wooden stool. He looked as if he had been sitting there since the Civil War and had come out of that badly."

Or this: "The bar entrance was to the left. It was dusky and quiet and a bartender moved mothlike against the faint glitter of piled glassware. A tall handsome blond in a dress that looked like seawater sifted over with gold dust came out of the Ladies' Room touching up her lips and turned toward the arch, humming."

Or even this: "We looked at each other with the clear innocent eyes of a couple of used car salesmen."

A day or two later, feeling perkier, I excavated my copies of *Raymond Chandler Speaking* and *Selected Letters of Raymond Chandler,* two invaluable adjuncts to the collected fiction, chockablock with reflections on writing. "All I'm looking for," austerely notes the author of *The Big Sleep,* "is an excuse for certain experiments in dramatic dialogue." Better yet, he maintains, "it doesn't matter a damn what a novel is about . . . the only fiction of any moment in any age is that which does magic with words . . . the subject matter is merely a springboard for the writer's imagination." For years I used to keep four improbable words from the creator of Philip Marlowe pinned above my desk: "I live for syntax."

Move over, Henry James.

Fantastic Journey

The World Fantasy Convention generally takes place on the weekend nearest to Halloween. Since no masquerades or role-playing games are permitted, the gathering is basically an opportunity for writers and serious readers to talk to each other about books. This year the convention took place in Baltimore, and I went up for a Saturday.

Once registered, I dropped in on a panel discussion devoted to the short story, featuring Lucius Shepard, Terry Bisson, and Howard Waldrop, the con's three guests of honor. Should these names be merely names to you, go immediately to your bookstore and ask for Shepard's *The Jaguar Hunter,* Bisson's *Bears Discover Fire,* and Waldrop's *All about Strange Monsters of the Recent Past.* If you can't find these titles, take any you can get and keep checking the used-bookshops for others. Shepard writes like Joseph Conrad on speed; Bisson can charm your toes off; and Waldrop is a Texas-style magic realist (see "Ike at the Mike," in which Sen. Elvis Presley attends a concert at the White House honoring the great old bluesman Dwight Eisenhower, or "God's Hooks!" wherein John Bunyan and Izaak Walton go fishing for Leviathan; both are in the hard-to-find but priceless collection *Howard Who?*).

Of the many rapid-fire, often very shrewd comments about the writing of fiction, I especially liked Howard Waldrop's definitions of the short story and the novel: A short story is "about the most important thing that will ever happen to that character in his life"; while a novel chronicles "the most important time in a character's life." Waldrop then added that by the story's end, "there must be some cost to the character."

Later, in a hallway, I overheard Joe Haldeman exclaim, "The guy asked, 'What's the world coming to?' I answered, 'How should I know? I'm only a science fiction writer.'" In the dealer's room, shelves weighty with expensive treasures, I found and bought the English proofs of Angela Carter's brilliant novel *Nights at the Circus,* surely a masterpiece if anything is. Later, over dinner, Edward Bryant, the convention's toastmaster, explained to me just how he used his own blood to stamp a lizard design on special editions of *Fetish.* At various cocktail parties, one might chat with novelists Elizabeth Hand, Gene Wolfe, and Stephen Donaldson, *Omni* editor Ellen Datlow, critic John Clute, steam-punk pioneer Tim Powers, and many others. At one point Michael Swanwick (*The Iron Dragon's Daughter*) insisted, clear-eyed and without the apparent encouragement of drink, that Gardner Dozois's opening pages to the forthcoming *City of*

God might well be "the best 4,000 words ever written in science fiction." Presumably the remaining words aren't half-bad either. By the end of the day, I just wanted to rush home and read.

Wondermonger

If the Library of America ever gets around to honoring a fantasy or science fiction writer—and I'm not precisely holding my breath here—my favorite-son vote would go to Jack Vance. (On later ballots I'd support Philip K. Dick, Theodore Sturgeon, and Ursula Le Guin.) Vance possesses one of the most distinctive voices in all fiction—languid, sardonic, wittily periphrastic. Think of a mixture of Gibbon and Wodehouse. This writer, still active after fifty years, is mainly known as a world-maker, expert at creating alien civilizations in all their gaudy, tawdry panoply. But I like him most for his velvety diction: "Toward the end of a stormy summer afternoon, with the sun finally breaking out under ragged black rain-clouds, Castle Janeil was overwhelmed and its population destroyed" (the opening sentence of "The Last Castle").

New readers should start with *The Dying Earth,* the novel that inaugurated Vance's impressive career, then go on to *The Eyes of the Overworld* (about a suave Kind-Hearts-and-Coronets-style con man named Cugel whose plans always go awry), *The Star King* (a thrilling tale of revenge), and the haunting *Lyonesse,* without overlooking the shorter fiction, especially "The Dragon Masters," "The Last Castle," and "The Moon Moth."

Listen to Cugel the Clever attempting a seduction: "Perhaps I am over-prompt; perhaps I overindulge my vanity; perhaps I contravene the normal decorum of the village—but is there reason why we should not repair to my chamber, and there amuse ourselves?"

As it turns out there isn't, though after the erotic exertions unpleasant consequences ensue. Certainly Jack Vance, like Raymond Chandler, is one of the most sheerly enjoyable writers in twentieth-century American literature. I'll be waiting for that call from the Library of America.

❧

When in doubt have a man come through the
door with a gun in his hand.
　　　　　　　　—Raymond Chandler

A Garland for Max

When a book of Max Beerbohm's caricatures was given by N. John Hall to the world, I looked eagerly in the acknowledgments for Lasner, Mark Samuels. I wondered if he would be there. He was there—along with Sir Rupert Hart-Davis, Lawrence Danson, and many other noted "Maximilians." In fact, Lasner was generously, and quite appropriately, denominated "a Beerbohm scholar and collector par excellence, whose sage advice and library of original drawings and reproductions have been of enormous help."

From time to time over the years I have presented after-dinner remarks to various book-collecting sodalities. These affairs are always congenial—the drink flows, the company soon grows animated, and conversation invariably turns on bibliophilic treasures glimpsed, yearned after, and duly acquired. On these evenings spent among the prominent bookmen and -women of Washington, I would occasionally discern, in a distant, smoky corner of the room, a reserved, well-dressed man in his thirties or early forties. Sometimes I noticed him chatting with Joshua Heller, a specialist in fine printing. I think it was the air of diffidence—uncommon among book collectors—that first intrigued me, and so I was pleased when we were finally introduced. Yes, he collected books; his name was Mark Samuels Lasner. "What sort of things do you go after?" I asked in my bluff manner. Oh, he murmured, late Victorian literature, 1890s material. Perhaps I'd like to see his collection sometime? I answered, "Of course," in that vague, careless way one does on such occasions.

The years, as they will, went by, and one day I received a small pamphlet in the mail. "England in the 1890s: Literary Publishing at the Bodley Head," by Margaret D. Stetz and Mark Samuels Lasner. The handsome booklet described Stetz as a professor of English at Georgetown University, while her co-author was simply called a collector and bibliographer. Alas, I glanced only casually through the pages, then shelved the book among my Oscar Wilde titles, churlishly failing to thank Lasner for his kind gift.

No matter. A few years subsequent I was honored with another publication from Lasner and Stetz: "The Yellow Book: A Centenary Exhibition" (held at Harvard's Houghton Library). This time I didn't fail to remark that a great many, a very great many, of the items lent to the show derived from the collection of . . . Mark Samuels Lasner. My curiosity was definitely piqued. Yet still I did nothing. Then a third item arrived: a private reprinting of "Enoch Soames," Max Beerbohm's classic memoir of a decadent poet, completely unappreciated in the 1890s, who sells his soul to the devil in exchange for a visit to the future. Soames plans to look up his name in the British Museum library catalogue and soothe his wounded self-esteem by gazing at the innumerable scholarly articles devoted to those masterpieces *Negations* and *Fungoids*. Needless to say, poor Soames discovers that he has been utterly forgotten; worse yet, he is even thought to be a fictional character created by Max Beerbohm. Of course, I truly meant to scribble some words of heartfelt appreciation. Alas, great is my shame. For even then I merely felt that I probably ought, someday, when it was convenient, to take a quick look at the Lasner collection.

In one of his essays Max Beerbohm observes, "I was a modest, good-humored boy. It is Oxford that has made me insufferable." I do not have that excuse. The lack of common civility, even the tacit condescension—they come back to me now, trailing clouds of ignominy. I had, it goes without saying, long prided myself on possessing one of the finer private libraries in the city. It might be disorganized, half the books might be in cardboard boxes, but it was . . . extensive. And I too had a special interest in the 1890s. Hadn't I reviewed Richard Ellmann's *Oscar Wilde*, Karl Beckson's life of Arthur Symons, and a reissue of Beerbohm's caricatures, *Rossetti and His Circle*? Indeed, didn't I own a first edition of Beerbohm's finest essay collection, *And Even Now*?

When Yale University Press dispatched to *Book World* an advance reading copy of Max Beerbohm's *Caricatures*, my heart leapt at the prospect of writing—more? yet again?—about this consummate stylist, master of the tongue-in-cheek essay, the literary parody (see *A Christmas Garland,* especially "The Mote in the Middle Distance," wherein two Henry Jamesian children try to decide whether or not to open their Christmas stockings), and the imaginary reminiscence (*Seven Men*), not to mention *Zuleika Dobson,* a somewhat brittle comic novel that concludes with the love-suicide of all the male undergraduates at Oxford University. This is, after all, the prose artist to whom waspish and arrogant Evelyn Waugh once wrote, meekly imploring him to accept a copy of *Brideshead Revisited.* "I can hardly hope you will read it, still less that you will approve any of it. I bring it like a terrier putting a dead rat on the counterpane—as an act of homage."

And so, one idle November weekend, while glancing through the preliminary matter of Hall's superb new album of Max's caricatures, I wondered if, by some chance, Mark Samuels Lasner's name might actually be there. It was, and this time I knew, indisputably, my course.

🌿

We had agreed that I should come round about 10 A.M. He was there waiting at the door, wearing—as I knew he would—an elegant and crisply knotted silk tie. They had, he explained while ushering me into the foyer, just returned from Japan, where he had lent a number of Beardsley drawings. They? "Margaret and I have been together for more than twenty years." So that explained that. Would I care for some tea? The ceilings were high, the walls painted yellow; dark Oriental rugs covered an expanse of even darker stained oak flooring. The large rooms felt quiet, orderly; I could see a leather sofa, beautifully arranged bookcases, many pictures. Even the dining-room tablecloth bore a flowery William Morris design. As we waited for the tea to steep, Lasner picked up a framed pencil drawing that had been lying casually on the table. "That looks like . . . " "It is. Enoch Soames." For all my enthusiasm for "the incomparable Max," I had never before seen the original of any of his two thousand drawings. And here was one of his most famous creations, the doomed Soames, that incarnate spirit of the fin de siècle.

I asked Lasner about his family, his past; he was forthright, yet strangely indefinite. The family money derived from, oh, patents of some kind; his early childhood had been spent in a twenty-seven-room 1880s house; even in college he had purchased "one or two Whistler etchings." But what, I persisted, had precipitated the passion for late Victoriana? Lasner smiled reminiscentially. As a young man, he had accompanied a friend to London, where he encountered Simon Nowell Smith . . . Bumptiously, I interrupted, "I know him. He edited that book of anecdotes about Henry James. *The Legend of the Master.*" "Yes." Simon, it turned out, possessed an extremely impressive library—"he had, for example, Virginia Woolf's copy of Eliot's poems, with a gift inscription"—and the young American soon found himself fired up by the romance of what bibliophiles call association copies. Before he left England, he had purchased Lionel Johnson's *The Art of Thomas Hardy,* presented by John Lane, publisher of the notorious *Yellow Book,* to George Meredith, the most revered novelist of the day.

We had by this time finished our Earl Grey. "Let me show you some things."

Displayed on the wall above the leather couch was a row of what Lasner called his "resting girls." A Whistler etching titled *Weary.* Two pre-Raphaelite stunners sketched by Rossetti. An Augustus John portrait of his first wife. In the corner a large, unmistakable drawing of the willowy, sloe-eyed Zuleika Dobson. As decorously seductive as these pictures might be, the high bookshelves opposite dominated the warmly lit room. His goal, said Lasner, was to create a "period library," to represent the artistic spirit in Britain between 1850 and 1900. In particular, he aimed to acquire at least one signed book or association copy from every important author of the time.

And thus quietly did the avalanche begin. As the morning progressed, I held in my hands Henry James's copy of his friend Turgenev's *A Lear of the Steppes*—with the chapter titles for *The Awkward Age* roughed out by the Master on the endpapers; a volume of Christina Rossetti's poems presented by their author to the Rev. C. L. Dodgson, aka Lewis Carroll; Ruskin's *Ethics of the Dust* inscribed to Jane Carlyle with "the old lecturer's love"; a poetry collection signed by Tennyson; *The Adventures of Sherlock Holmes* inscribed by Conan Doyle to the editor of the *Strand* magazine, which first published these immortal stories; and, not least, a copy of the atmospheric melodrama *The Lost Stradivarius,* signed by its one-time owner Thomas Hardy, with a tipped-in autograph of its author, John Meade Falkner, followed by a long inscription from novelist Hugh Walpole and the ownership stickers of the great Victorian expert Michael Sadleir, the collector Bradley Martin, and, not least, Mark Samuels Lasner.

Yet even this was not all, by any means. Lasner showed me books from Max's library, among them *The Quest for Corvo* with an elegantly calligraphed homage from A. J. A. Symons; he pointed out Beerbohm caricatures hanging in his halls of artist Will Rothenstein, self-promoting novelist Hall Caine, theater director Harley Granville-Barker, actor (and Max's half-brother) Herbert Beerbohm Tree, and numerous others. One groaning bookcase held multiple copies of all Beerbohm's published work—I noticed at least forty editions of *Zuleika Dobson*. "I've been working on a Beerbohm bibliography for more than ten years," said Lasner, in a resigned tone.

❧

The sunny morning faded into gray afternoon, and I recall the remainder of my visit as a kind of blur. Back at the dining room table, Lasner suddenly unveiled both the rough, much-inked-out pencil draft and the fair copy of the story now known as "Felix Argallo and Walter Ledgett." Max, it turned out, used heavyweight drawing paper for his writing and could be almost snippy with printers: "Please follow my punctuation exactly. . . . Trust me to have known what I wanted every time." Here were photographs snapped in 1913 of Max's young bride, Florence Kahn; a copy of *A Christmas Garland*, "improved" with caricatures of nearly all the parodied writers and inscribed "For Mamma, from her loving son, Max, 1912"; and even the original of Beerbohm's most famous letter, in which he refuses to help his biographer Bohun Lynch and actually asks that his artistry be underrated, "so that those who don't care for my work shall not be incensed, and those who do shall rally round me."

Overstimulated like a 5-year-old who's devoured all his Halloween candy, I somehow happened to mention Max's old friend Aubrey Beardsley. Beardsley! In a trice Lasner had flung open a closet door, and there, piled higgledy-piggledy next to the umbrellas, stood scores of framed prints: self-portraits of Max; Beerbohm's naughty caricature of a naked Frank Harris (who sometimes told the truth "when his invention flagged"); and somewhere—yes, here's one or two—a cache of Beardsley drawings, including one for the title page of that shocking bestseller, Grant Allen's—be still my beating heart!—*The Woman Who Did.* "Stop!" I cried. "Hold, enough." What might I see were I to murmur William Morris or Robert Browning or . . . ? But it was past 2, and I felt utterly exhausted. With all the Maximilian courtesy I could muster, I bade goodbye to Mark Samuels Lasner, and drove home to my own, once-treasured books. I couldn't help but feel that they looked altogether dowdy on that misty late November afternoon.

Read at Whim!

While section-surfing through the *Post* one Sunday in 1995, I happened upon a fine Metro story by Dan Beyers about area high schools requiring students to do a certain amount of summer reading. At Winston Churchill High School, for instance, juniors were being asked to read any four of the following books: Russell Baker's *Growing Up*, William Styron's *Sophie's Choice*, Lorene Cary's *Black Ice*, Mark Mathabane's *Kaffir Boy*, Shakespeare's *Henry IV*, James Michener's *Chesapeake*, Barbara Kingsolver's *The Bean Trees*, Beryl Markham's *West with the Night*, Michael Dorris's *Yellow Raft in Blue Water*, and Amy Tan's *Kitchen God's Wife*.

Now, anyone who loves books must, of necessity, feel ambivalent about "required reading." By and large, if you force a kid to open a particular book, he or she will do so grudgingly. Occasionally a good novel can win over even the recalcitrant, but most of the time an unwilling reader will merely slump down before the required text with a kind of deep-space weariness: Another book! There have been so many, many books already. Will there be no end? Other kids will approach the chosen volume gingerly, as though it were some alien artifact they had never seen before and that was liable to inflict a sudden and hideous form of disabling injury. And yet still others will display the time-honored adolescent combination of boredom, lethargy, and free-floating belligerence which makes abundantly clear that the actual turning of a page is an unfathomably complex process almost certainly foredoomed to utter and complete failure.

Books, it has always seemed to me, must be read with passion, or they are hardly worth reading at all. The boy or girl who eagerly devours Mad magazines, X-Men comics, and the statistics on the backs of baseball cards may come to love books. All those compelled to read—whether the terminally bored or the goody-goody A student who dutifully follows the official curriculum—will probably grow up to regard viewing public television as the absolute acme of cultural achievement. In summer I think young people should be encouraged to visit the library regularly or to browse occasionally at a favorite bookstore. (If you don't have a favorite bookstore, get one.) Let Hillary or Owen pick out some appealing titles. Then leave the kids alone. In general, summer oughtn't be an extension of school: It should be a time for idleness and part-time jobs and hanging out, for mowing grass or souping up cars, for rainy-day Monopoly games and Dr. Moreau–like experiments on hapless insects ("The House of Pain!"), for getting bored and exploring what used to be called one's inner resources. And for reading purely, solely, entirely for the fun of it.

Back to Basics

But my dismay about the Churchill High School list went beyond the mere idea of such required reading. I also felt uneasy about the titles chosen. Except for the Shakespeare and Markham, all the books were published during the past twenty-five years. They also represent a transparently multicultural smorgasbord: If you are Asian, African, or Native American, Southern or Jewish or Anglo-Saxon, there is at least one title Just For You.

As it happens, I know some of these selections and recall the reviews of most of the others: In general, they're very good books. Yet aren't such contemporary, not to say trendy, novels and autobiographies just the ones that young people ought to be reading on their own? Several have made the bestseller list or won prizes. Why should they be "required"? I can only imagine that the school picked them because they were "youthful" or touched on current social concerns. I know that people will bark at me, but I still think schools should mainly teach established masterpieces, the older the better. The Bible, Homer, Plato, Ovid, Augustine, Dante, Shakespeare —these are the classics I would like my children to know and know well. Not because they are the best or because they offer uplifting moral lessons, but because the *Iliad* and the *Confessions* and the *Divine Comedy* are among the great patterning works of western culture. They are the wells to which later writers go for examples and allusions, for inspiration, for the deeper textures of their own lesser books, even when these are such impressive achievements as, say, Gloria Naylor's *Linden Hills* or Jane Smiley's *A Thousand Acres* or Donald Hall's *The One Day*. Schools should first teach the books that matter most. If you insist on some kind of required summer reading, why not—as a former president once remarked—the best?

Still Listing

Of course, high-school kids will grumble that Plato is too hard for a lazy day at the pool. Maybe. But he's never going to get any easier. Besides, if young people are only half as smart as they think they are, *The Republic* should be a snap.

Nevertheless, I was recently daydreaming—my only real hobby—and concluded that a useful high school or college course might be built around a handful of uncanonical but vastly influential modern books: those early modern "masterworks" that helped establish the conventions, if not the archetypal patterns, of current popular fiction. To narrow a vast field somewhat, I decided to restrict this imaginary curriculum to British titles of the twentieth century (though one could easily select a parallel set of American books). Without such a limitation, one might choose *Don Quixote* as the template for virtually every kind of fiction since the sixteenth century.

Romance: Georgette Heyer's *Devil's Cub*. Ask any romance writer to name the godmother of the field, and Heyer's is the name you will hear. She specialized in witty "regency romances," in most of which the course of true love, between rakish men and self-possessed women, never runs anywhere even close to smooth. Heyer looks back to Jane Austen and forward to half the fiction on the bestseller list. Other equally good titles include *Cotillion, A Civil Contract, Sprig Muslin,* and *Regency Buck*.

Adventure: Rafael Sabatini's *Captain Blood*. In this swashbuckling, albeit somewhat stiffly written classic we see a quiet, underestimated man survive an ordeal to emerge an avenging angel, his oppressor's worst nightmare, the modern avatar of the Count of Monte Cristo. In the wake of Sabatini's dashing buccaneer come C. S. Forester and Patrick O'Brian, but also James Bond and Dick Francis. Alternate title: Geoffrey Household's *Rogue Male*—the tale of the hunter who tries to assassinate Hitler, only to find himself become the hunted. The greatest chase novel of all time.

Spy story: Somerset Maugham's *Ashenden, or The British Agent*. Modern espionage fiction is laced with agents who are world-weary, inefficient, burned out, cynical. Such sentiments must be endemic to this genre, for *Ashenden* is one of the earliest spy novels (actually a collection of stories) and displays most of the familiar trappings. See "The Hairless Mexican," about a cool, professional assassin who murders the wrong man.

Camp comedy: Ronald Firbank's *The Flower beneath the Foot.* No question here about the master of this genre. Firbank is silly and naughty, and his prose actually minces: "Neither her Gaudiness the Mistress of the Robes nor her Dreaminess the Queen were feeling quite themselves." But he is also a major influence on a whole line of writers from Evelyn Waugh and Anthony Powell to W. M. Spackman and Alan Hollinghurst. More than just a model of one kind of gay literary sensibility, Firbank taught fiction how to leave out the inessential, to be fast-moving and airy, to reflect the fragmented way people actually talk. For more farcical comedy, the master is, of course, P. G. Wodehouse, and the richest single work *Leave It to Psmith.*

Science fiction: Olaf Stapledon's *Last and First Men.* Science fiction typically seeks to provoke "the sense of wonder." No one has ever done this better than Stapledon. In this novel he foretells the history of mankind from the present into the far, far distant future. He creates a score of different civilizations, set on various planets throughout the galaxy, and shows how men struggle, flourish, and destroy themselves, time after time after time. His paragraphs contain novels in embryo. H. G. Wells is certainly the greatest name in British sf, but Stapledon is a close runner-up.

Historical novel: Robert Graves's *I, Claudius.* This superb book made history contemporary, showing us that the great figures of the past were living, scheming, and flawed—just like ourselves, only more so. Graves took one of the monuments of antiquity—the grandeur that was Rome—and revealed the backside of the whitewashed marble. Such demystification led to a liberation of historical fiction, replacing the overwritten, highly colored example of Scott. Only a step separates *I, Claudius* from *Burr* and *Possession.*

Children's literature: Beatrix Potter's *Peter Rabbit.* Virtually all of modern-day children's literature can be found here in seedling form: the cozy home, the runaway free spirit, the misadventures in an adult world, the attendant helpers, the hard-won wisdom of experience, pictures that complement and enrich the often witty text. Potter's classic is even the first in a series, that favorite form of modern readers, followed by *Benjamin Bunny* and *The Flopsy Bunnies.*

Horror and fantasy: Lord Dunsany. Any representative collection. Dunsany could write every sort of fantasy perfectly: "The Three Sailors Gambit" is the greatest of all chess stories; "Two Bottles of Relish" is a masterpiece of black humor; the Joseph Jorkens club stories are the best of the "a strange thing once happened to me in the Punjab" style of tall tales. In his early stories Dunsany created an entire universe of awesome gods and would-be heroes, depicted in gorgeously evocative prose: "Toldees, Mondath, Arizim, these are the Inner Lands, the lands whose sentinels upon their borders do not behold the sea." Dunsany never plumbed the depths of real horror—the great early exemplar here is Arthur Machen —but he did provide fantasy with its frequent mix of humor, heightened style, and operatic flourish.

Mystery: Dorothy Sayers's *Gaudy Night.* From Christie, Marsh, and Allingham to James, Highsmith, and Rendell, the English mystery/thriller has long been dominated by women. To me, *Gaudy Night* is clearly Dorothy Sayers's most influential masterpiece: an ingenious whodunit, a brilliant social comedy about an Oxford women's college, a moving love story, and a serious novel about issues of class-consciousness and the place of women in modern society. Plus there's none of that damn change-ringing you get in *The Nine Tailors.*

Well, there's the start of my curriculum, though I've had to leave out several gems: Travel writing would be represented by Robert Byron's effervescent *Road to Oxiana;* realist fiction by V. S. Pritchett's short stories; biography by A. J. A. Symons's *Quest for Corvo*—this last the work that transformed a stately, seamless genre into the self-aware, anxiety-ridden form we know today. For an American-anchored list, I'd include Dashiell Hammett, S. J. Perelman, Margaret Mitchell, and Alfred Bester (*The Stars My Destination*—the science fiction masterwork behind the New Wave, the Cyberpunks, and much else). I could go on. Still, this is a start toward a course devoted to "patterning" works. Maybe I should call up the University of Maryland and see if they'd let me teach it.

✎

> . . . the irregular crab,
> Which though't goes backward
> Thinks that it goes right,
> Because it goes its owne way
> —John Webster

Comedy Tonight

Now that the Modern Library's controversial ranking of the twentieth century's greatest novels in English has been shown to be largely a work of fiction (or even fantasy), it struck me that the time was right for another, more useful tally. As the famous Victorian classicist Benjamin Jowett once remarked, "We have sought truth, and sometime perhaps found it. But have we had any fun?" Instead of the Great Works, the school texts and established classics, how about a list of the 100 most amusing comic novels, the ever-reliable masterpieces of humor and high spirits? After all, these are the books we actually like, that make us laugh out loud and lift our hearts. Some readers even call such titles comfort books, for they tend to be the ones we turn to when the world is too much with us or, as is more often the case, against us.

The following 100 titles—all published in English in the twentieth century—appear roughly as they suggested themselves to me, certainly not in order of merit or hilarity. The list adopts a one author/one book rule; otherwise half the selections would be written by P. G. Wodehouse, Evelyn Waugh, and Terry Pratchett. Nearly all the items are works of fiction, mainly novels, but I have waffled a bit and smuggled in a few humorous travel classics, some essay collections, and even one or two autobiographies: compiler's privilege. Also, only books I can personally vouch for were eligible, which accounts for the absence of several titles that surely belong here—Joyce Cary's *The Horse's Mouth,* Anthony Powell's *From a View to a Death,* something by Muriel Spark. (Even now these glare at me from a To Be Read pile substantial enough to stock a small bookshop.) To spark interest, jog memories, or suggest something of a work's general character, I append a very brief description for each book. But remember: In comedy, style and timing are everything; don't judge any of these classics by its summarizing phrase.

1. *Leave It to Psmith,* by P. G. Wodehouse (shenanigans at Blandings Castle)

2. *Crome Yellow,* by Aldous Huxley (country house intellectuals trade repartee)

3. *The Pyrates,* by George Macdonald Fraser (dazzling send-up of high-seas swashbucklers)

4. *Augustus Carp,* by Himself (Henry Howarth Bashford) (unconscious moral hypocrite: brilliant control of tone)

5. *The Trials of Topsy,* by A. P. Herbert (bouncy Valley Girl talk, 1920s London style: irresistible)

6. *The Unfortunate Fursey,* by Mervyn Wall (medieval monk tempted by debonair Satan)

7. *Gentlemen Prefer Blondes,* by Anita Loos (Lorelei Lee—gold-digger of 1925)

8. *Mapp and Lucia,* by E. F. Benson (clash of social titans in Tilling)

9. *What a Life!,* by E. V. Lucas and George Morrow (masterpiece of dadaist collage)

10. *The Young Visiters,* by Daisy Ashford (a 9-year-old looks at love)

11. *Appleby's End,* by Michael Innes (a wry detective among rural English eccentrics)

12. *Tik-Tok,* by John Sladek (a courteous robot kills his way to the top)

13. *The Pot of Gold,* by James Stephens (blarney and fairies)

14. *The Travel Tales of Joseph Jorkens,* by Lord Dunsany (tall tales told over whisky)

15. *His Monkey Wife,* by John Collier (callow Brit marries sensitive chimp)

16. *Lucky Jim,* by Kingsley Amis (red-brick university phonies)

17. *Decline and Fall,* by Evelyn Waugh (a twentieth-century *Candide*)

18. *Cold Comfort Farm,* by Stella Gibbons (sophisticate among British hill-billies)

19. *Party Going,* by Henry Green (Bright Young Things flirt and carry on)

20. *An Armful of Warm Girl,* by W. M. Spackman (December–May romance)

21. *Imaginative Qualities of Actual Things,* by Gilbert Sorrentino (savage satire of '60s art/literature scene)

22. *Catch-22,* by Joseph Heller (war is hell—and hilarious, sort of)

23. *Amphigorey,* by Edward Gorey (Gothic sensationalism/Edwardian backdrops)

24. *Pictures from an Institution,* by Randall Jarrell (captious urban intellectual at small Southern women's college)

25. *Bullivant and the Lambs,* by Ivy Compton-Burnett (brittle drawing-room black humor)

26. *A Severed Head,* by Iris Murdoch (incest and samurai swords: her tightest, most outrageous novel)

27. *Lolita,* by Vladimir Nabokov (European suavity confronts American vulgarity)

28. *Alan Mendelsohn, the Boy from Mars,* by Daniel Pinkwater (misfits discover their supernatural powers)

29. *The Catcher in the Rye,* by J. D. Salinger (the voice of a generation)

30. *The Night Life of the Gods,* by Thorne Smith (Roman statues come alive; ribaldry ensues)

31. *The Sword in the Stone,* by T. H. White (Wart among the Arthurian anachronisms)

32. *God Save the Mark,* by Donald E. Westlake (scams, quips, and capers)

33. *Murphy,* by Samuel Beckett (deadpan philosophical humor)

34. *The Eyes of the Overworld,* by Jack Vance (misadventures of a thief/con man in the far future)

35. *Cakes and Ale,* by Somerset Maugham (secret life of Edwardian men of letters)

36. *Oranges Are Not the Only Fruit,* by Jeanette Winterson (growing up lesbian and evangelical)

37. *The Silver Stallion,* by James Branch Cabell (tongue-in-cheek adventures in medieval Poictesme)

38. *The Napoleon of Notting Hill,* by G. K. Chesterton (London neighborhoods at war)

39. *All about H. Hatterr,* by G. V. Desani (Indian English in excelsis)

40. *Seven Men,* by Max Beerbohm (includes "Enoch Soames" and "Savonarola Brown")

41. *The Sirens of Titan,* by Kurt Vonnegut (gallows humor/galactic farce)

42. *The Chronicles of Clovis,* by Saki (the master of the sardonic tale)

43. *South Wind,* by Norman Douglas (decadent expatriates in fictional Capri)

44. *The Flower beneath the Foot,* by Ronald Firbank (camping it up)

45. *The Gate of Angels,* by Penelope Fitzgerald (smiles of a summer night)

46. *You Know Me, Al,* by Ring Lardner (tales of the vernacular)

47. *The Locusts Have No King,* by Dawn Powell (love and power plays among 1940s literati)

48. *A Fan's Notes,* by Frederick Exley (his tawdry career)

49. *The Phantom Tollbooth,* by Norton Juster (words and numbers frolic and quarrel)

50. *Lady into Fox,* by David Garnett (wife metamorphosizes)

51. *Letter to Lord Byron,* by W. H. Auden (wisecracking verse epistle— from Iceland)

52. *Too Many Cooks,* by Rex Stout (gourmets, guffaws, and Archie Goodwin at his fizziest)

53. *Portnoy's Complaint,* by Philip Roth (angst, Momma, and shiksas)

54. *The Thurber Carnival,* by James Thurber (drawings, stories, "My Life and Hard Times")

55. *Guys and Dolls,* by Damon Runyon (raffish present-tense escapades of '30s crooks)

56. *The Thin Man,* by Dashiell Hammett (witty where-is-he)

57. *Or All the Seas with Oysters,* by Avram Davidson (tales of the curious and curiouser)

58. *Two Serious Ladies,* by Jane Bowles (hothouse humor and languorous eroticism)

59. *At Swim-Two-Birds,* by Flann O'Brien (characters turn on author)

60. *Flaubert's Parrot,* by Julian Barnes (cracking up the critics)

61. *The Road to Oxiana,* by Robert Byron (waggish spirits in Middle East)

62. *On the Shoulders of Giants,* by Robert K. Merton (scholarship for the fun of it)

63. *Little Big Man,* by Thomas Berger (the decline of the West: a masterpiece)

64. *Candy,* by Terry Southern and Mason Hoffenberg (Good grief!)

65. *Federigo,* by Howard Nemerov (delicious farce of marriage and adultery)

66. *Thus Was Adonis Murdered,* by Sarah Caudwell (erudition, eccentric barristers, elegantly witty mystery)

67. *Wise Children,* by Angela Carter (Carter's *Midsummer Night's Dream*)

68. *Tropic of Cancer,* by Henry Miller (obscenely hilarious: expat in Paris)

69. *The Pursuit of Love,* by Nancy Mitford (outrageous English clan)

70. *Animal Farm,* by George Orwell (all animals are equal, but . . .)

71. *The Tin Men,* by Michael Frayn (computers, corporations, uproarious chaos)

72. *Christie Malry's Own Double-Entry,* by B. S. Johnson (quiet clerk seeks revenge)

73. *Up in the Old Hotel,* by Joseph Mitchell (wistful and humorous profiles: New York bohemians)

74. *A Frolic of His Own,* by William Gaddis (litigiousness and slapstick)

75. *The Most of S. J. Perelman* (language runs amuck)

76. *The Moving Toyshop,* by Edmund Crispin (madcap mystery set in Oxford)

77. *A Confederacy of Dunces,* by John Kennedy Toole (ranting against the world)

78. *Enderby,* by Anthony Burgess (misfortunes of a poet)

79. *Sixty Stories,* by Donald Barthelme (the comedy of clichés)

80. *Life among the Savages,* by Shirley Jackson (family zaniness)

81. *The Many Loves of Dobie Gillis,* by Max Shulman (love goes wrong, repeatedly)

82. *Lake Wobegon Days,* by Garrison Keillor (Our Town, Minnesota)

83. *Will This Do?,* by Auberon Waugh (waspish and wicked autobiography)

84. *Man and Superman,* by Bernard Shaw (rapier wit and diabolical philosophy)

85. *Riotous Assembly,* by Tom Sharpe (savage, vulgar farce about South Africa)

86. *Mort,* by Terry Pratchett (Death takes an apprentice)

87. *Is That What People Do?,* by Robert Sheckley (science fiction's great satirist of the '50s)

88. *Five Children and It,* by E. Nesbit (misadventures and wishful thinking)

89. *The Rebel Angels,* by Robertson Davies (scholars, pedants, and gypsies in love)

90. *A Glass of Blessings,* by Barbara Pym (domestic and ecclesiastical intrigue)

91. *Hindoo Holiday,* by J. R. Ackerley (Indian love song, but very funny)

92. *Small World,* by David Lodge (hip literary theorists at play)

93. *The Dick Gibson Show,* by Stanley Elkin (behind the mike on talk radio)

94. *The Mezzanine,* by Nicholson Baker (humor is in the details)

95. *Expecting Someone Taller,* by Tom Holt (nice guy acquires Ring of the Nibelungs)

96. *The History Man,* by Malcolm Bradbury (serio-comedy about '60s academic life)

97. *A Short Walk in the Hindu Kush,* by Eric Newby (fools rush in)

98. *Rumpole of the Bailey,* by John Mortimer (the law is an ass, but not Horace R.)

99. *United States: Collected Essays,* by Gore Vidal (the pleasure of his company)

100. *Ulysses,* by James Joyce (a comic masterpiece, among other things)

So there you are: 100 very amusing books, some of the best literary entertainment of the century. As usual, several titles may prove hard to find—particularly three of my current favorites: *Mapp and Lucia, Topsy,* and *Augustus Carp.* Devastatingly funny, they will cheer you through many a hard night.

Light of Other Days

"Tell me where all past years are. . . . The captains and the kings depart.
. . . This same flower that smiles today / Tomorrow will be dying. . . .
Where are the snows of yesteryear?"

St. Augustine used to say that he thought he understood time—until
you asked him to define it. Surely, many people must feel—on a birthday,
at the beginning of summer—an occasional twinge of chronological surprise: "Me? Me? Nearly 50 years old. This must be some kind of joke."
Maybe it is. Though, as Melville observed, the wit thereof we but dimly
discern and more than suspect is at nobody's expense but our own. These
days I look in my bathroom mirror and remember my father, staring in
another mirror and murmuring to himself, in the grave histrionic way he
had, "The tragedy is not that we are old, but that we are young."

Does anyone ever think himself mature? Most of the time we feel like
overgrown kids pretending to be adults. We put on business suits and
dresses, and the winking world, like a parent at Halloween, agrees to go
along with the ruse that we are Real Grownups. Of course, deep down we
know that this is all just play-acting, and that come Saturday afternoon
we'll hike to the park for a game of kickball or, if it rains, put on a show in
the garage and . . . About then, we realize that we aren't in fact 11 or 14
anymore, and that this Saturday afternoon we'll have to drive our own 11-

year-old to soccer practice or swim-team tryouts in a $20,000 mini-van that is almost paid off. But not quite.

There is, I suppose, in each of us an eternal summer, always beckoning, "Come away, come away." Outside of dreams, apart from the sudden ache of a Proustian flashback—tasting caramel syrup on vanilla ice cream after many years, discovering a workbook from second grade and remembering the assignments—we have all agreed to accept the routine, the utter dailiness of grown-up things. Yet we yearn. Is this really all there is? Just this? All life, wrote Yeats, seems at times "a preparation for something that never happens."

Romantic Lies

When we are young, books act upon us like oracles. "Here," they say, "is a glimpse of your life." We read *Pride and Prejudice* and know that one day Darcy or Elizabeth will stroll by our side through the gardens at Pemberly. We finish an espionage novel and imagine ourselves as suave and deadly James Bond on a swaying luxury train hurtling across Eastern Europe. When we look up from *Microbe Hunters,* we picture our own face peering through a microscope at the cure for cancer. Little wonder that most of us can hardly wait to grow up. For never do we conceive that we will, in fact, turn out to be the gardener pitching mulch behind the rosebushes, or a harried accountant for Amtrak, or the high-school general science teacher, explaining how to dissect a still-twitching frog to a class of appalled ninth-graders.

From *Don Quixote* to *The Great Gatsby,* one of the great themes of western literature is this power of fiction to set us up for a fall. As a girl, Emma Bovary reads romantic novels and daydreams of elegant balls and sumptuous dinner parties; as a woman she finds her fantasies reduced to desperate adultery. Her life has been poisoned by a vision she could never forget, nor ever quite fulfill. Or has it?

Critics might dismiss Emma or Jay Gatsby or Don Quixote as naive readers, overly susceptible to the written word. After all, they foolishly believed in the green light, felt that next time they needed only to stretch out their arms a little farther to realize their sentimental dreams. Yet for many of us such characters seem surprisingly admirable. At least they refused to put away childish hopes, refused to sell out. The people around them are perfectly sensible and realistic—people like our grown-up selves—and their lives are dull, venal, bourgeois, and routine. Like Monsieur Homais, most of them, most of us, will eventually receive a little ribbon from the Legion of Honor. Or a pin from the twenty-year club.

Looking Backwards

At a certain point in life, one's gaze shifts from the future to the past. Instead of looking forward to new bestsellers, we yearn to go back to childhood favorites. Rather than spend an evening with Don DeLillo or A. S. Byatt, we think it would be fun to reread some of the Tarzan books. "I had this story from one who had no business to tell it to me, or to any other." Booksellers know that elderly men will suddenly call up and ask for all the issues of *Amazing Stories* from 1934 to 1938, the years when the eminent surgeon or retired executive was only a teenager who used to stare, dimeless, at the chrome spaceship or tentacled monster on those shiny pulp covers. Past 70, that boy still dreams of galactic adventure. Or rather he dreams of his youth. We hope by opening again *The Adventures of Sherlock Holmes* or *Rebecca* or *Tik-Tok of Oz*, that we somehow, if only for an hour or two, can erase the passage of years. "Backward, turn backward, O Time, in your flight, / Make me a child again just for to-night!" It never really happens. Adults know too much. In a sense, our lives have poisoned the books that formed us. We may still admire and appreciate a great or even shlocky classic from the golden age of reading—early adolescence—but it can never again be a waking dream, a preview of the wonders that lie hidden behind Curtain No. 3. Art, we have learned, always exaggerates. No Ruritania awaits our derring-do. Only some Bosnia, with its carnage and horror.

Names to Conjure With

A few years ago I bought for $5 an old copy of *Twentieth Century Authors: A Biographical Dictionary of Modern Literature,* edited by Stanley J. Kunitz (the poet) and Howard Haycraft (the mysteries expert). This massive tome, published in 1942, is one of the standbys of the 1950s library reference shelf. You would recognize its green cover. Unlike Benet's indispensable *Reader's Encyclopedia,* it encouraged living writers to contribute short first-person accounts of their careers. The editors then added some strictly factual material, enlivened with quite personal, often slyly humorous judgments and anecdotes. For anyone of a literary bent, it is a splendid book for browsing, as good in its way as Britain's famous, but multi-volumed, *Dictionary of National Biography.* Here, for instance, are the summarizing sentences in the entry on T. S. Eliot:

"Eliot has been described as an Arrow Collar man. He is darkly handsome, sensitive, extremely subtle, always ironical. He wears his handkerchief in his cuff, drinks burgundy and sherry, plays chess (not so well), and is afraid of cows and high places. He prefers to mingle with the nobility, with church dignitaries and genteel spirits. . . ." Isn't that charming? Percy Lubbock, we read, "cannot write a great deal more. He has little to do with the fleeting and mediocre, with the hasty and frivolous." John P. Marquand, it turns out, "figured as the murderee in Timothy Fuller's thinly disguised mystery novel of the Boston literary scene, *Three-Thirds of a Ghost.*" (Must look for this book.) And the last sentence for the write-up on Martha Gellhorn is deliciously sexist: "The author is slim and blonde." Still, it isn't long before a browser's smile starts to grow wistful. Take the entry for Clyde Brion Davis: "Still in his early middle age, Mr. Davis bears careful watching; he is one of the most unexpected and unpredictable of current writers." Perhaps so, but I have only met one person who has ever read *The Great American Novel—*. Orrick Johns, we are told, "was one of the pioneers of the new poetry in America." Orrick Johns? "Some of the pleasantest novels in print would have been lost to us had William De Morgan died at 65." Tell me, who reads those pleasant, long out of print, novels now?

And who reads Emil Ludwig or F. Van Wyck Mason, Louis Bromfield or Manuel Komroff? Yet even in my childhood these were stalwarts of the library shelf and the monthly book club. All virtually forgotten. Still, they are "twentieth-century authors," and they stare out at us—did I mention that each entry comes with a one-inch-square photo of the honored writer? —while we, half a century later, look back into their serious and hopeful faces. Shrewd people thought their work mattered, was important. We peer again into their faces. Did they know their fate? Could they have suspected?

The Old Illusions

Nevertheless, I cannot quite forget or dismiss these fading figures. I own several novels by Clyde Brion Davis, once read Van Wyck Mason with pleasure. They, as much as Pound or Ellison or Colette, make up my literary experience. Maybe yours, too. Louis Bromfield was from my home state of Ohio. Manuel Komroff edited my edition of Marco Polo's travels. And, of course, in ancient reveries, I once aspired to be like them, burned to see my name casually mentioned in the *Saturday Review of Literature* as "one of our most promising younger novelists." Alas, the gentlemanly literary culture I dreamed of joining, and probably half-imagined, had already begun to disappear. "The thoughts of youth are long, long thoughts." Sometimes they last a whole lifetime. Even now, like characters out of a Jack Finney time-travel fantasy, some of us still yearn to ride the 20th-Century Limited into an art deco New York, check into the Algonquin, stroll down Fifth Avenue to see our new books in the Scribners' shop window, and then go out for drinks with . . . Well, I'd be embarrassed to tell you. But you'd recognize the names.

Sigh. As Conrad knew, we never really learn, do we? "And we all nodded at him: the man of finance, the man of accounts, the man of law, we all nodded at him over the polished table that like a still sheet of brown water reflected our faces, lined, wrinkled; our faces marked by toil, by deceptions, by success, by love; our weary eyes looking still, looking always, looking anxiously for something out of life, that while it is expected is already gone—has passed unseen, in a sigh, in a flash—together with the youth, with the strength, with the romance of illusions."

Data Daze

For those of us who suffer from Researcher's Syndrome, sometimes known as Graduate Student's Disease, the Internet—once promised as a palliative, if not a miracle cure for this mental illness—has actually worsened our pitiable condition. In years past when a restless soul grew interested in, say, the art of the mystery story or John Webster's tragedy "The Duchess of Malfi" or the study of Late Antiquity, he or she could spend a few years in the library and emerge, admittedly a gray and broken shell, knowing nearly all that could be gleaned about the chosen subject. I say nearly all, for the essence of this scholar's malady lies in its perfidiousness: Its sufferers can never fully finish their research. Always, like the elusive blue flower of the German romantics, there beckons yet one more important text to peruse, just a few more documents to consult: Try as they may, the afflicted can never shake off a vague malaise, the sense that somewhere the key work awaits, that single reference that will turn the lock and open a new era in the appreciation of Lydgate's *Fall of Princes* or Milne's *House at Pooh Corner.*

But now, with the advent of chatrooms and e-mail lists, Web sites and home pages, research has entered a head-spinning era of constant flux, of permanent revolution. There can be no end to one's studies these days except through sheer exhaustion. Not merely do hot buttons and hypertext links entice us on Möbius trips through cyberspace, but the very nature of knowledge acquisition has altered. Instead of internalizing written texts, we engage in endless conversations, non-stop seminars wherein gossip and pedantry commingle. Consider: Every day fans of Patrick O'Brian's historical novels and James Joyce's *Finnegans Wake* go on-line to clarify some factual point or register a query about these masterpieces. Subscribers to these groups may stay only a while and then depart, but each contributes his little ort of understanding. Yet who would have thought that at the end of the millennium, exegesis would again be a flourishing genre? But then a fully loaded Web site resembles nothing so much as a page from an illuminated Bible, a few lines of text surrounded by swirls and layers of minutely focused commentary, most of it deeply learned, some of it positively demented.

Reading Readiness

All this was brought home to me recently while I was reading E. F. Benson's six comic novels about that irresistible force of nature Mrs. Emmeline Lucas, known as Lucia, and that immovable rock of malice, Miss Elizabeth Mapp. Little did I suspect that these perennially rediscovered masterpieces of English humor—largely about thrusts and parries for dominion among a group of well-to-do Britons—would lead to the transformation of my summer. But attend! My story follows, and all is true.

The tale begins innocently enough on one of those cold, rainy afternoons that mark April in Washington. Seeking refreshment from my editorial labors, I'd gone for a cup of coffee and then wandered blithely into the Book Room to check out the day's deliveries. Here were stacked page proofs of the usual forthcoming novels, military biographies, and compendia of soupy peasant wisdom. (Dale Carnegie—thou shouldst be living at this hour!) Just as I was about to return to the exciting task of editing a review about tax reform in post-1980s Ukraine—such a joy!—I noticed a slender tome titled *Queen Lucia*. Pouncing like a rabid marmoset, I snatched at the precious volume, and by so doing felled a precarious stack of the fall's more academic titles: I vividly recall *And Smiles to Go: The Female Gaze in the Modern Highway Billboard; A Micro-Analysis of the Macrobiotic: A Keynesian Looks at Tofu;* and, a bit late in the season, *Diamond Sutra: The Zen Way of Baseball.* As I picked up this last, the slender instruction manual fell open and I read, "First, said the Master, the acolyte must surrender his will to the varnished wood. He and the bat—One being!" No doubt you'll want to look for all these at your better university bookstores.

Queen Lucia, originally published in 1920, I knew was the first install-ment in a series of novels revered by Edward Gorey, Nancy Mitford, W. H. Auden, Auberon Waugh, and Noel Coward. On my subway ride home that night, I gobbled up the new edition's winsome introductory reminis-cence by Patrick O'Connor, the crusading editor who had first reprinted the Benson novels in paperback and later bound them together as a hard-cover omnibus entitled *Make Way for Lucia.* (In due course, I learned that O'Connor had eventually chucked publishing to work as a ski instructor in New England—very Bensonian.) Since the Lucia books, in any form, were now out of print, Moyer Bell was planning to republish the lot, in cor-rected texts, over the next year or two. All this was good news, except for that tiresome bit about spacing out the republication. Those who follow moderation and the golden mean in their reading habits—and I salute you sturdy souls—might be able to wait patiently like the Zen masters of base-ball, but I wanted all the books, and I wanted them now. So I began my usual search-and-acquire campaign in the Washington area's secondhand bookstores.

This may have been a mistake. I now own seventeen books by or about E. F. Benson (1867–1940), as well as one or two by his brothers, Robert Hugh Benson (author of theological fantasies and a friend of the notorious Baron Corvo) and A. C. Benson, a donnish essayist and inveterate keeper of diaries. Besides the subsequent Lucia novels (*Lucia in London; Miss Mapp; Mapp and Lucia; The Worshipful Lucia; Trouble for Lucia*), highlights of my unexpected collection include a beautiful copy of *As We Were,* Benson's memoir of his privileged Victorian childhood (his father became Archbishop of Canterbury), and firsts of *Spook Stories* and *More Spook Sto-ries,* essential volumes for any good fantasy collection. Lest the censorious imagine that I have the willpower of a willow branch, let me assure them that I waved aside at least a half-dozen other Benson titles, partly because even I couldn't contemplate gradually acquiring all eighty or so of his popu-lar biographies and sentimental novels. Yet I'd still happily take home the two "mysteries," *The Luck of the Vails* and *The Blotting Book,* as well as a nice copy of the comic *Secret Lives.*

Well, now I was certainly ready to read Lucia. Or was I?

Matters Worsen

Since the Christmas when my sportive infants implored Santa to bring them a spanking-new computer, our household has resounded to the mar-tial music, deafening explosions, and annoying catchphrases of Red Alert and Command and Conquer. But one lonely night it suddenly struck me that this very same machine could do more than play simulated war games. With a few adjustments, it could scuttle around the World Wide Web; it could send e-mail hither and yon. And so before you could say "A Luddite Discovers the Internet," I was on-line, searching for Bensoniana. The .com bookstores soon told me that only a few Benson titles were currently available. Better for my purposes, Interloc, Bibliofind, and some other used-book search services displayed dozens of Benson titles, at prices ranging from $8 to several hundred. I was sorely tempted by one or two items but concluded that I had more than enough of this prolific writer's oeuvre. Especially since I had yet to read a word of it, apart from a few ghost stories (don't miss "Caterpillars," "Mrs. Amworth," and "Negotium Perambulans").

Meanwhile, feeling increasingly overconfident about my computer dexterity, I distinctly recall fantasizing that I might learn a little programming, even write some code in my spare time, maybe tinker with the hardware. But for the moment I contented myself with calling up a search engine and cautiously typing in Benson's name; after a few seconds of microchip suspense, there gradually unfurled before my astonished eyes the E. F. Benson home page. There were photographs of the man himself—movie-star handsome; little wonder that he enjoyed so much social success, especially with rich dowagers—and summaries of the six Lucia comedies and views of Rye (fictionalized as Tilling) and links to both the E. F. Benson Society and the Tilling Society. There was even a sampling of favorite passages from Benson—though most of my own, not-yet-enjoyed favorites were apparently overlooked, including this gem from *Queen Lucia:* "My life has been guided by only one principle, and that is to finish a game of croquet whatever happens."

I diligently followed up all the EFB links, as well as bypaths now lost in time's mist, and somehow found my confused way to a Benson discussion group. With due circumspection, I thoughtfully drafted my first message, merely identifying myself and asking for answers to the usual FAQs (Frequently Asked Questions). Answers came bouncing back from Mrs. Titus W. Trout, Lord Tony, Blue Birdie, Pug (of nearby Poolesville), Mr. Hopkins, and a dozen others, all of whom I eventually deduced—following a smoke-filled night of Sherlockian ratiocination—were "noms de liste," drawn from the Lucia books. To bring me up to date, the unpugnacious Pug sent a selection of past postings, and before long I felt part of a closely knit group whose 100 or so members just happened to live in Scandinavia, Australia, Britain, and North Dakota. I began to look forward to my nightly visits with this urbane set (some of whom wrote in the voice of their chosen characters): Discussions of *As We Were* followed recollections of charming hostelries in Rye; plans for a cyber tea party on Benson's birthday vied with naughty limericks; arguments broke out over whether to read *Colin* or *Paying Guests* next; there was talk of Charles Kingsley and Oscar Wilde, Elizabeth Peters and Avram Davidson.

Pleasant as all this was (and is), E. F. Benson seemed mainly a springboard for all kinds of witty, bookish conversation. Pug shrewdly observed that the group's dynamics—its liking for gossip and news and squabble—mimicked that of the citizens of Riseholme and Tilling, who are always eager to hear the latest about Lucia or Miss Mapp. Whatever the case, one can grow surprisingly fond of people known only through blips on a computer screen.

About this time I actually opened *Queen Lucia*. And even read the first chapter, with growing pleasure. Unfortunately, I couldn't prevent myself from wondering how Benson's book (and its successors) would compare to other British classics of pre–World War II comic fiction. I knew Ronald Firbank's novels, as well as P. G. Wodehouse's and Waugh's, but shouldn't I read A. P. Herbert's *Topsy* and W. W. Jacobs's short stories and the famous *Diary of a Nobody* and go back to Daisy Ashford's *The Young Visiters* and look again at *Cold Comfort Farm,* and fish out my copy of *Augustus Carp,* once described as "the funniest unknown book in the world"? After all, one could fully appreciate Benson's genius only in context.

Well, I reasoned, the whole summer lies ahead of me. I have time to enjoy a half-dozen very pleasant novels before returning to *Queen Lucia.* And then—heavy sigh here—I learned of the existence of a five-part *Mapp and Lucia* video. Obviously I had to see it, but couldn't decide whether to wait until I'd read the novel (fourth in the series) or simply plump down immediately and enjoy the production on its own merits. Prunella Scales—a wonderfully Bensonian name—was reportedly a perfect Mapp. Maybe I could watch a couple of installments on nights when I felt particularly tired. Or maybe . . . just maybe . . . I could simply spend the rest of my life getting ready to read the Lucia books. Hmmm, would that be so bad?

Four-Leaf Clovers

Everyone knows who the great modern Irish writers are—Shaw, Yeats, Joyce, Beckett—a quartet of such eminence that none of them needs a first name to be instantly recognized. Next come the merely colossal, though still giants in their genres: the playwright Sean O'Casey, the short-story writer Frank O'Connor, the novelist Elizabeth Bowen, the Nobel Prize-winning poet Seamus Heaney. These are the Irish authors taught in classrooms, literary figures known the world over. Which is, paradoxically, the problem. Though I like a great man (or woman) at least as much as any Thomas Carlyle, as a reader I sometimes find such elevated literary company almost too stellar. To say that you love Joyce is to be just one more moo in the penman's lowing herd. Better to turn to the margins of literature, where the field is less crowded and the pleasures—of, say, the humorous fantasies of Irish literature's minor masters—deserve rediscovery. In such cases it is nearly always the style that first steals our affections—a certain hauteur in the authorial voice, perhaps an elaborate syntax or unusual diction, that edge of sardonic humor. Listen:

"In the centre of the pine wood called Coilla Doraca there lived not long ago two Philosophers. They were wiser than anything else in the world except the Salmon who lies in the pool of Glyn Cagny into which the nuts of knowledge fall from the hazel bush on its bank. He, of course, is the most profound of living creatures, but the two Philosophers are next to him in wisdom."

When reading this passage for the first time—they are the opening sentences to James Stephens's *The Crock of Gold* (1912)—I recognized one of my favorite kinds of prose: elegant blarney. To me, such high-toned diction elicits that shivery tingle one feels when sinking into a hot bath at the close of a sorely trying day. As to its actual plot, however, *The Crock of Gold* turns out to be something of a farrago: A local farmer discovers the hiding place of some leprechauns' gold; the farmer's daughter runs off with the great god Pan; the Philosopher seeks out the Gaelic deity Angus Og to rescue the girl; the leprechauns, angered over the loss of their treasure, falsely inform the local constabulary that the Philosopher has murdered his comrade; and, finally, the entire Celtic pantheon gathers to re-enter the secular world and presumably restore Eire to its ancient glory. Not surprisingly, *The Crock of Gold* displays many styles, and can be, by turns, didactic, touching, naturalistic, sentimental, and tiresome, as well as utterly magical. Maybe this range, as well as a common birthday, explains why James Joyce once chose Stephens as the right man to finish *Finnegans Wake* if he couldn't do it himself. In fact, I wonder if James Stephens might not be one of those Unacknowledged Influences on several later writers. Some of the Philosopher's logic-twisting dialogues with travelers met on empty roads sound like Beckett, while the shtick with slapstick policemen and Gaelic mythological beings recalls Flann O'Brien, who plays marvelous games with these in his tricksy novels *At Swim-Two-Birds* (1939) and *The Third Policemen* (1960, but written c. 1940). I checked Anthony Cronin's biography *No Laughing Matter,* but there is only a note that O'Brien probably read Stephens in his youth.

Cronin's invaluable book deftly chronicles the rather sorrowful life of civil servant Brian O'Nolan, aka Flann O'Brien, aka Myles na gCopaleen, this last being the name under which Dublin's answer to S. J. Perelman contributed a column to the *Irish Times:* I own four copies of *The Best of Myles* (1968, drawing on material from 1940s), two in hardcover, and would buy a fifth if I found one:

"I see that the collected letters of Cezanne have been published. Believe me, they are not half as interesting as the letters of Manet, which I am editing for publication at present. The title of the volume will be 'Littera Scripta Manet.' Limited edition of 25 copies printed on steam-rolled pig's liver and bound with Irish thongs in dessicated goat-hide quilting, a book to treasure for all time but to lock away in hot weather."

Perhaps O'Brien's most famous pieces describe professional book-handling—trained technicians who dog-ear and scribble in your books so that you appear more intellectual than you are—and an escort service staffed by ventriloquists for those who wish to seem witty without effort. Yet best of all are his effortless send-ups of sentimental Irish clichés:

"Remember the last time we played these little games when we were all together? Remember the yellow lamplight, Spot with his torn ear, the shutters with the iron bar across them; the black kettle hanging from the old smut-furred chain in the chimney and the delicate fluted china teacups made in Belleek? Poor George was alive then and Annie was only a little girl, little thinking she was soon to marry. That was over twenty-one years ago, in Newcastle West, where daddy's column of the Black and Tans was stationed. Dear old dead days, gone beyond recall. . . ."

Of course, the author who specialized in "dear old dead days, gone beyond recall"—at least of a sort—was Edward John Moreton Drax Plunkett, 18th Baron Dunsany. In collections like *The Sword of Welleran* (1908) and *A Dreamer's Tales* (1910), Dunsany, writing in a highly decorated, opulent style (with a quill pen), related Arabian Nights–like tales of sorcery, trickery, and wonder. Consider these opening sentences:

"When Thangobrind the jeweller heard the ominous cough, he turned at once upon that narrow way. A thief was he, of very high repute. . . ." "The Gibbelins eat, as is well known, nothing less good than man." "When the nomads came to El Lola they had no more songs, and the question of stealing the golden box arose in all its magnitude." If you can willingly stop reading stories with such beginnings, you must have the soul of an insurance salesman.

Of Dunsany's few novels, the most famous is *The King of Elfland's Daughter* (1924), a book that relies on neither plot nor characterization nor action to keep the reader's interest, but on lyrical description. Young Prince Alveric crosses into timeless faery, "beyond the fields we know," and wins the love of Lirazel, the king of Elfland's daughter; later her distraught father—half Zeus, half Buddha—resorts to one of his last two runes to waft his beloved child home; Alveric then searches after his fairy-wife for more than a dozen years; their son grows into a mighty hunter of unicorns; and eventually Lirazel returns to our world, bringing the other world's magic with her. One might read all this as the eventual harmonizing of the inner self, or even as a unifying of traditional archetypes, the Anglo-Saxon (practical, restless, conventional) and the Celtic (indolent, dreamy, poetic). Dunsany particularly excels at depicting landscapes of yearning, stasis, and reverie. Here is Alveric on his forlorn quest:

"Whether Elfland always lay over the next horizon, brightening the clouds with its glow, and moved away just as he came, or whether it had gone days or years before, he did not know but still kept on and on. And he came at last to a dry and grassless ridge on which his eyes and his hopes had been set for long, and from it he looked far over the desolate flatness that stretched to the rim of the sky, and saw never a sign of Elfland, never a slope of the mountains: even the little treasures of memory that had been left behind by the ebb were withering into things of our every day. Then Alveric drew his magical sword from its sheath. But though that sword had power against enchantment it had not been given the power to bring again an enchantment that was gone; and the desolate land remained the same, for all that he waved his sword, stony, deserted, unromantic and wide.

"For a little while he went on; but in that flat land the horizon moved imperceptibly with him, and never a peak appeared of the Elfin Mountains; and on that dreary plain he soon discovered, as sooner or later many a man must, that he had lost Elfland."

At one point Alveric goes to visit the witch Ziroondel and finds her on the heath with her broom. When questioned about what she's doing, she answers, "Sweeping the world." Alveric asks her, "Why are you sweeping the world, mother witch?" and she replies, "There's things in the world that ought not be here." In that eerie simplicity lies Dunsany's extraordinary imaginative power.

Dunsany could be funny as well as numinous, especially in the tall tales told by Joseph Jorkens in his London club (see, especially, *Jorkens Remembers Africa,* 1934). But the real masterpiece of post-war Irish humor is Mervyn Wall's *The Unfortunate Fursey* (1946). Set in the tenth century, the novel opens with the diabolic invasion of the monastery of Clonmacnoise by the forces of evil: poltergeists, succubi, demons, even Satan himself. When temporarily thwarted, these infernal shock troops take refuge in the cell of a 40-year-old lay brother: "Brother Fursey possessed the virtue of Holy Simplicity in such a high degree that he was considered unfit for any work other than paring edible roots in the monastery kitchen, and even at that, it could not be truthfully claimed that he excelled."

The Devil—as usual in such fantasies—is a courteous gentleman of impeccable manners and delicious wit. When Fursey is thrown out of Clonmacnoise, the prince of darkness accompanies him on the road to the city of Cashel. En route Satan mentions that the bishop of Cashel is trying to execute a certain old lady, a longtime friend. "'Himself and the King are intent on burning her as a witch. Did you ever hear the like?' said the Devil, and a hard note crept into his voice. 'If there's one thing I can't stand,' he said, 'it's superstition.'" As the novel proceeds, Fursey quite unwillingly becomes a wizard, acquires a long-suffering familiar, and in due course finds himself on trial for sorcery. Happily, his old friend the Devil— "always helpful, if a little headstrong"—comes to his rescue, actually conducting the ex-monk's defense. Much more happens in this satirical poke at Irish folkways, and all of it is delightful. In fact, *The Unfortunate Fursey* and its 1948 sequel, *The Return of Fursey* (which I'm saving for summer reading), have been called the Irish equivalent to T. H. White's *The Once and Future King*.

If you enjoy the dry, ironic humor of John Collier, Roald Dahl, Saki, or Jack Vance (and you should), you will like Fursey—provided you can find a copy of his misadventures. Exert yourself. The victory, as the Devil reminds us, "is not to the strong, but to the crafty." Or sometimes to the speedy: I noticed only one copy of Wall's masterpiece for sale on the Internet.

Sez Who?

Afternoon Delight: "OK," says my 7-year-old. "But first the Beanie Baby store, and then the bookstore. And you have to buy me two Beanies." "One." "Two." "All right, two. But not a word to Mom about the bookstore. That'll be our little secret." A strange light glints in suddenly cunning blue eyes. "Two Beanies, and an ice cream sandwich." Resistance, as they say, is futile.

Smoochie the Frog and Rainbow the Chameleon in hand, the child of my heart studies the jewelry cases at the front of the thrift store/book shop. He peers closely at a gaudy multicolored pin in the shape of a parrot. "Mom would like that for her birthday." $16. This is getting to be a costly escapade. But then . . . there on the shelf are first English editions of George Painter's two-volume biography of Proust ($4), pristine copies of the initial two volumes in the standard set of Henry James's short stories ($2 each), and a beautiful English hardcover of Mario Praz's *The Hero in Eclipse in Victorian Fiction* ($3). Poor Mario. The century's leading Italian interpreter of English literature, Praz is one of my favorite critics, not least because he was thought to possess the Evil Eye. People would cross themselves when he looked their way. Colleagues would avoid meeting him. His autobiography, *The House of Life,* is basically a description of the furnishings in his apartment. Another book rants about the sheer awfulness of Spain and Spanish culture. And his most famous work, *The Romantic Agony,* remains a wonderfully lurid study of sexual excess in the nineteenth century.

Friendly Visit: "You need to cull," says my London friend John, possessor of the finest private library I know. "Get rid of the paperbacks and later printings." He pulls out three or four G. K. Chesterton titles from my shelves. "All the Father Browns should go; none is right." He approves, with mildly covetous eye, the American first of *The Napoleon of Notting Hill.* "But what," I splutter, "should I do if I want to read some Father Brown stories?" My friend looks perplexed, then stern. "Better to forgo a temporary pleasure than to muck up your library with . . . clutter." For a moment he might be a Puritan divine.

The next day we go booking. At a local used-book warehouse I seize upon a lovely copy of the English edition of John Collier's *His Monkey Wife,* a fizzily satirical jeu d'esprit about a man who marries a chimp. Alas, it's the second printing. On the other hand, it's only $7, and I daydream about rereading this witty novel, turning its slightly stiff, creamy pages while sipping gin and tonic. A much prettier volume than my American reprint. "Put that back," insists my friend, as he checks out my small pile of possible purchases. "Clutter." But I mew, piteously, that it's such an attractive book. "A true collector ought not to be swayed by mere looks. Either a book is right or it's not." Cowed, I slowly replace the Collier on the shelf. Who would have thought that collecting books could be such a spiritually rigorous calling?

Pulp Nonfiction: "Earthworms," says the tiny ad at the back of the January 1969 issue of *Ellery Queen's Mystery Magazine.* I've recently bought $5 worth of back issues dating from the 1960s and '70s—10 cents apiece— and have been idly turning the pages, reading John Dickson Carr's "Jury Box" review column, laughing at Robert L. Fish's brilliant Schlock Homes parodies, wondering if a certain Thomas Flanagan could be the future prize-winner for *The Year of the French.* In particular, I've been setting aside any months featuring crime stories by Avram Davidson, one of my favorite writers, best known for his quirky, humorous, and utterly original fantasy fiction (in "Or All the Seas with Oysters" we learn that clothes hangers are the larval state of bicycles).

These old magazines, with their grainy paper stock, double columns of type, and back cover advertisements for the Detective Book Club ("$40.75 worth of Perry Mason mysteries for only $1"), provide a dose of powerfully concentrated nostalgia: They carry me back to the basements of yesteryear, where one could always unearth moldering stacks of *True, Modern Romance, Life,* and *EQMM,* usually in some dark corner or right under the shelves lined with Reader's Digest Condensed Books and the bestsellers of Thomas B. Costain. *The Black Rose*—now, there was a novel!

In particular, the Ellery Queen classifieds sound a last huzzah for the era of door-to-door salesmen and mail-order, get-rich schemes: "Hypnotize Strangers in Seconds! Most Powerful Device Created! Amazing Hypnodisk only $2"; "Guaranteed Home Income Raising Chinchillas"; "Save hundreds of dollars!!! Make your own S&M Densitometer" (whatever that is); "Buried Treasure Is Everywhere: New Map Book Shows over 400 U.S. Locations"; "ESP laboratory"; "Root Beer Formula—family secret, only $3"; "Over 60 Peanut Butter Sandwich Recipes." Still, of all these my favorite has to be: "Earthworms. BIG Money Raising Fishworms and Crickets. Free Literature. Carter Farm, Plains, Georgia." Note the name and address. Obviously, our thirty-ninth president was somewhat more than just a peanut farmer. I wonder if any of that free literature is still available.

At the Library: "Beautiful day," says the librarian, as I dry my wet glasses. Is there a better place on a rainy afternoon than a library? I stop by my local branch at least once a week, and sometimes don't even check out a book. I might buy a paperback for a quarter from the little on-sale cart; rent a video for my children; possibly do some research for a review. Of course, being list-mad, I always pick up those photocopied handouts and bookmarks of Recommended Readings, the ones headed "If You like Anne Tyler . . . " or "If you like Stephen King . . . " Now and then I even think of surreptitiously replacing the official lists with my own counterfeits: "If You Like *Layamon's Brut,* be sure to try *Alcuin's Hymn* and *The Dream of the Rood*"; "If You Like *Fanny Hill,* don't miss *The Pearl* and *The Tides of Lust.*"

Bad Timing: "This?" says the elderly gentleman at the secondhand bookshop. "Why, I just found it on the New Arrivals shelf. I'd read some of the stories and thought I'd give this a try." I stifle my greed and angst. This is *The Five Jars,* the only novel by the ghost-story master M. R. James. I've been wanting a copy for years. The white-haired usurper—a double for one of James's mild-mannered antiquaries or doomed clergymen—allows me to look at the book. Though not a first (sorry, John), it is an early edition, cheap at $8, and a hard item to find in cloth. I think of offering to buy it from him—or of simply bolting out the door while tossing a ten-spot to the store's cashier. But I can see that Canon Alberic, as I've mentally dubbed him, is already staring at me warily. "You know," I say nonchalantly, "that it's a children's book." I emphasize the word "children's." "Not really for grown-ups. For kids. Ju-ve-nile readers." The elderly man brightens. "Why, I didn't know, but thank you for telling me. I'll just give it to my granddaughter."

Visit Home: "Why don't you," says my mother, "sort some of those boxes of books up in the attic?" Sort is a maternal code word for get rid of. Packed under the eaves are maybe a dozen cartons. Here, I soon discover, are my paperback copies of the mysteries and thrillers that succored me through early adolescence: Sax Rohmer's *The Insidious Dr. Fu Manchu* and its innumerable sequels, a half-dozen of Donald Hamilton's Matt Helm adventures, various spy thrillers by Edward S. Aarons, James Munro, and numerous half-forgotten paperback novelists: *Assignment: Sulu Sea; The Man Who Sold Death; The Silken Baroness Contract* . . . No way am I parting with any of these treasures.

On the other hand, several boxes spill over with French *livres de poche,* acquired during a year spent in Marseille (my gun-running days, about which I preserve a discreet silence): Sartre's earnest *Chemins de la Liberté* sequence, regional fiction by Francis Carco and Henri Bosco, a historical novel by Jean de la Varende . . . They all make the short car journey to the local Goodwill. Maybe, I reflect, some high school kid, taking French IV, will ride over on his bike and grab a couple for a quarter apiece. In a moment I flash back to my own younger self, peddling from Amvets Value Village to St. Vincent de Paul's Opportunity Shop to Clarice's Values to the Salvation Army outlet, in search of something good to read. Something, ideally, like *Murderer's Row* or *My Gun Is Quick.*

In the Wheaton Library Sale Room: "Got in a nice classical collection," says the record expert when I ask what's new. Wonderful discs, many by my favorite performers: pianist Sviatoslav Richter, tenor Jussi Bjorling, violinist David Oistrakh—not that it takes any special skill to appreciate such virtuosi. There's even a recording of Mozart's *Magic Flute* conducted by George Szell—something I'd never seen before and which isn't mentioned in any of my music reference books. Doubtless true audiophiles know all about it. I wander along the shelves, searching for paperbacks of E. F. Benson's Lucia books, Tom Sharpe's comic novels, further installments in Terry Pratchett's Discworld series. Tragedy tomorrow, comedy tonight. Am planning to spend a lot of the summer on light reading and have already set aside James Anderson's *The Affair of the Blood-Stained Tea Cosy* (a pastiche of the classic country house mystery), Joe Keenan's two Wodehouse-like comedies about a pair of gay blades in modern New York, some Ivy Compton Burnett, and a one-volume compilation of E. Nesbit's novels about the Bastable family.

Suddenly, what to my wondering eyes should appear but an entire bookcase stocked with past numbers of *Gramophone,* the classical music magazine. There must be two hundred issues, some going back to the early 1950s. For a dizzying moment I think of buying them all. Five for a dollar.

What a bargain! But—the voice of reason making a rare, one-performance-only appearance—where would I put them? Instead I shrewdly take every single December issue: December is when the magazine's various critics choose their favorite records of the year. I also look for the months announcing the annual music awards. I will lie by swimming pools this July and read—against the shrill counterpoint of children shouting Marco Polo—about Emil Gilels playing Grieg, the Hungarian Quartet performing Beethoven, the Tallis Scholars singing Palestrina.

At the Café: "We've had books for sale here for a while," says the young guy making up double iced caffe lattes and other confections. I order a small black coffee, which costs $1.32. There's a stack of the latest titles for Oprah's Book Club. I try to imagine the talk-show diva announcing that this month's discussion will focus on *The Brothers Karamazov.*

Smiling to myself, I choose a seat in a corner away from the loudspeaker emitting country-western sounds. Then I open my notebook, and think about my next "Readings" column. I scribble an idea, then another. I sip my coffee. The world is good.

Lament for a Maker

In the great fifteenth-century poem "Lament for the Makers," William Dunbar reflects on the deaths of his poetic contemporaries, most of them now forgotten but one or two, including Chaucer, among the glories of English literature. Drawing on traditional views of life's uncertainty ("this fals world is bot transitory"), Dunbar lists the ravages of time, names the friends who have died, and confesses his own fears, even as a Latin phrase from the Office of the Dead rings at the end of each quatrain like a tocsin:

> The stait of man dois change and vary,
> Now sound, now seik, now blith, now sary,
> Now dansand mery, now like to dee:
> Timor mortis conturbat me.

"The fear of death troubles me."

We have all experienced such intimations of mortality, usually after awaking from uneasy dreams, when we are jabbed into sudden consciousness by the irrefutable, ice-cold realization that someday we too must die. Lying there in the tremulous darkness, our minds find the prospect inconceivable, terrifying, and for a shuddering moment, astonishingly close at hand. But the spiritual vertigo eventually passes, and we return to our sleepy lives, once more temporarily forgetful of death's bright dart.

Dunbar's lamentation for the poets of his age came sadly to mind just before Christmas of 1996, when I learned of Ross Thomas's death. For many readers Ross Thomas has long been one of the most entertaining writers of our time, his fiction a tart mixture of crime caper, spy thriller, and political novel, frequently set in such exotic places as a semi-imaginary Africa or an all-too-real Washington. With their sardonic tone, crisp sentences, and original and engaging characters, Thomas's two dozen or so novels can be quite literally irresistible.

That Christmas I casually took up my old copy of *Chinaman's Chance* and read again its opening sentences: "The pretender to the Emperor's throne was a fat thirty-seven-year-old Chinaman called Artie Wu who always jogged along Malibu Beach right after dawn even in summer, when dawn came round as early as 4:42. It was while jogging along the beach just east of the Paradise Cove pier that he tripped over a dead pelican, fell and met the man with six greyhounds. It was the sixteenth of June, a Thursday." A few hours later I turned, regretfully, the last page.

In fact, I find aspects of this particular novel's denouement somewhat farfetched—too many people seem to be related—but then *Hamlet* or *Crime and Punishment* can be farfetched too. The deep pleasure of *Chinaman's Chance* derives from its intricate exposition, its roguish heroes, and a glistening diction. An ex-Marine who has just had his thumb broken because he is behind on his loan payments shakes his head "as though suddenly struck by the realization that all was perfidy." A ruthless crime boss is discovered reading Rilke when visited by his former roommate (from Bowdoin!), now a renegade CIA agent. Both men are utterly amoral, yet one possesses a wistful romantic courtliness and the other a refined demeanor and beautifully tailored manners.

Of course, for me Ross Thomas has long been more than the author of *The Seersucker Whipsaw*, the Edgar-winning *Briarpatch*, or *Ah, Treachery!* (his last novel, wherein the protagonist spends Christmas Eve happily rereading Freya Stark's *The Valleys of the Assassins*). For nearly eighteen years I periodically telephoned Malibu to ask Thomas to review something or other. The man was always, invariably, at his desk. He would pick up the phone on the second ring, agree to write about the book (usually a thriller or Washington novel), and three weeks later send in an immaculately typed, absolutely perfect critique or appreciation, precisely 750 words long. No reviewer was ever more professional.

Eventually, I met Thomas a few times—one memorable evening in the company of Elmore Leonard—and liked him a lot. He possessed an appealingly dry sense of humor, the kind where you have to think twice to pick up on the ironies, and he told wonderful anecdotes about the idiocies of Hollywood hotshots and entrepreneurs. Tradition asserts that writers put the best of themselves into their work. Perhaps so. But in this case I, like many others, deeply miss the man himself.

Of Time and the Rolodex

Holden Caulfield famously observed that what he wanted, after reading a good book, was to be able to call up the writer on the phone. When I first came to *Book World,* I did just that: telephoned my heroes, ostensibly (and sometimes successfully) to ask them to review, but really just to hear their voices and, in the best sense, pay my respects. A good many of these eminences were then elderly and—as is natural, alas—have now died. In fact, my friend and colleague Reid Beddow once jokingly called my Rolodex a necropolis, for the cards of the glorious dead are still in it.

Here at the beginning, for instance, is Isaac Asimov, who wrote for an education supplement, many years ago, about "science and the sense of wonder." Like Ross Thomas he was always at his desk; like Balzac he believed that constant work was the law of art as it is of life. The Bs cast up the polymathic novelist Anthony Burgess, who struck me as having read everything, and most of it twice. For a while his Italian wife acted as his agent, and the contessa, as I always thought of her, demanded double our usual reviewing fee for her husband. She got it. Next comes my much-missed Angela Carter, with her devil-may-care iconoclasm and the prose of an angel (or even of an aerialiste with real wings: see *Nights at the Circus*). Our book business finished, we would usually exchange anecdotes about our growing sons. Flipping through the cards at random, I glimpse the names of Robert Penn Warren, who sent *Book World* a poem that we featured on the front page, and Sir John Pope-Hennessy, the distinguished art historian of the Renaissance, who once reviewed a lavish edition of Vasari's *Lives,* and Sir Harold Acton, dedicatee of Evelyn Waugh's *Decline and Fall* and later the genial grandee of the Villa La Pietra, which he invited me to visit. I never did.

The names of favorite science fiction greats whiz by: the eccentric, antiquarian Avram Davidson, as mordantly funny as John Collier or Roald Dahl; the kindly Theodore Sturgeon, surely one of America's best short-story writers; Fritz Leiber, who praised Stephen King's *Danse Macabre*. Here too is Terrence des Pres, dead a week after agreeing to review a book by Primo Levi, who had himself just committed suicide; and Professor Warren Ault, who at 102 wrote about a new biography of his friend T. E. Lawrence, in whose company he had made brass rubbings at Oxford a mere eighty years previous. Ault died quietly in his sleep only a few days before his memoir appeared in print. Then there is the gentlemanly John D. MacDonald, whose thrillers about Travis McGee I could never really like but whose high-quality prolificness I admired unconditionally, and the gravel-voiced Charles Willeford, revered by the cognoscenti for his Hoke Mosely thrillers, especially *Miami Blues.*

Of fiction writers there is no end. Robertson Davies, who also died in 1996, wrote regularly for *Book World* in the '80s and once contributed a ghost story, an updated *Christmas Carol,* for a special holiday issue. A cluster of shades circles around the name of John Gardner, author of *Grendel* and other novels but best known for the once-notorious *On Moral Fiction.* Not long before his motorcycle death, Gardner reviewed *Dubin's Lives* by Bernard Malamud. Later that year I glimpsed the aged Malamud at a literary cocktail party talking quietly with spymaster James J. Angleton: I stood shyly in a corner and gazed my full at them, in thrall to wonder and surmise. Not far from Gardner's Rolodex card peacefully lie those of his former student Raymond Carver, the finest short-story writer of the '80s, and of his old friend the late Stanley Elkin, whose early fiction he published. Carver kept promising to review but never did: He was probably too sick with cancer to bother about such frivolities. Elkin appeared twice in *Book World*—once in an essay he wrote for the series The Writing Life, and once in a conversation with William Gass on the art of fiction: They argued a lot about John Gardner.

And yet another turn of the wheel yields up James Merrill, whose death cast a pall over the spring's poetry, and classicist Robert Fitzgerald, who translated the ancients (Homer, Virgil) and befriended the moderns (John Berryman, Flannery O'Connor). At Paul Monette's name I pause, thinking of his death at 49 from AIDS and recalling the screwball humor of his first novel, and my second major book review, *Taking Care of Mrs. Carroll.* More happily, Christopher Isherwood's card reminds me of a forty-five-minute conversation about the character and crotchets of W. H. Auden. For literary thrills, though, none has yet equaled meeting Virgil Thomson, whose hand I actually shook. That was like touching Moses, for not only was Thomson a great composer and music critic, he was also the friend of Gertrude Stein, James Joyce, and other gods of modern art.

Yet of all the cards still reposing on my Rolodex, two in particular elicit thoughts that lie too deep for tears. One belongs to my own mentor in the literary life, Robert Phelps, expert on Colette, Auden, Cocteau, and the art of friendship. The other is that for my *Book World* colleague Reid Beddow. Shortly after my father's funeral, Reid comforted me with apt, consoling words, all the while knowing that he himself was dying. Such selflessness was characteristic of the man. Ah, Reid! Good friend, superb editor, lover of books and Irish setters, be with me during this gloomy season of the year. *Timor mortis conturbat me.*

Last Things

The literary often turn to words for comfort, and a theme like death brings out the deepest poetry. I'm very fond of the Roman swagger of the dying Bosola in Webster's "Duchess of Malfi." He is asked, "How came Antonio by his death?" and answers with these proud and somber words:

> In a mist: I know not how
> Such a mistake, as I have often seene
> In a play: Oh I am gone—
> We are only like dead wals, or vaulted graves,
> That ruined, yeildes no echo: Fare you well—
> It may be paine: but no harme to me to die,
> In so good a quarrel: Oh this gloomy world,
> In what a shadow, or deep pit of darknesse,
> Doth (womanish, and fearful) mankind live!
> Let worthy minds nere stagger in distrust
> To suffer death, or shame, for what is just—
> Mine is another voyage.

My every third thought will be the grave, asserted the retired magician Prospero, and he might have been echoed by the philosopher Pascal: "The last act is bloody, however wonderful the rest of the play." William Temple, in an essay on poetry, offers a more comforting, if rather quietistic, view: "When all is done, human life is at the greatest and the best but like a froward child, that must be played with and humoured a little to keep it quiet till it falls asleep, and then the care is over."

The final sentences of George Eliot's *Middlemarch* may seem a bit fustian, but they build to a magnificent final cadence: "For the growing good of the world is partly dependent on unhistoric acts; and that things are not so ill with you and me as they might have been, is half owing to the number who lived faithfully a hidden life, and rest in unvisited tombs."

"And rest in unvisited tombs." Am I wrong to hear in this lovely phrase a mournful Biblical echo? No scriptural verses are as lonely as these: "As for man, his days are as grass: as a flower of the field, so he flourisheth. For the wind passeth over it, and it is gone; and the place thereof shall know it no more."

Clubland

In P. G. Wodehouse novels, Bertie Wooster often repairs to the Drones Club, there to launch a deadly breadstick at Tuppy Glossop or to confer about matters of the heart with Gussie Fink-Nottle, the noted newt-fancier. In Dorothy Sayers's *Unpleasantness at the Bellona Club,* an elderly member is found in his usual leather chair, slumped behind a copy of the *Morning Post,* quite dead. But for how long? That's the mystery. In biographies and memoirs, English notables are always enjoying bibulous lunches at White's and then penning a scathing letter to the club secretary about the churlishness of the younger members or the completely reprehensible conduct of Maj. Cholmondley, he of the loud, booming voice.

They may be hives of privilege and wealth, but private clubs have long cast a siren-spell on those of us whose idea of paradise is a faded leather armchair, some late afternoon sunlight streaming through a window, an amusing book to read, and the distant promise of a good dinner with lively company. Of course, we could never actually afford or justify the annual fees, let alone find the time to steal away from our jobs or families for an afternoon; and if we did, our hearts would soon be troubled by the thought that we really should be up and about, engaging in some Type-A behavior or doing our part for the Protestant work ethic. Not everyone can be a Drone who aspires to that coveted and enviable condition.

Still, now and again, it is pleasant to pretend. Recently I was an overnight guest at the Yale Club in New York. Even without crossing its threshold I could tell that this was a serious place: A notice on the door stated that gentlemen were required to wear jackets and ties in all public rooms. I duly strolled around the corner and surreptitiously slipped on a tie, fortunately one of a sober regimental character. I then sauntered back, allowed the door to be opened for me by an eager minion, and approached the front desk with what I hoped was the jaunty nonchalance of Raffles, the gentleman-cracksman. I signed my name with a calligraphic flourish and forthwith received my guest membership card, with all attendant privileges.

Privileges. My mind seemed to dwell on that word. While riding the elevator to my room, I noted various floors that provided a steam room, several restaurants (including one on the rooftop), health-club facilities, a library. Naturally the hallways sported architectural prints of New Haven and portraits of distinguished Yalies; in the distance I could almost certainly hear the susurration of chambermaids and the comforting ring of heavy silver on china plates. "Come the revolution," I murmured quietly as I later dried my face with a fluffy towel, unobtrusively stamped with the club's initials, "come the revolution, all this will go." But then I stopped by the Grill Room for lunch: a buffet with a choice of veal or fresh fish, delicately prepared vegetables, all kinds of rolls (several suitable for tossing), raspberries or cheesecake for dessert. In the middle of the dining area stood two green-felt billiard tables, and I could picture old duffers being taken for thousands by pencil-mustached foreigners in ill-fitting evening clothes. Nearby I noticed a chess corner and bridge nook, as well as an expensive backgammon set tucked near a silent television. All around there were small groups of people, to all appearances networking, cutting deals, rekindling old romances. One could, I thought, get used to this.

Then I saw the library. Long mahogany tables. Individual reading lamps. Soft carpeting everywhere. Row upon row of dark wooden shelves. All at once, my populist convictions, already beginning to buckle, utterly collapsed. I wanted this room. I resolved to amend my life and grow rich beyond the dreams of avarice, just so I could own a library exactly like this one. Suddenly I knew just how Scarlett O'Hara felt, standing at night in that field of turnips.

Still reeling from this sudden flush of materialist desire, I proceeded to wander into a large common room, where I immediately paused in silent wonder, dumbfounded: For there they all were, the living descendants of Mervyn Keene, Clubman. At the center of the room loomed a vast table, barely suitable for the wedding feast at Cana; upon its polished brown surface lay folded newspapers from around the world. Nearby, stuffed deep in armchairs or half-reclining on leather sofas, there relaxed more than a dozen substantial men in soft gray suits, their stomachs valiantly supporting watch chains and Phi Beta Kappa keys; several were smoking cigars of a fragrance that even Fidel would envy, while others sipped thoughtfully from tumblers of single-malt scotch or brandy. A few spoke in hushed tones with companions, no doubt discussing the fate of the Dow or the finer points of a newly acquired spaniel, and one looked like George Will. For all I know, it might have been George Will.

A day later my guest membership in the Yale Club came to an end. I rode the train back to Washington in a pensive mood, basking in the afterglow of my brush with clubland. At home in Silver Spring, once the intended site of the nightmarish megamall, I walked across my weedy lawn, up the steps of a porch badly in need of fresh paint, and into a hallway strewn with schoolbags, plastic weaponry, and a cat mewing to be let out. A rush of children soon swarmed about me and sternly demanded presents. My beloved spouse glanced up from a dining-room table covered with invoices and bills, then gazed reproachfully at my loot from the Strand bookstore. I gave a faint, Walter Mittyish smile.

Of my idyll in the early paradise, nothing remains now but the warm memory, like that of a child for a long-ago visit to Disney World.

The Learning Channels

February always felt bleakest in Oberlin—cold rain alternated with wet snow, the gray sky never changed for weeks, and we would shiver in our swampcoats and parkas while wading across the muddy quad toward the breakfast line at Dascomb. After wolfing down some cereal and coffee, most of us would then race—nearly always late—to an 8 o'clock art class in Hall Auditorium, a practice room at the Conservatory, a lecture in Peters or King.

For a long time I thought about my friends when I remembered my days at Oberlin, some thirty years ago. But more recently I've started recalling my teachers. Most are retired now, some are dead, and I feel—perhaps a sign of my own middle-agedness—a bittersweet solicitude when I picture them: gripping lecterns, scribbling formulas on blackboards, desperately questioning an honors seminar about the motivations for Emma Bovary's adultery. They tried so hard! I want to tell them, now that it is for the most part too late, how much I loved their courses; above all, I want to thank them for opening my mind to history, literature, art, philosophy, music, and so much else.

But would they, I sometimes wonder, even remember me? An average college professor must teach two or three courses a semester, from 100 to 1,000 students a year. A few cutups and whiz kids doubtless stand out, but ultimately one 19-year-old must be much like another. More than most people, professors lead inherently tragic lives: They grow old while all around them swarm the eternally young. Though they plant and scatter seeds aplenty, nearly all their harvests remain unseen.

I was lucky enough to attend a college where captivating teachers were the norm. Sometimes you didn't even have to take a class to be inspired by them. The retired and distinguished Professor Frederick B. Artz, author of standard works on medieval history and revolutionary Europe, lived in an ordinary-looking house behind the old Carnegie Library. I met him, very briefly, only once. But I have never forgotten his study. Dark bookshelves along the walls. Worn volumes—hardcovers, sets—standing in serried rows. The kind of antique globe Prince Henry the Navigator might have daydreamed over. Oriental rugs, of course, and Renaissance prints, even a green-globed library lamp in the center of a massive desk. Throughout, the holy hush of ancient sacrifice. Many years afterward, I acquired a copy of Sandys's *Short History of Classical Scholarship,* with Artz's bookplate in it. Even now I occasionally pick up the book just to stare at the scribbled date —"Cambridge, October, 1921"—while trying to imagine the meeting of the young scholar with the eminent Sir John Edwin Sandys, whose calling card is pasted on the flyleaf. Alas, the several thousand other books and works of art live only in my memory, and I have long known that "Freddy" Artz's study will haunt me all my life: a vision of Pisgah.

As an undergraduate I took several courses in European history, and all of them were superb. Barry McGill, sandy-haired, tall, and thin, would stride into the lecture hall and immediately begin talking. He invariably wore dark, crisply pressed three-piece suits; favored dashing rep ties with quietly assertive stripes of burgundy; and always kept his dressy black wingtips polished and spotless. There was no nonsense about him. He lectured, we took notes. But such a mind! Such clarity in his exposition of anything from nominalism to the course of the Thirty Years' War! As he spoke, in crisp, Gibbonian sentences, one felt awe at the precision of his intelligence. Imagine Sherlock Holmes as a history prof and you will have an inkling of McGill's charisma. Alas, I now cringe to recollect the subject of my term paper for his class in early modern European thought: a psychoanalytic interpretation of the nineteenth-century anarchist Mikhail Bakunin ("The passion for destruction is a creative passion"). What can I say? It was 1968. In one self-destructive moment I managed to send a solid A average plummeting to a C-plus for the semester. I am grateful only that my research led me to several books by E. H. Carr, including his wonderful account of Alexander Herzen, Bakunin, and friends, *The Romantic Exiles.* McGill died a couple of years ago, and I never saw him again after I graduated. But there was obviously far more to the man than an Ohio college instructor with the dry manner of an Oxford grandee. I was told that, following the death of his wife, the long-retired McGill, restless and lonely, took a part-time job without pay shelving books in the college library. A former colleague asked him why, and he reportedly answered, "I began my academic life as a student working in the library, and I can think of no better way to end it." I hope this story isn't apocryphal.

In those days Oberlin—living up to the old ideal of a liberal arts college—swarmed with professors who poured their energies into the classroom and never quite got around to writing that major work of scholarship. We students benefited, of course. Immensely. There was my revered English teacher Andrew Bongiorno, who taught Dante and Metaphysical poetry. When he gently elucidated a line of Donne or Herbert, you felt the irresistible authority that always accompanies deep learning tempered by spiritual humility. Bongiorno died in 1999 at the age of 98. There was Robert Neil, who specialized in German history and who sometimes wore suspenders and lederhosen to class. Funny, worldly, and very smart, Neil had studied with Crane Brinton at Harvard and, according to rumor, had there dispensed fabulous sums on wine for his college dining club. And then there was Mathis Szykowski, an expert on the nineteenth-century French novel. A Polish Jew in World War II France, he lost most of his family to the Holocaust, emigrated to America, married a black woman, spent five years on a socialist farm, and earned a B.A. in night school while working by day as a typesetter in New York City. He came to Oberlin on a short-term appointment with only an M.A., and seven years later, well into middle age, was granted tenure. Without a Ph.D. The college didn't really have a choice: Anyone with a smidgen of French took his courses to see, as one student evaluation had it, "a genius in action." When Szykowski spoke about war or politics or art or ideology, you could look into his eyes—unnervingly large and probing behind his thick glasses—and know that he wasn't just getting this stuff from books.

In those now-ancient days, courses focused on major texts and were serious about study. For one French class—with wry, quick-witted New Yorker Vinio Rossi—we read *À la recherche du temps perdu* in a semester; in another, all of Montaigne's essays. For a required religion course, I took "Old Testament Literature," and we started with Genesis and ended with Zechariah and Malachi. Since our teacher, Herbert Gordon May, was the Old Testament editor of the Revised Standard Version of the Bible, it was a little like learning from God himself. In "Shakespeare" students gradually went through the complete works in a year. Tests were rigorous: Warren Taylor, who taught the later plays, would ask exam questions such as "What happens when Hamlet visits his mother in her bedroom? Quote as much of the dialogue as you can in your answers." The fiery, Lear-like Taylor, who was then a year from retirement, maintained that interpretations of Shakespeare changed like fashions, but there was no substitute for simply knowing the plays inside out. (As indeed there isn't.) For a class on Yeats and Stevens—under the direction of poet and professor David Young —we read not only all the verse of these two demanding poets but whole volumes of their prose: Yeats's *A Vision*, Stevens's *The Necessary Angel*, raftloads of miscellaneous essays, criticism, and letters.

Despite an emphasis on good teaching, Oberlin also boasted some older scholars of international reputation besides Artz and May. Several belonged to the art department. The courtly Wolfgang Stechow—the great authority on Northern baroque art—spent half the year at the Allen Art Museum and half the year at the National Gallery here in D.C. To the rigorous Stechow, the only scholarship that really counted was archival research and work with primary materials. Modern art professor Ellen Johnson—a powerful advocate of new painting—donated much of her own collection, often work given to her by now-famous artists, to establish a program through which students could "rent" a real painting or etching for a semester; I can vividly remember a Sol Lewitt print and an Andy Warhol "Marilyn" in my future wife's dorm room. Back then a young scholar, Richard Spear, allowed me to audit his classes in baroque art: They were the most cultivated and informed art lectures this side of Kenneth Clark. Last month he brought out a massive study of the Renaissance painter Guido Reni.

🐛

But doubtless there are great and eccentric teachers at every college, no matter how small or grand. Like Virgil with Dante, such masters lead us slowly up out of the intellectual darkness—and then we leave them behind with scarcely a backward glance, let alone a proper thank you. I can't let that happen with Marcia Colish.

Professor Colish taught the richest, most mind-expanding course of my entire academic career: "The Intellectual History of the Middle Ages." Many people know a little about the thought and literature of the modern world, but Colish introduced her students to Augustine's apologetics and philosophy, Bede's *Ecclesiastical History*, the educational achievements of

Alcuin, the soaring theological intellects of Anselm and Bernard of Clair-
vaux, the romances of Chrétien de Troyes, Abelard's razor-sharp mind, the
ecstatic visions of the Victorines, St. Thomas Aquinas's rigorous scholasti-
cism, and that summa of medieval culture, Dante's *Divine Comedy.*

I realize now that she could scarcely have been more than 30, but there
was no doubting her vast learning even then. She spoke machine-gun fast
in a brassy voice, and you had to focus to keep up with her plum-packed
lectures. Gnosticism. Avicenna. The Other World. Universals. Andreas
Capellanus's *Art of Courtly Love.* Hroswitha's plays. And her assignments!
Read E. K. Rand's *Founders of the Middle Ages.* Read M. L. W. Laistner's
Thought and Letters in Western Europe, A.D. *500–900.* Read Charles Homer
Haskins's *Renaissance of the Twelfth Century.* Read the entire *Divine Com-
edy*—by next week.

Exhilarating hardly describes Colish's class, but a course, no matter
how good, is almost as evanescent as a ballet. Once it's over, it's over. Or so
I thought until 1998, when Yale brought out the first volume in its new
series "The Yale Intellectual History of the West." *Medieval Foundations of
the Western Intellectual Tradition, 400–1400,* by Marcia L. Colish, is clearly
based on the class I took so many years ago, and it should instantly become
the standard introduction to its subject. Colish's prose is hardly sparkling,
and she can be acutely demanding at times (she loves medieval philosophy
more than most of us ever will), but between the covers of this hefty,
densely written volume is a whole lost world of culture and wisdom. I've
read two-thirds of the book, and my copy is already stippled with stars,
checks, underlinings, and all the other ornamentation of intensive study.
What's more, every so often a phrase or fact suddenly delivers a minor
epiphany, and I can hear Colish's voice and feel myself—for a brief, cozy
moment—scribbling away in my college notebook. It's a good feeling, especially on a cold, gray winter morning in February.

Guy Davenport

In a preface to *The Hunter Gracchus,* his third collection of essays and reviews, Guy Davenport points out that he is not writing "for scholars or fellow critics, but for people who like to read, to look at pictures, and to know things." Should you count yourself among this apparently happy few (few because Davenport would otherwise be a bestseller, as he deserves), you won't want to miss *The Hunter Gracchus and Other Papers on Literature and Art,* in which Davenport provides 300 pages of scholarly entertainment, impassioned views (on society and politics, as well as the arts), and loving appreciation of books and paintings and the people who create them.

Unusually for me, I read most of these pieces when they first appeared; in fact I actually took the trouble to look for many of them, in some cases to buy entire books to acquire them. For years I believed that a muted admiration for "The Ransom of Red Chief" and "The Gift of the Magi" had exhausted my personal need for O. Henry—until I learned that Davenport had edited, with substantial introductions, a volume of selected stories and an edition of the novel *Cabbages and Kings.* Had to have them both. Hurried to the bookstore that very afternoon. Each month I still scan the *New Criterion* for Davenport's name among the contributors:

From time to time he has reviewed books on Hawthorne, Darwin, Stephen Crane, Thoreau, Proust. One bumper issue printed a series of reflections on Kafka's enigmatic "The Hunter Gracchus," a story which, till then, I remembered mainly because of my own pitiful attempts to read it in German. Best of all, a special number of the much-missed *Antaeus* published the autobiographical "On Reading." Was it Auden who said that the true sign of devotion to an author is a willingness to collect his periodical journalism?

To my mind, Guy Davenport is the best literary essayist since Randall Jarrell and Cyril Connolly; like them, he possesses an original critical intelligence, a sensibility appealingly out of step with our debased times, and, most important of all, a distinctive and congenial voice, a unique sound. We turn to such writers in part just to listen to their printed conversation. Here, for instance, is Davenport remembering his early years in Anderson, South Carolina, sometime during the early 1930s. A neighbor is visiting:

"Before Mrs. Shiflett's son, as good a boy to his mother as ever was, fell into some snare of the law, he had been a great reader. And one fateful day Mrs. Shiflett, who wore a bonnet and apron to authenticate her respectability as a good countrywoman, brought with her, on one of her many visits to set a spell with my mother, a volume of the Tarzan series, one in which Tarzan saves himself from perishing of thirst in the Sahara by braining a vulture and drinking its blood. She lent it to me. Hit were one of the books Clyde loved in particular.

"I do not have an ordered memory, but I know that this work of Edgar Rice Burroughs was the first book I read. I was thought to be retarded as a child, and all the evidence indicates that I was. I have no memory of the first grade, to which I was not admitted until I was seven, except that of peeing my pants and having to be sent home whenever I was spoken to by our hapless teacher. I have even forgotten her appearance and her name, and I call her hapless because there was a classmate, now a psychiatrist, who fainted when he was called on, and another who stiffened into petit mal. I managed to control my bladder by the third grade, but the fainter and the sufferer from fits, both classmates of mine through the ninth grade, when I quit school, kept teachers edgy until graduation."

This is Davenport at his folksiest and most autobiographical. The details, the mimicry, the tantalizing throwaway about quitting school in ninth grade—all conspire to make the listener beg, like Oliver Twist, for more. With his usual flair for the unexpected juxtaposition, Davenport ends this essay with a glimpse of himself in Paris exploring, improbably, "the Cimetiere des Chiens et Chats," where he comes upon "the grave of Rin-Tin-

Tin, Grande Vedette du Cinema." He grows reflective: "I'm old enough to know that all things are a matter of roots and branches, of spiritual seeds and spiritual growth, and that I would not have been in Paris at all, not, anyway, as a scholar buying books and tracking down historical sites and going to museums with educated eyes rather than eyes blank with ignorance, if, in the accident of things, Aunt Mae and Mrs. Shiflett had not taken the responsibility of being custodian of the modest libraries of a brother and a son, so that I could teach myself to read."

As a critic, Davenport shines as an intrepid appreciator, an ideal teacher. By preference, he likes to walk the reader through a painting or a poem, teasing out the meaning of odd details, making connections with history and other works of art. His previous, must-have essay collections, *The Geography of the Imagination* and *Every Force Evolves a Form,* display his range: With a rainwater clarity, he can write about the naturalist Louis Agassiz or ancient poetry and thought (his *7 Greeks* gathers his translations of the poets Archilokhos, Sappho, Alkman, and Anakreon, the sayings of the philosophers Heracleitos and Diogenes, the surviving mimes of Herondas). He can account for the importance of prehistoric cave art to early modernism or outline the achievements of Joyce and Pound (about whom he composed, respectively, an Oxford thesis while a Rhodes scholar and a Harvard dissertation). He can make you yearn to read or look again at neglected masters like the poets Charles Olson and Louis Zukofsky and the painters Balthus and Charles Burchfield. He can send you out eagerly searching for C. M. Doughty's six-volume epic poem, *The Dawn in Britain,* and for the works of Ronald Johnson, Jonathan Williams, and Paul Metcalf.

In all this, his method is nothing other than the deep attentiveness engendered by love—that and a firm faith in simply knowing things. He conveys, to adopt his own words about painter Paul Cadmus, "a perfect balance of spirit and information." Whitman, he reminds us, "walked on the Boston common with Emerson, exchanged greetings with Lincoln on Washington streets, heard Agassiz lecture on geology, attended Poe's reburial in Baltimore, and held a kind of salon in Camden in his old age, eating doughnuts with a circle of young men, sitting for a portrait by Eakins." Davenport is a library of such out-of-the-way yet telling facts. He begins one journal entry with a characteristic anecdote: "Protagoras sold firewood. Democritus liked the way he bundled it for carrying and hired him to be his secretary. Mind is evident in the patterns it makes. Inner, outer. To discern these patterns is to be a philosopher." In "Civilization and Its Opposite in the 1940s," Davenport points out, while writing of ancient cave art, that "it was a little girl who first noticed the painted ceiling at Altamira in northern Spain (her father had been studying its floor for years; she, on her first visit, looked up)." Lascaux, he notes, "was a munitions cache for the Maquis until 1944."

❦

Davenport's own prose suggests the Shaker cleanness and earthy factuality of a Thoreau. "Tidy your sentences. If you're going to write English, write it idiomatically. Be as plain as you can but don't leave anything out." Such compactness leads easily to the epigrammatic: "Ruskin is the philosopher of clutter." But Davenport, on occasion, can grow fierce when denouncing the automobile as the destroyer of cities, or outraged at the way our humanity has been warped by technology, repressive religion, and impersonal government.

In the early 1960s, this then-mid-fortyish college professor at the University of Kentucky gradually began to write fiction. These stories, too, were acts of homage, illuminations, by other means, of the sensibilities and achievements of favorite writers and artists. His first collection, *Tatlin!*, appeared in 1974 and more and more seems one of the secret masterpieces of our time. In "The Aeroplanes at Brescia," set in 1907, Kafka unknowingly glimpses Wittgenstein at a flying competition among pioneer aeronauts like Bleriot and Curtiss. Any sentence here may be as pithy as a journal entry, as sensuous as Scott Fitzgerald: Rougier's "craft droned above them like a wasp at the end of a long afternoon at harvest time, drunk with its own existence and with the fat goodness of the world." In the title story, Davenport relates, through a series of vignettes, the tragic history of Soviet art; nearly a hundred historical personages—Mayakovsky, Mandelstam, Father Gapon, the architect Tatlin himself—appear in these fifty-one pages.

As Davenport's essays make clear, he reveres the French philosopher Charles Fourier, "whose ideas inspired Marx and Lenin, our own New England transcendentalists, and many American communities on the frontier. His radical idea was to retribalize humanity into small agricultural communities, or harmonies—pure little democracies in which everyone was friend (and lover) of everyone else." For many readers, that parenthetical phrase hints at a problematic element in some (by no means all) of Davenport's fiction. In several stories he describes the easygoing, somewhat polymorphous, sex play of pubescent boys and girls.

Davenport rightly bristles at the insinuation of any "salacities": His fiction clearly implies a kind of Fourierist (or at least Danish) Utopia where body is not bruised to pleasure soul; his preternaturally intellectual kids even talk a little like those from Ivy Compton-Burnett. In Davenport's artwork—he is as passionate a painter as he is a student of literature—he also occasionally depicts adolescents, especially young boys, unclothed or in underwear; iconographically, they function as daimons of the spiritual, embodiments of the natural and unfallen. In *A Balance of Quinces: The Paintings and Drawings of Guy Davenport,* Erik Anderson Reece discusses Davenport's pictorial imagination and reproduces dozens of his pictures (including a few covers for the classical magazine *Arion* and one of the comic illustrations for Hugh Kenner's *The Counterfeiters*). Because Davenport admires the witty, undervalued American realism of Grant Wood, the grid-tableaux of Mondrian, and the collage-like paintings of Picasso and Klee, he turns out striking works in all these styles, producing realistic portraits (of Pound, Joyce, Robert Walser), geometrical acrylics, exuberant trompe l'oeil abstracts such as "Orpheus Preaching to the Animals."

"Literature," Davenport has said, "is a complex dialogue of books talking to books." Just so his art constantly quotes and alludes to earlier paintings and texts. For a writer as productive and learned as this one, the handsomely designed *Guy Davenport: A Bibliography* by Joan Crane is a luxurious necessity, if only for the listing of early and uncollected pieces (many for the *National Review*). No Davenport fan will want to be without this guide to his oeuvre.

Happily, that oeuvre is still being created. Now retired from the university but still living in Lexington, Kentucky, Davenport, says Reece, divides his days "among reading, writing, painting, keeping up a voluminous correspondence, and carrying on a twenty-five-year-long conversation over dinners with Bonnie Jean Cox. . . . Most of his traveling is done on foot in his hometown. His house is a monument to high modernism. Most of his tables are replicas of one Ezra Pound built for his Paris apartment, modeled on a De Stijl simplicity. Bookshelves are everywhere. Tan burlap covers the walls, but it is barely visible under the gallery of etchings, calligraphy, prints, photographs and paintings (very few of his own). This is not a Mondrian's austere studio but rather a personal museum, filled with Rilkean objects that Davenport has invested with his own poetic sensibilities." To me it sounds pretty close to heaven.

Eros by Any Other Name

Early one Saturday morning, when I was about 14 or 15, I decided to take a walk up to Central Park, about two blocks from my Ohio home. Why, I no longer have any clear idea, though I may have been intending a little jogging as part of some ambitious physical fitness regimen (ah, the dreams of youth!). It was, I remember, a cool, damp morning, for there had been a thunderstorm the night before and everything still glistened with rain. After reaching the park, I began to cross a gravel lot—a favorite trysting spot for local teenagers—when I noticed a whitish splotch on one of the big boulders along the edge of the parking area. I strolled over for a better look and discovered that the splotch was a book, turned face down. I flipped it over with my foot. Its title was *Candy*.

The book was entirely soaked through with rain, and its pages were a solid brick of wet pulp. Still, I was able to tell that this must be a seriously dirty novel, nothing less than pornography. There was, I believe, the imprint of red lips on the otherwise virginal white cover. There was also a rather official-looking notice that this paperback by "Maxwell Kenton" was an unexpurgated reproduction of the original Paris edition published by the Olympia Press. Those infinitely suggestive words, "unexpurgated" and "Paris," convinced me that this had to be a treasure worth saving.

To sneak such a book past the baleful eye of my mother required me to stuff the wet glob under my shirt. After a cheery "I'm back," I immediately scurried off to my room. My bedroom door, of course, couldn't be locked—we never did that sort of thing in my family, and it would have aroused immediate suspicion that Something Improper was going on—so I proceeded without delay to the bathroom. Its door, of course, had a latch, and I used it, yelling out to my mom that I was going to take a quick bath after all my sweaty exercise. While I ran water into the tub, I dug out my trusty Boy Scout knife and unscrewed the metal vent of the heat register, then carefully laid the book inside the duct. Not only an ideal hiding place, the register would also provide the means to dry out the sodden pages. I need wait only a few hours for the furnace to do its work. I turned the thermostat up to 80.

Later that afternoon, after my parents and sisters had gone out, I retrieved the concealed volume only to discover that it had accordioned out to three times its original thickness. The pages were rippled, and the binding was loose. However, the text was dry and, most important of all, completely readable.

Nowadays, *Candy* is regarded as something of a '60s classic, a comic novel that exaggerates and undermines many of the conventions of pornography. Doubtless the book is studied in university classes while teachers and students chuckle over the darling girl's encounters with Professor Mephesto ("the burdens—the needs of man are so deep and so—aching") and with the hunchback, Uncle Jack, Dr. Krankheit, the guru Grindle, and many others; the words "Good grief—it's Daddy!" have even become, if not quite famous, then at least vividly remembered and fondly recalled. But when I read the book, lying on a bathroom floor as hot air blew on me from a ventless register, I utterly missed the humor. My blood was racing and my heart was pounding; my hands felt clammy and my face flush. Here was the stuff that adolescent dreams were made of.

I rushed through the novel, eyes growing wide and wider, all the way to Candy's erotic epiphany on its final page. Finished, I slipped the sinful text back into its hiding place and immediately felt myself awash in shame and guilt. It was one thing to glimpse curvy pin-ups, like those on the Ridge Tool calendar in a neighbor's garage. But to read scenes of quite unspeakable deliciousness, indeed to see them quite vividly in one's mind's eye, was quite another. What should I do?

If I kept the book around, eventually I would yield to its corrupt allure and read it again. That obviously wouldn't do. Yet it seemed unthinkable to destroy a book. Maybe I should just return it to the park? But what if a younger or less iron-resolved kid discovered it and surrendered to slobbering depravity as a result? God, what if a girl found it! Or even one of my sisters! No, I had to get the book out of the house. So naturally I gave it to my friend Tom.

Who, of course, read it and passed it on to Ray, who read it and recommended it to Ed, who read it and lent it to Lance, who . . . Eventually, all my buddies had ravenously devoured *Candy.* Tom alone thought it quite funny—he must have been more sophisticated than the rest of us.

Soon afterwards rumors began to circulate about other Dirty Books. Down in dank basements, piled under old issues of *True* and *Cavalier,* one might find ancient paperbacks with suggestive covers, leggy blondes or big-breasted babes looking for trouble. Once somebody showed me a novel about how an innocent sorority girl was transformed into a sex-mad lesbian. I didn't even dare to open that. One had, after all, to preserve a few decencies lest civilization itself fall prey to the unrestrained lust of frenzied maenads and slavering maniacs. That would be terrible—though my uneasy dreams suggested that I might secretly feel somewhat otherwise.

A year or so after discovering *Candy,* I was elected my school's representative to Boys' State. This was, and perhaps still is, a mock government in which 16-year-olds campaign for state offices, establish laws, and generally learn how our legislators supposedly work. It was an honor to be chosen, though I soon felt it to be of paramount importance not to sully the reputation of Admiral King as the toughest high school in Ohio. So along with my dressy clothes I packed a quart bottle of homemade wine, courtesy of my friend Ray (who had swiped it from his father), and a paperback of *Fanny Hill.* Both of these, needless to say, were strictly verboten by the straight-arrow organizers of Boys' State.

After more than thirty years, I can no longer remember where I acquired that copy of *Fanny Hill.* I certainly wouldn't have had the nerve to buy it at Rusine's cigar store, a smoky haven for shrink-wrapped paperbacks, alluring manuals on how to fight with razors, and what were then called "men's magazines." I probably unearthed the paperback on one of my periodic visits to the thrift shops of Lorain (my hometown), most likely Clarice's Values or the Salvation Army. There one might turn up anything, from an early edition of *Ulysses* to the latest whiz-bang adventures of Rick Brant, Ken Holt, or Tom Swift. Doubtless I hid John Cleland's underground classic in among a stack of Tarzans and Agatha Christies, all priced at a nickel or a dime apiece.

Boys' State was held during the summer at Ohio University, famous in that halcyon era as a party school ("If you kick the bushes, the bushes kick back"), and I soon surrendered to the hedonistic spirit of this *locus amoenus.* On my second day there, my roommate—an earnest young fogey with serious political ambitions—returned from a hard day on the convention floor to find me sitting at my ease, sipping red wine from a jelly jar, while intently perusing Miss Hill's autobiography. He reacted with a satisfying gasp of horror and immediately began to splutter that I was a disgrace and deserved to be thrown out of Boys' State. Indeed, he felt morally obligated to turn in such a miscreant as myself, obviously not of the mettle worthy of our juvenile government. He was certainly right about that.

By this time, however, half the dorm seemed to know that Dirda possessed both alcohol and filth, so my tiny room rapidly filled up with model students eager for a sip of nectar and the chance to read a page or two from the "Memoirs of a Woman of Pleasure." Seizing my chance, I sold shots for 50 cents and ten minutes with the book for a quarter. Had I been just a tad smarter, I would have swapped my contraband for votes and gotten myself elected Boys' State governor, the highest office in the land. That, after all, is the American way.

I must say, however, that *Fanny Hill* proved rather a disappointment after the gladsome delights of *Candy.* The formal and somewhat euphemistic language struck me as tiresome, while the brutally frank presentation of various sexual tableaux lacked what one might call, strangely enough, romance. I didn't even finish the book, finding it, all in all, repetitive and slightly boring. Perhaps I would feel different now, but I have never looked into John Cleland's novel again.

My Sin, My Soul

These days, of course, you can order *Candy* from the Book-of-the-Month Club in a handsome trade paperback with its actual authors' names emblazoned on the cover: Terry Southern and Mason Hoffenberg. *Fanny Hill* has been published, with scholarly apparatus, as an Oxford World's Classic. Of course, our current bestsellers are far more sexually explicit and know how to arouse the reader with just a flick of the whip, uh, wrist. While editing a review of Judith Krantz's novel *Spring Collection,* I was checking a quote when I happened upon an extended lesbian love scene. Before long, I felt it my duty, as a conscientious editor, to study the passage in some detail. We've undoubtedly come a long way, baby.

Yes, indeed. Consider Vladimir Nabokov. Over the years I have picked up every edition of *Lolita* that I can find. I don't own the expensive Olympia Press first edition, published as part of the notorious Traveler's Library, but I know that it appeared in subdued light-green covers, without art: a starkly innocent look for a series that included such notable titles as *White Thighs, The English Governess,* and *The Loins of Amon.* The early American hardcovers of *Lolita* similarly downplay the novel's "forbidden" content:

Just the word "Lolita" appears on the Putnam dust jacket in black letters against a white background. For the paperback, the title was only marginally more daring: The letters were colored in red and yellow, as if with crayons.

However, matters heated up a bit once the now-classic film appeared. For the 1961 *Lolita: A Screenplay*, the O has been transformed into a heart with a safety pin through it. A 1962 English paperback offers a still of Sue Lyon wearing heart-shaped sunglasses and sucking languorously on a cherry lollipop. A later Fawcett paperback, no date given, adds a small photograph to the lower right corner, revealing a sultry, dark-tressed beauty (not Lyon) leaning on her arm and looking out at the reader seductively. The 1982 Greenwich Press cloth edition depicts a seriously brazen man-eater, hardly a nymphet, peeking out of the O in "Lolita" with the wet-lipped, come-hither look of a topless dancer.

Now that erotic literature has become widely acceptable, provided it looks relatively "tasteful," a recent Vintage trade paperback proffers a misty, soft-focused photograph of a young girl dressed in a halter top and shorts, standing behind an old-fashioned bicycle. Still, the most provocative image may be that found on the Largely Literary T-shirt: A leering Nabokov drapes his knobby hand on Lolita's naked shoulder; the pigtailed young girl, with her back to us, wears only a thin-cotton, polka-dot summer dress. Nabokov's masterpiece is, of course, much more than an erotic fantasy, so the cover of the most recent edition of *The Annotated Lolita* again adopts an austerely typographical design, highlighting the editor's introductory essay and the abundant scholarly endnotes.

Alas, at the age I first read *Lolita,* I found Nabokov's luscious language the sexiest aspect of the book. And it was so funny! *Lolita* may be a tragic love story or the portrait of a monster or both, but I still laugh aloud at the death of Clare Quilty. Good grief! Maybe I really should give *Candy* another whirl. This time I might actually notice the jokes.

❧

To give of oneself—fully—is not merely a
duty prescribed by an outmoded superstition,
it is a beautiful and thrilling privilege.
                                    —Candy Christian

Frank Confessions

There's an old saying, "as happy as God in France," and most of us know instinctively what this means: wine, cheese, fresh bread, cafés near splashing fountains; a perfect climate, wide boulevards for window-shopping, sexy people beautifully decked out, bookstores at every other street corner. Of course, Washington has nearly all these too, except the perfect climate. But while the Parisian strolls through life, the Washingtonian hustles. We yearn for money, power, and fame; the French prefer a game of dominos or boules after work, six-week vacations, and lots of time for love, reading, and good food. Long ago in France I knew a poet, unpublished, who, to support himself and his family, just happened to work in a bank. In America he would be nothing but a teller with a useless hobby.

Nowadays, among intellectuals France holds an ambiguous position. For many conservative thinkers it is the source for most of what has gone wrong with American higher education. One need only murmur a few names or phrases: Foucault, Derrida, Althusser, Sade; post-structuralism, deconstruction, *la différance,* the Annales approach to history; and, *bien sûr,* the seemingly crazed literary cultists of the nouveau roman, Tel Quel and Oulipo. Yet none of this is really new. France has been blamed for its revolutionary ideas for hundreds of years. The troubadours upset the Church with the cult of passionate courtly love; the philosophes overturned centuries of tradition by insisting on political and intellectual freedom; surrealists gave art a shake from which it has never quite recovered; and the existentialists, with their berets and black turtlenecks, made every postwar teenager a philosopher.

While Americans naturally tend to be docile and meek about culture, the French live for the thrust and parry of argument: Theirs is a society based on oral sparring. In England, family and school are still vitally important; in America, money and connections count most; but in France the only thing that really matters is intelligence. Voltaire is, for this reason, the archetypal Frenchman. What other country could have produced *Apostrophes,* a weekly television program of immense national popularity, entirely given over to the serious discussion of new books? What other country would have a day of national mourning following the death of a novelist (Colette) or a philosopher (Sartre)? And where else would a minister of culture actually be one of the nation's most cultured people (André Malraux)?

Alas, except for one long weekend, I haven't visited France, let alone lived there, in almost twenty-five years. And yet hardly a week goes by that I don't think of the tree-lined main street of Aix and the glint of the light on the water of Marseille's Vieux Port, or taste in my mind *steak-frites* and *pâté* sandwiches and *menthe à l'eau.*

Some of this nostalgia obviously derives from the normal wistfulness of the middle-aged. Still, anyone who has been to France can match my memories with his or her own. I will always count among my red-letter days that in which I first sat down, in ninth grade, and learned to say "J'entre dans la salle de classe." It was my introduction to a new world. Or rather to an old one, of irresistible glamour. As Thomas Jefferson used to say, every man has two countries—his own and France.

Such Gall

Like many people, I have kept up my love affair with France through reading. I myself prefer classical prose, beautifully balanced sentences, the ice-water diction of a Mérimée. But I am convinced that literature regularly needs risk, excess, and experiment. If books don't surprise or shock some people, they just aren't doing their job. "Etonne-moi!" said Diaghilev to Cocteau. That should be every artist's aim, the words inscribed above his desk: Astonish me.

Recently several astonishing French books have come out in English. Each provides a sudden access of vision, a glimpse into new ways of creating art, or of thinking about it.

1. *An Anecdoted Topography of Chance,* by Daniel Spoerri, with Robert Filliou, Emmett Williams, Dieter Roth, and Roland Topor. Many of the great experimental novels attempt to undercut the merciless domination of plot: *Tristram Shandy,* for instance, but also late James, Proust, and Joyce. In general, these books are endlessly digressive or essayistic, replacing the propulsiveness of narrative with the leisurely play of consciousness. A few contemporary works, such as Nabokov's *Pale Fire* or Nicholson Baker's *The Mezzanine,* go so far as to employ footnotes and to obsess about the seemingly trivial; before long the wise reader learns that the real action of these "novels" lies in the interruptions.

One afternoon in 1962, artist Daniel Spoerri made a rough diagram of all the objects on his worktable—a paintbrush, a jar of paprika, a Magic Marker, a clock, a glass of wine, etc. Spoerri then wrote a sentence or a page about each of these objects: how it had come into his life, why it was on the table, who had been using it last; in short, whatever associations struck his fancy. These comments were then passed among his friends, who could, as they chose, footnote any element in them and add their own reflections. Since *An Anecdoted Topography of Chance* has gone through several editions over the years—in German, French, and English—its authors have gradually added detailed cross-references and footnotes to their footnotes. The latest and momentarily definitive version works something like computer hypertext, with little essays constantly branching off and begetting other mini-essays. Because of its catchall character, Spoerri himself calls the *Topography* a "human garbage can."

The success of such a formula naturally depends on the degree of one's interest in the commentary. In this instance the co-creators generate a wonderful feeling of bonhomie: Spoerri gradually discloses the story of his life and art; his German friend and translator Dieter Roth indulges in philosophical flights and extravagant wordplay; and everyone tries to be amusing, taking up such vexed matters as the naming of toilet papers, a mother's disappointment in her artist-son, the invention of a perpetual motion machine, and the dangers of maps. "From a button," says Spoerri, "you can explain the world."

Besides its various levels of texts, the *Topography* regales one with quotations, aphorisms, lots of illustrations, cameos of the famous (John Ashbery, Robert Rauschenberg). Even the index is a hoot: "Alexander the Great, husband of Roxana"; "Albers, Josef, whom I have owed a letter since 1960"; "Gide, André, who could easily have got an annulment"; "Hecht, Anthony, who patronized Lionel Trilling's dentist." In short, for many this will be a book to treasure, even perhaps to annotate.

2. *How I Wrote Certain of My Books and other Writings of Raymond Roussel,* edited by Trevor Winkfield. Raymond Roussel (1877–1933) is one of the strangest and most influential of all modern French writers, once dubbed by poet Louis Aragon the "president of the Republic of Dreams" and a major influence on such modern American writers as John Ashbery, Kenneth Koch, and Harry Mathews (all of whom provide translations for this anthology).

Like the members of Oulipo (see next entry), Roussel established elaborate constraints for the composition of his novels, plays, and poems. For instance, he constructed much of his fiction according to exacting wordplay. He would take a phrase like "Tu n'en auras pas" (You will not have any), then slur it into "Dune en or a pas" (golden dune with footsteps); from this he would set up a scene in which a character kisses footprints on a dune. By employing a series of homonyms and skewed phrases, Roussel created the component elements for strange, somewhat surreal stories, which he then composed in a classically pure French. For his long poem *Nouvelles Impressions d'Afrique,* consisting almost entirely of parentheses inside parentheses, the millionaire-author commissioned fifty-nine illustrations "through the intermediary of a private detective agency." A hack artist was obliged to create pictures according to brief written instructions, without any knowledge of the poem they would illustrate. The resulting images are utterly banal in themselves, but in conjunction with their captions oddly unsettling. By the way, the hyperexperimental Roussel believed that the greatest writer who ever lived was Jules Verne.

3. *Oulipo Laboratory,* texts from the Bibliothèque Oulipienne translated by Harry Mathews and Iain White. The Oulipo (Ouvroir de Littérature Potentielle, Workshop for Potential Literature) is a group of mathematicians and writers who adopt various arithmetical formulas and self-imposed restrictive systems as aids to the writing of poetry and fiction. The group's most famous success, Georges Perec's *La Disparition,* relates a story of some 200 or so pages without using the letter E (this dazzling tour de force was dazzlingly Englished by Gilbert Adair as *A Void*).

In this little anthology of Oulipo booklets, Jean Fournel goes Perec twenty-five better: He has created a novel whose main text eschews all the letters of the alphabet. "Suburbia" consists solely of the peripheral aspects of any book: a title page, copyright page, contents, preface, footnotes, index, blurbs. Yet with these alone Fournel unfolds a thrilling, if rather somber, story. Take the dedication: "For Marie-Laure, with whom we dallied so long on the periphery of love, this fiery tale." Because this particular edition of "Suburbia" is intended as a school text, the footnotes sound a pedagogical air: e.g., "What intention on the author's part does this brutal opening suggest?" or "In which human drama is Robert actually trapped? Drugs, alcohol, violence, lovelessness, alienation: does the context allow a choice?" A brilliant send-up of literary conventions, and more daringly provocative than *Trainspotting*.

Parenthetical digression: Fournel's experiment reminded me of a similar work by Jean Ferry, an expert on Roussel (and a satrap of the zany College de Pataphysique, but that's another column). Rather than type up a whole novel, which would take far too much time, Ferry simply composed its single key sentence or paragraph. "They met for the last time in January's dark twilight, on the terrace of the café All-Goes-Well, which is in fact the one spot in Paris where things can be counted to go badly. Never had she appeared to him so pale, so gaunt." What more does one need? Among his other condensed novels, Ferry includes "Driver, a thousand francs for you if we reach the Gare de Lyon in time for the Marseille express!" and "The monster of Gevaudan laughed in the shadows." Surely anyone can imagine all the travail and heartbreak and final triumph preceding the four words that sum up virtually all pastoral fiction: "Bring in your calves!"

Oulipo Laboratory also reprints "How I Wrote One of My Books," Italo Calvino's description of the algorithm used in the composition of his masterpiece, *If on a winter's night a traveler*. The Italian fabulist's admirers, who are legion, might also want to look for *Playtexts: Ludics in Contemporary Literature*, by Warren Motte. *Playtexts* covers, albeit rather academically, such games-playing authors as Gombrowicz, Perec, Harry Mathews, Nabokov, and Eco, with a particularly good essay on Calvino's most obviously Oulipian novel, the Tarot-based *Castle of Crossed Destinies*. Harry Mathews, the sole American member of Oulipo, may also be enjoyed in Sun and Moon's republication of *Selected Declarations of Dependence*, an entire book of poems and stories built around "perverbs," the unnatural crossing of two proverbs: e.g., "You can't make an omelet with good intentions" or "Let the dead bury the things which are Caesar's."

Such books may not always be what many of us think of as fiction or poetry, but then that's the point. It goes without saying that in their playfulness, wit, and intelligence they strike me as deeply, enviably French.

Mememormee

As it happens, there was a time when I read scores of autobiographies, anything from Augustine's *Confessions* to *True Confessions*. I even consulted books about the genre, starting with Georg Misch's *History of Autobiography in Antiquity*, a two-volume work of minute German scholarship devoted to a period largely devoid of any confessional writing whatsoever. Misch opens his study with hieroglyphic inscriptions, in which the unspoken essence of much autobiography—self-glorification—is made explicit: "Nebuchadnezzar, King of Babylon, the rightful ruler, the expression of the righteous heart of Marduk, the exalted high priest, the beloved of Nebo, the wise prince—am I." Even in English this has an impressive ring.

The confessional impulse got its first really good boost from Christianity, a religion that emphasizes the inner life, the examination of conscience, and the retrospective glance over one's doleful and sinful past. St. Augustine's classic account of his progress up from paganism is conceived as an exemplum of the soul's restlessness until it rests in God. Because Augustine deems his acceptance of Christianity the major event of his earthly existence, he selects from his past just the steps that lead toward a climactic moment of spiritual agony in a garden (a setting rich with figural associations from both Old and New Testament). There Augustine, wracked with indecision, suddenly hears an angelic voice say, "Tolle, lege" (Take, read), and he reaches for his mother's Bible. A saint is born.

After Augustine, autobiography languished until the Renaissance, when Man with a capital M again became the measure of all things. Popes and poets wrote the stories of their lives because, in Cellini's simple words, "they had done something." More than any other, my favorite Renaissance autobiographer is the cranky mathematician, doctor, and astrologer Girolamo Cardano, once thought to possess the greatest mind since Aristotle. Instead of relating his life in a chronological fashion, Cardano divides *De Vita Propria Liber* (The Book of My Life) into categories. Chapters bear titles such as "Stature and appearance"; "Those things in which I take pleasure"; "Things in which I feel I have failed"; "Testimony of illustrious men concerning me." Cardano's faith in astrology reputedly led him to commit suicide so that he might die on the very day predicted by his horoscope. In *The Book of My Life* he reveals a winningly dour personality: "Although various abortive medicines—as I have heard—were tried in vain, I was normally born on the 24th day of September in the year 1500. . . . I was not maimed, save in the genitals, so that from my twenty-first to my thirty-first year I was unable to lie with women, and many a time I lamented my fate, envying every other man his own good fortune."

His father, Cardano informs us, often turned for help to a "demon which he openly confessed attended him as a familiar spirit"; he adds coyly that this was "a relationship the significance of which I steadfastly refrained from investigating." The Renaissance magus—I picture him as resembling Merlyn from *The Sword in the Stone*—grumpily complains that he becomes "the owner of all sorts of little animals that get attached to me: kids, lambs, hares, rabbits, and storks. They litter up the whole house." He discloses that he devoted himself to serious study—his writings run to 7,000 folio pages—"as a counterpoise to an insane love for my children." (Alas, one son poisoned his wife and was beheaded.) Throughout a checkered life, Cardano preserves an attractive realism: "I am by no means unaware that these afflictions may seem meaningless to future generations, and more especially to strangers; but there is nothing, as I have said, in this mortal life except inanity, emptiness, and dream-shadows."

Passing reluctantly over Montaigne—my choice to represent mankind on the Intergalactic Council of Planets: surely he and Sei Shonagon embody the acme of humane self-understanding—I want to commend John Bunyan's *Grace Abounding to the Chief of Sinners,* a masterpiece of both spiritual autobiography and plain prose. The seventeenth century reintroduced the autobiography as a tool for self-scrutiny, following the injunction of Lamentations 3:40: "Let us search and try our ways, and turn again to the Lord." At one point, Bunyan is condemned to a long spell in prison and must leave behind his blind daughter: "Poor child, thought I, what sorrow art thou like to have for thy portion in this world? Thou must be beaten, must beg, suffer hunger, cold, nakedness, and a thousand calamities, though I cannot now endure the wind should blow upon thee. . . ."

As so often with this great writer, that last clause movingly raises the homely to the sublime.

From the eighteenth century on, the autobiography flourishes like the green bay tree: Rousseau's *Confessions* opens with a trumpet blast: "I am beginning an enterprise without precedent and which will never have a successor. I want to show the world a man in all the truth of his nature, and that man is myself." The pages that follow make up the world's finest autobiography, not least because its author reveals himself—in beautifully limpid, declarative sentences—as delusional, hypocritical, absolutely shameless, irresistibly human. Rousseau can talk of urinating in a neighbor's cooking pot or allowing a servant girl to be fired over a theft he committed; he will confess to suffering from both premature ejaculation and deepseated paranoia. But then he will pause and ask: Are you, dear reader, any better than I?

In the title to his somberly impressive and underappreciated *Aus Meinem Leben: Dichtung und Wahrheit* (From My life: Poetry and Truth), Goethe indicates the twin poles of all modern autobiography: the tension between the claims of truth and the need for artistry. The Sage of Weimar portrays himself as a daemonic figure, a summing-up in his own person of the forces that run through the history of his time; he and Germany are one, both suffused by the same Zeitgeist. Perhaps.

Yet another great Romantic autobiography is sometimes overlooked because it's written in blank verse: *The Prelude,* William Wordsworth's epic about the growth of a poet's soul, an invigorating, and only occasionally tedious, account of "those recollected hours that have the charm / Of visionary things." With a typical outrageousness the philosopher Nietzsche gave his short account of his intellectual development the sacrilegious title *Ecce Homo;* he blithely titles one chapter "Why I write such good books." Freud maintained that Nietzsche possessed "a more penetrating knowledge of himself than any other man who ever lived or was ever likely to live." This dangerously exhilarating thinker himself declared, "I am no man, I am dynamite."

Which conveniently leads us to that substance's inventor, Alfred Nobel, whose name adorns humankind's greatest public honor—and who composed a minimalist autobiography of consummate despondency: "Alfred Nobel—his miserable existence should have been terminated at birth by a humane doctor as he drew his first howling breath. Principal virtues: keeping his nails clean and never being a burden to anyone. Principal faults: that he has no family, is bad-tempered and has a poor digestion. One and only wish: not to be buried alive. Greatest sin: that he does not worship Mammon. Important events in his life: none."

In the twentieth century, autobiography has become the last refuge of semi-successful novelists. Not that there aren't exceptions. A well-read friend maintains that Anthony Burgess's two rumbustious volumes—*Little Wilson and Big God* and *You've Had Your Time*—compose the greatest English autobiography since Gibbon's urbane masterpiece of self-complacency. I myself regard V. S. Pritchett's *A Cab at the Door* and Sartre's *Les Mots* (The Words) as twin peaks of childhood memoir—and quite likely the finest achievements of these two disparate authors.

Much as I love certain autobiographies, I still don't quite trust the form. Maybe I haven't gotten over being taken in by Bruce Chatwin's *The Songlines*—a baggy, philosophical fiction disguised as fact. Or maybe, having tried to write about my own early life, I realize how much of the past remains fuzzy, partial, elusive. With the best will in the world, autobiographers can't truly record the past; they can only re-create a certain image of it. The gates of ivory and of horn ultimately are one.

Tomes for Tots

Okay, the kids want new video games and CD-ROMs and all sorts of computer gimcrackery for Christmas. If I may be so bold as to quote an authority on the holiday spirit—Bah, humbug! Not, of course, that I won't be buying just this stuff for my own Tiny Tims: Who am I to bear the burden of utterly ruining three childhoods by depriving my progeny of expensive electronic doohickeys, invincible plastic warriors, and an arsenal of weaponry that would make Rambo drool and slaver? Yet just as mothers have always slipped in sweaters among the cap-guns and Barbies, so I will wrap up a few books for my local tough guys, whether they want them or not. A bookman's gotta do what a bookman's gotta do. I say, Send the CD-ROMs back to the Romulans.

It struck me recently that other folk may wish to be so old-fashioned as to give children books as Christmas presents. There are, of course, hundreds of good titles available: Check your local bookstore. Just don't pick up anything too prosaic, such as "A Child's First Book about Floor Wax" or "A Day in the Life of the Department of Commerce." There's a reason why kids glom on to R. L Stine's Goosebumps titles and the Harry Potter books: They're scary and exciting. Only grown-ups wistfully yearn to go back to the days of Christopher Robin and Pooh.

Having read and reviewed crates of children's books over the years, I have naturally kept a bookshelf of favorites, sure-fire winners, especially for kids under 10. Here is a briefly annotated list, roughly arranged from toddler to pre-teen and excluding some obvious classics like Dr. Seuss titles and *Charlotte's Web*. Many of these are the books I plan to keep around even when my own children are grown.

Over in the Meadow, illustrated by Paul Galdone. The most restful of nursery rhymes, illustrated by a versatile artist who also painted covers for P. G. Wodehouse novels. Ages 2 and up.

How Hippo!, by Marcia Brown. Baby hippo saved from alligator's jaws by his formidable mamma. Great woodcuts, especially that of Mrs. Hippo with her enormous mouth wide open. Ages 2–5.

Each Peach Pear Plum, by Janet and Allan Ahlberg. Simple rhymes, ingenious puzzle pictures. See if you can find the Three Bears on their first appearance. The delight of 3-year-olds.

Oh, Were They Ever Happy!, by Peter Spier. An almost wordless masterpiece about what happens when three siblings decide to paint the house while their parents are away. Take a look at the bathroom after the kids have cleaned up themselves and their tools. Just as good: *Bored, Nothing to Do,* in which two brothers build an airplane out of parts from around the house. Ages 3–7.

The Travels of Babar, by Jean de Brunhoff. Pachyderm honeymoon interrupted by natural disasters and rhino insurrection. An indisputable classic (though the "savages" are a regrettable stereotype). Look for the big elephant-folio edition. All ages.

The Story of Ferdinand, by Munro Leaf; pictures by Robert Lawson. The classic exposition of nonviolence as a way of life. All ages.

The Big Orange Splot, by Daniel Pinkwater. What Ferdinand is to nonviolence, this book is to nonconformity. When a seagull drops a bucket of paint on an ordinary house, Mr. Plumbean is led to create the home of his dreams—to the consternation of his neighbors. Ages 2 and up.

Anansi the Spider, by Gerald McDermott. When Anansi is swallowed by Fish, it takes all five of his sons—and their special talents—to save his life. A neat fable about cooperation, with bizarrely appealing geometrical illustrations. Ages 3–7.

Mike Mulligan and His Steam Shovel, by Virginia Lee Burton. An old steam shovel races the clock to show a doubting town her true worth. Both little kids and their parents will find this book touching, in different ways. Ages 2–6.

We're Going on a Bear Hunt, by Michael Rosen; pictures by Helen Oxenbury. This singsong ballad, replete with onomatopoeic sounds, follows a family facing the elements in the hopes of capturing a bear. "We're not scared. We're going to catch a big one." A shrewdly structured book, especially in its interplay of text and pictures. Ages 4–9.

Boney-Legs, retold by Joanna Cole. The tale of the little girl who outwits Baba Yaga, the Russian witch with iron teeth. Love this story. Ages 4 and up.

My Mama Says There Aren't Any Zombies, Ghosts, Vampires, Creatures, Demons, Monsters, Fiends, Goblins or Things, by Judith Viorst; illustrated by Kay Chorao. A mom assures her son that there's nothing to be afraid of, but the boy remembers that "sometimes even Mamas make mistakes." Viorst's other books are also delightful, especially *Alexander Who Used to Be Rich Last Sunday.* Ages 4–8.

Sing a Song of Sixpence. A tried-and-true collection of poetry for younger kids, illustrated by a dozen of the best artists in the business: Leo and Diane Dillon, Trina Schart Hyman, etc. Don't miss Ogden Nash's "Adventures of Isabel." Ages 4 and up.

Brave Irene, by William Steig. My favorite of Steig's score or so of picture books: A young girl braves a snowstorm to deliver a dress from her seamstress mother. Fierce blizzard; dauntless fortitude. A Steig alternate: *Rotten Island,* where delicious ugliness rules until, alas, a flower appears. Ages 3–7.

That Terrible Halloween Night, by James Stevenson. When the kids try to scare grandpa, he tells them about the shocking thing that happened to him in a forbidding old house many years before. One of a series of fine tall tales related by Grandpa. Ages 3–8. Two other pre-K chillers: Ruth Brown's *A Dark, Dark Tale,* an atmospheric classic that leads a child through a dark, dark wood to a dark, dark house to a dark, dark room; and Brinton Turkle's *Do Not Open,* in which Miss Moody inadvertently releases an evil demon from a sealed bottle. Parent alert: Sensitive little ones may find the monster here a little too vivid.

The Hat, by Tomi Ungerer. A magical top hat helps an impoverished one-legged war veteran to become the toast of society. A witty and captivating tale, as is Ungerer's more Gallic *The Beast of Monsieur Racine.* Ages 4–8.

A Day with Wilbur Robinson, by William Joyce. A kid visits a friend at home—and discovers man-eating tigers, flying saucers, singing frogs, and mad scientists. We should all be so lucky. See also Joyce's *Dinosaur Bob* and his holiday picture book, *Santa Calls.* Ages 4–10.

The Cut-Ups, by James Marshall. Two happy-go-lucky buddies run afoul of Lamar J. Spurgle, a former principal who hates children. Marshall was so distinctive and prolific an artist that even grownups like to collect his many books. His most famous creation, for Harry Allard's *Miss Nelson Is Missing!,* remains the most dreaded substitute teacher of all time, Viola Swamp. Ages 4–8.

How Tom Beat Captain Najork and His Hired Sportsmen, by Russell Hoban; pictures by Quentin Blake. Freewheeling kid rebels against battle-axe aunt, who sends for Captain Najork to teach the boy a lesson. But Tom's fooling around has prepared him to be a master-player of "womble, muck and sneedball." Younger kids will enjoy Hoban's endearing Frances the Badger series (e.g., *Bedtime for Frances*), while older brothers and sisters should try the beautifully written, wistful allegory of life's vicissitudes, *The Mouse and His Child.*

The Juniper Tree, translated by Lore Segal and Randall Jarrell; pictures by Maurice Sendak. The most elegant compilation of Grimm fairy tales. All ages.

Jumanji, by Chris Van Allsburg. A brother and sister discover a jungle adventure game in which the imaginary becomes all too real. One of Van Allsburg's four or five masterpieces, along with *The Garden of Abdul-Gasazi* and *The Mysteries of Harris Burdick*—picture books from the Twilight Zone. Ages 4 and up.

The Devil's Storybook, by Natalie Babbitt. Lighthearted tall tales about the devil, in most of which he is thwarted by his intended victims. Sequel: *The Devil's Other Storybook.* Ages 7–12.

June 29, 1999, by David Wiesner. Young girl sends plants into space; gigantic vegetables unexpectedly appear all over the country. Surreal images. As good as Wiesner's Caldecott winner, *Tuesday.* Ages 4–8.

The Hobbit, by J. R. R. Tolkien. Bilbo, Gandalf, Smaug—and a certain mysterious ring with a promising future. Perfect for reading aloud to elementary-school-age children.

The Phantom Tollbooth, by Norton Juster. Milo travels through a wonderland of puns and odd creatures in his attempt to bring back Rhyme and Reason to the world. Almost as good as Lewis Carroll. Ages 6–12.

Homer Price, by Robert McCloskey. A nostalgic classic: cozy tall tales about small-town life. Imagine Jimmy Stewart as a 13-year-old boy. Sequel: *Centerburg Tales.* Young kids shouldn't miss the author-illustrator's *Make Way for Ducklings.*

The Witches, by Roald Dahl; illustrated by Quentin Blake. Dahl's most thrilling story. Ten-year-olds will read it wide-eyed until late into the night, while looking anxiously over their shoulders. Ages 8 and up.

A Wrinkle in Time, by Madeleine L'Engle. "It was a dark and stormy night." So opens this exciting novel of precocious children, witches, interplanetary adventure, and moral responsibility. Ages 8–12.

Alan Mendelsohn, the Boy from Mars, by Daniel Pinkwater. If I could have written any children's book in the world, this is the one I would choose. Two misfit kids wander into a rundown part of town, purchase the Klugarsh mind-control system from a mysterious shopkeeper, and then embark on a series of hilarious and surprising adventures. Boyhood dreams come true. Ages 8 and up. Almost as good: *The Snarkout Boys and the Avocado of Death.*

Three Classics

As fall approaches, a reader's fancy naturally turns to thoughts of mysteries, ghost stories, Victorian novels, and other autumnal fare. This is the time when Miltonists put away "L'Allegro" and pick up "Il Penseroso." Yet before we all surrender to the louring melancholy of October, let us enjoy the best season of all, Indian summer. During my holidays I read a good many comic novels, but none more outstanding than *The Trials of Topsy,* by A. P. Herbert, *Augustus Carp,* by Himself, and *Mapp and Lucia,* by E. F. Benson.

A prolific contributor to *Punch,* A. P. Herbert is little read these days, but on the basis of *The Trials of Topsy* and its companion, *Topsy, M.P.,* he was obviously a man ahead of his time. For Topsy, a London debutante who writes breathless letters to her friend Trix, is nothing less than a Jazz Age Valley Girl. Imagine a blend of Lorelei Lee and Alicia Silverstone of *Clueless:*

"Because my dear as I've been trying to tell you all this time, two nights ago we went over to the Hunt Ball of the Yealm Vale and Fowkley, my dear pronounced Yaffle, Mr. Haddock and me and that rather antiseptic young Guardee I told you about, Terence Flydde by name, my dear too Etonian, my dear utterly clean-limbed, washes all over and flawlessly upholstered, but of course the cerebellum is a perfect vacuum, well, my dear, I've always fancied he was rather attracted and of course he's absolutely baneless but of course a girl would just as soon marry a pedigree St. Bernard dog, so I didn't exactly propose to dedicate the evening to him though I must say those red coats are rather decorative. . . ."

In the course of her adventures, Topsy writes about country weekends, charity bazaars, art shows, Christmas, dieting, and even politics. While working on Mr. Haddock's parliamentary campaign, our heroine prints up her own views on social issues and foreign affairs: "Of course don't think I don't adulate the poor because I simply do only the people I pity are the Middle Classes who of course pay for everything and get nothing and why they do it I simply can't imagine and my advice to them is to pay no Income-Tax until they've one foot in the jail." Elsewhere Topsy notes, with her usual impeccable logic, "Of course, I adore Peace and Disarmament and everything, but what I always say is well, what about pirates?" What indeed?

Augustus Carp, Esq. appeared in 1924 anonymously but is now known to be the work of a distinguished physician named Henry Howarth Bashford. Anthony Burgess considered it "one of the great comic novels of the twentieth century," as will anybody else who finds and reads the book. Like other classics of English humor (*Vice Versa; The Diary of a Nobody*), *Augustus Carp* is the tale of a father and son. The two Carps are models of unconscious hypocrisy; that is, each imagines he behaves as a perfect Xtian (always so spelled) even while exploiting loved ones, blackmailing teachers, bringing suit for minor infractions, and wrecking lives. In particular, young Augustus's narrative voice is a masterpiece of controlled irony. One revels in every word and turn of his elegant syntax:

"From the time of his marriage to the day of my birth, and as soon thereafter as the doctor had permitted her to rise, my father had been in the habit of enabling my mother to provide him with an early cup of tea. And this he had done by waking her regularly a few minutes before six o'clock. . . ." Note that devastating use of "enabling"—sheer genius.

The Carps always find excuses. "But to become ordained presupposed an examination, and I had been seriously handicapped in this particular respect by a proven disability, probably hereditary in origin, to demonstrate my culture in so confined a form." After finagling his Xtian way into a job with a religious publisher—they distribute books with titles like "Gnashers of Teeth" and "Without Are Dogs"—Augustus comes to know the Stool family, fanatically devoted to stamping out drink, dancing, and tobacco. Here is son Ezekiel:

"No taller than myself, and weighing considerably less, he had suffered all his life from an inherent dread of shaving, and the greater portion of his face was in consequence obliterated by a profuse but gentle growth of hair.

His voice, too, owing to some developmental defect, had only partially broken; and indeed his father Abraham (afterwards removed to an asylum) had on more than one occasion attempted to sacrifice him, under the mistaken impression that he was some sort of animal that would be suitable as a burnt offering." Later, Augustus meets this father: "Mr. Abraham Stool, indeed, who had not then been segregated, but who was already under the impression that he was the Hebrew patriarch, several times insisted upon my approaching him and placing my hand under his left thigh, after which he would offer me, in addition to Mrs. Stool, a varying number of rams and goats." *Augustus Carp, Esq.* should be returned to print immediately. I aim to buy every used paperback I come across. Gifts for my Xtian and non-Xtian friends.

All six books in E. F. Benson's cycle about Emmeline Lucas and Elizabeth Mapp are quite irresistible, but their humor—subtle, malicious, everfresh—emphasizes situation as much as language. In each novel (except *Miss Mapp*) Lucia finds her dictatorship of local society threatened, and she must outmaneuver adversaries on many flanks.

In *Mapp and Lucia,* Benson brings his two greatest characters into direct conflict. After the death of her husband, Lucia decides to leave the village of Riseholme and move to Tilling, a port city rather like Rye (where Benson lived, eventually becoming mayor). Before long, Tilling's resident queen, Elizabeth Mapp, is launching foul plots to prevent the dynamic Lucia from further captivating Major Benjy, the Padre (a clergyman who chatters away in a comic Scots dialect), and Quaint Irene (based on the famous lesbian Radclyffe Hall), among others. Inevitably, dinner parties, art competitions, bridge games, and catty conversation drive the novel to its famous climax, in which the two rivals are swept out to sea while clinging to a kitchen table. It's hard to quote from *Mapp and Lucia,* for so much of the book's tone depends on context. But here's Mapp, on her way to purloin the closely guarded recipe for the scrumptious "Lobster à la Riseholme": She passes some servants on their way to a whist drive and "wished them a Merry Christmas and hoped they would all win. (Little kindly remarks like that always pleased servants, thought Elizabeth; they showed a human sympathy with their pleasures, and cost nothing; so much better than Christmas boxes)."

But really one needs to read all these novels, masterly send-ups of the syrupy civilities and hypocrisies of daily life. Who can forget Lucia's kitschy Shakespearean garden? Or how she pretends to take a lover so as to seem more attractive to London society? In *Miss Mapp* the huffing Navy man Captain Puffin suffers a seizure, falls forward into his soup—and drowns. And here, at the opening of *Lucia in London,* Benson describes Georgie

Pillson—Lucia's epicene neighbor and ally—visiting his soulmate after the death of her wealthy aunt:

"Georgie held her hand a moment longer than was usual, and gave it a little extra pressure for the conveyance of sympathy. Lucia, to acknowledge that, pressed a little more, and Georgie tightened his grip again to show that he understood, until their respective fingernails grew white with the conveyance and reception of sympathy. It was rather agonizing, because a bit of skin on his little finger had got caught between two of the rings on his third finger, and he was glad when they quite understood each other."

There are people who reread the Lucia books every year. Wise are they, and very happy.

Vacation Reading

The bags are nearly packed, and you are already starting to daydream about beach blankets, that cabin in the mountains, or Mom's home cooking. Vacation. Two glorious weeks of lolling about, sipping cool drinks, eating both unwisely and too well, maybe reading a book or two. Ah, yes, no August holiday is ever complete without the obligatory Beach Read, the latest paperback mega-hit, the sizzler or shocker of the season.

As a longtime Reader and Advisor (D.C. license pending), I have come up with a few guidelines for choosing your summer vacation books. You may want to clip this and tape it to the refrigerator.

1. You should always take more books than you can possibly get through. Who knows? It could rain every day at Ocean City, there might be a National Beer Alert (syringes? locusts? diseased hops?), you may discover that you can't quite lose yourself in Gil Orlovitz's *Milkbottle H.* A good rule of thumb is: Pack twice as many books as changes of underwear.

2. Make sure to bring something by a writer you know you like. If you've read, say, P. G. Wodehouse's *Right Ho, Jeeves* and can say with confidence that you never had such a good time in your life—this is, by the way, the Correct Critical Response—you ought to lay in *Uncle Fred in the Springtime* or the complete Mulliner stories.

3. Make at least one of your books a classic you have always hoped to read. Odds are you'll still be toting it along ten summers from now, but maybe, just maybe, you'll open *Middlemarch* and be swept away. (Once again: CCR—Correct Critical Response.) Then this fall when you bump into George Will—a devotee of Eliot's novel—you can say something like, "George, do you ever see yourself as Casaubon?" Be prepared to duck.

4. Include a good collection of poems. In lots of ways poetry makes ideal vacation reading: Unlike a novel or biography, you can actually finish a poem in a few minutes, then go out for a hike or a hamburger with something to think about. Moreover, poets are continually going on about nature, mountains, the sea, the search for love, the relentless passage of time; in short, the typical elements of a summer holiday. Who, before the Dewey Beach sirens and Rehoboth studs, would not sympathize with Tennyson's "Tears, Idle Tears," especially the bit about kisses "sweet as those by hopeless fancy feigned / On lips that are for others"? Or, if spurned by a flaxen-haired beauty, fail to find consolation in Yeats's "Never shall a young man / Thrown into despair / By those great honey-colored / ramparts at your ear / Love you for yourself alone / and not your yellow hair"?

5. Take something Really Serious. As Lorelei Lee used to say, "Fun's fun, but a girl can't go on laughing all the time." Suppose you've always liked that observation by Heraclitus about a person not being able to step into the same river twice. Now is the time to learn more about the pre-Socratics and their thought. Buy the Penguin *Early Greek Philosophy;* add volumes 1 and 2 of W. K. Guthrie's *History of Greek Philosophy.* Plan a little mini-seminar of one. When you get back to the office, you'll dazzle your co-workers as you contrast Heraclitus with Parmenides—and later confess to your minister or rabbi that you've been converted to Pythagoreanism. Of course, low-level bureaucrats will find the slightly later philosophy of Epicurus even more appealing: To be happy, one should choose an obscure life and try to avoid as much pain as possible.

6. Pack up some trash. After all, you are wallowing, aren't you? Out there, in your tent or camper, a zillion miles from the cultural watchdogs, no one will know that you're indulging in solitary vice, slobbering over John Grisham or Judith Krantz or the latest techno-porn. In fact, you should go all the way here, and make this session a real show: Knock off a six-pack, gobble M&Ms, scratch, belch, and worse. Get it all out of your system until next year. Then, purified of these shameful urges, you can go forth this fall to help make the bestseller list into something a tenured professor of English could be proud of. So what if it's boring? Long live the Modern Library!

7. Buy the cheapest copies you can find of the books you want. Don't take your signed first of Robert Penn Warren's *All the King's Men* anywhere that isn't climate-controlled. Buy a paperback. Better yet: Buy a used paperback at a secondhand bookshop, or from the nearest Salvation Army or Goodwill. We're talking expendable here, not collectable. Ideally, you should discard your books as you finish them: Agatha Christie's *Death in the Air* should be left on the plane; *The Portable Chekhov* abandoned at the seaside resort (the page folded down at "The Lady with the Dog"); *Lolita* tossed onto the unmade bed of a western motel.

Well, there you have them: Seven tips for holiday reading. Of course, I've left my most important recommendation for last. Never, ever take *Remembrance of Things Past, War and Peace,* or *The Decline and Fall of the Roman Empire* on a summer vacation. At some point in life, you will be tempted into thinking that you might actually get through one of these monuments while swinging in a hammock or relaxing in a deck chair. Vanity of vanities! Upon these three rocks have foundered some of the best vacation readers of our time. As everyone should know, these books can be read only in late fall or early winter, when the days have grown short and our evenings are filled with firelight and melancholy.

Found in the Stacks

Following my own rule no. 3, during the summer holidays I usually pack a bagful of those books that I really should have read long ago and am too embarrassed to confess that I haven't read yet. The only person that I can think of without any such biblio-lacunae is E. F. Bleiler, who has read virtually everything. And a lot of it twice. For years Bleiler was responsible for the Dover reprints of Victorian and Edwardian detective fiction, ghost stories, and suspense novels. He later compiled three mammoth reference works, *The Guide to Supernatural Fiction, Science Fiction: The Early Years,* and *Science Fiction: The Gernsback Years,* all wonderfully browsable, stuffed with pungent brief descriptions of books that once were as popular as the latest from Alice Walker or Stephen King. Though his scholarly interests lie mainly in Victorian genre fiction, Bleiler has also read obscure works in dozens of languages, written a Japanese grammar, and produced a scholarly edition of Nostradamus (which was reviewed in the *Times Literary Supplement* by the doyenne of Renaissance occult studies, Frances Yates). I once asked him to suggest a few truly neglected books that the adventurous might look for in libraries and used bookstores. Here is a selection from a much longer list:

Thomas Love Peacock, *Headlong Hall* (1815) and *Nightmare Abbey* (1818). "Perhaps these comic novels are too well known, but they are Peacock's best. The stuffy pronouncements of the Byron and Coleridge characters are wonderful."

Mrs. Henry Wood, *The Shadow of Ashlydat* (1863). "Hauntings, scandals, thrills. The best of the Victorian lady mysteries, after Mary E. Braddon's *Lady Audley's Secret* (1862) and Wood's own *East Lynne* (1861)."

Thomas Surr, *A Winter in London* (1806). "Perhaps the best of what are sometimes called the Silver Fork novels, emphasizing high society, social intrigue, gaming in Regency England. Artificial style, but enjoyable."

Geoffrey Dennis, *Bloody Mary's* (1934). "The finest school story that I know, with remarkable character studies, typical of British masters and pupils."

Mervyn Wall, *Leaves for the Burning* (1952). "This has been called the best novel to emerge from de Valera's Ireland. It is almost unknown in this country. Wall is known, though, for two very fine fantasies, *The Unfortunate Fursey* and *The Return of Fursey.*"

Arthur Machen, *Hieroglyphics* (1902). "The manifesto of the Aesthetic Movement in fin-de-siècle Great Britain. Beautifully written, and a cogent, clear, anti-naturalistic statement."

Bleiler also recommends the travels of George Borrow (especially *Wild Wales*), Basile's *Pentameron* ("the Neapolitan versions of the familiar fairy tales are far more earthy and punchy than the German or French"), and the Shakespeare Apocrypha, those plays once attributed to Shakespeare, such as *Sir John Oldcastle* and *Arden of Feversham*. Now, if only a vacation could last about two years instead of two weeks.

One More Modest Proposal

Early in the summer of 1993, a newly birthdayed 9-year-old began a campaign to persuade his mother to allow him to see *Jurassic Park*. Normally "Chris," as we shall call him, would have directed all such maneuvers at his fond and indulgent father, but the old bookworm—in fact, a youthful 44-year-old of exceptional charm and intelligence—had long ago made clear that if the family never went out to the movies again, Dad, at least, would count it no great loss. Mom, by contrast, was known to be exceedingly fond of action films, and just might be turned.

The time-hallowed arguments, passed down the millennia from generation to generation, soon made their scheduled appearance: "Adam saw it, and he wasn't scared at all." "I promise to make my bed for a week." "I'll do anything, *anything*, if you take me to *Jurassic Park*." "You and Dad are the meanest parents in the world." Neither promises nor imprecations availed. Mom wouldn't change her mind. So our enterprising lad, hungry, yea ravenous, for blood and gore, actually undertook the unthinkable: He unearthed one of the eight million copies of Michael Crichton's novel and slowly read the entire thing. We are talking, I should point out, about a normal kid who, given the choice between eating his green and leafy vegetables and reading any book whatsoever, would rather have asked for seconds on broccoli. For a week a mute and dumbstruck family would stumble across the future fourth-grader sprawled on the floor in front of a silent television, turning pages, rapt over imaginary parks with real raptors in them. There were, to be sure, the recurrent nightmares. But what the hey, no pain, no gain.

All of which merely provides some background for my proposed Jurassic Reading Plan. It's really quite simple: We persuade the various literacy councils, the Center for the Book, and Reading Is Fundamental to contribute their entire budgets to publicizing all the Merchant-Ivory films (*Howards End*, *The Bostonians*) and selected Masterpiece Theatre series, such as *The Pallisers* and *Pride and Prejudice*. Through spooky spot-ads, gothicky billboards, chatty Cathy Morland dolls, and fast-food giveaways, we make every 8-to-16-year-old in America absolutely frenzied to rent and watch, say, *Northanger Abbey*. And then we don't let them. Absolutely, unconditionally refuse. Instead, parents will be required to leave the major works of Austen—or Forster, Trollope, and James—lying casually at the common domestic bottlenecks: near the television, telephone, and refrigerator. Brilliant, no? Ah, but you may ask, what about James's late novels, those marvels of serpentine syntax and torturous lucidity? Not to worry. What we do here is send ringers into the schools with tattered copies of *The Wings of the Dove*. Teachers, livid with feigned shock, should seize these on sight and dramatically lock them in their desks next to old paperbacks of *The Amboy Dukes* and *Peyton Place*. Any copies of *Dove* that escape confiscation will be furtively, surreptitiously read to pieces. I really don't understand why no one has ever thought of this before.

Shake Scenes

Some years ago, in one of those inexplicable enthusiasms that sometimes overwhelm even the most disciplined readers, I started to devour everything I could find about *Hamlet*. I accumulated a dozen editions of the play (best is Harold Jenkins's Arden), studied its textual history (lost Ur-Hamlet, the 1603 First or Bad Quarto, the 1604 Second Quarto, the 1623 Folio), skimmed through a couple of dozen essays and books, rented Laurence Olivier's Oscar-winning film, and generally carried on like a frisky graduate student.

It was, however, difficult to explain to innocent bystanders that I was actually reading Shakespeare for fun—and during August, no less, when the rest of the world was eagerly buying up books about how to live forever, weigh less, find inner peace, land a better-paying job, and make love like a professional. Not that any and all of these aren't consummations devoutly to be wished. After all, Hamlet himself reflects deeply on most of these matters: He worries incessantly about that bourn from which no traveler returns, his own mother calls him "fat" near the play's end, and he is assailed by a "sore distraction," visions of ghosts, and thoughts of murder. He even complains that he lacks "advancement" and that his uncle "popped in" and stole the crown that should have been his. Not least, the erstwhile "glass of fashion" shows himself quite rudely and lewdly obsessed with "country matters." Still, as I tried to make clear at a dinner party to some kin (who were being less than kind), you can't really blame me for enjoying Shakespeare: There's a divinity that shapes our reading tastes, rough-hew them how we will.

Like most Americans of my generation, I first became aware of Shakespeare by watching "Our Gang" comedies. In one classic episode, Spanky and Darla mutilated the balcony scene from *Romeo and Juliet* and Alfalfa vainly tried to recite Mark Antony's "Friends, Romans, countrymen" speech—while dodging rotten fruit thrown by an audience that chanted "We want the Flory-Dories," a pubescent version of the Rockettes. Shakespeare, I had strongly impressed upon me, could be funny as well as peculiar.

Some years later, at the age of 11 or 12, I found myself lounging in our family car awaiting my mother, who was busy picking up Krazy Day bargains at the local Penney's department store. Near me stood one of those massive industrial dumpsters, from which I soon detected unexpected rustlings. Suddenly, what to my wondrous eyes should appear but three kids my age scrambling from the trash bin with their arms heavy-laden with long-playing records. It appeared that someone—no doubt a disgruntled, larcenous employee—had secreted the new LPs, which the three treasure-hunters grudgingly agreed to share with me. When I got home, I discovered that along with Vincent Price reciting the poems of Shelley, Renata Tebaldi singing her favorite arias, and an album entitled *Dream Dancing*—this last to provide background music to my early adolescence— there was an abridged audio version of John Gielgud's *Richard III.* As is universally acknowledged, Gielgud possessed the most entrancing speaking voice in the world. From his very first syllables as Richard—"Now is the winter of our discontent"—I was mesmerized. For the next week or so, I took to commandeering the bathroom, where I would declaim to the surrounding tiles, in tones aspiring to the mellifluous and orotund, "A horse, a horse, my kingdom for a horse!"

Shortly after I found the Gielgud LP, my eighth-grade teacher announced that he was going to play for the class a recorded version of *Macbeth.* In a moment the bright day was gone, replaced by the sounds of storm and battle, the dull clang of swords, thunder booming and lightning crackling, the wind rising, falling. And then, emerging above the din, voices that chilled the blood: "When shall we three meet again?" "When the hurly burly's done / When the battle's lost and won." And then, "Double, double, toil and trouble / Fire burn and cauldron bubble." The weird sisters were clearly the scariest witches this side of Oz. Moreover, what kid could resist their double-edged prophecies, especially that "none of woman born" will ever harm Macbeth? Even when Macduff finally stands before the usurper, like some ancient Scottish Terminator, declaring that he was from his dead mother's womb untimely ripped, Macbeth still goes down swinging: "I will not yield, / To kiss the ground before young Malcolm's feet / and to be baited with the rabble's curse." Everyone in our class agreed that the guy had style. Looking for more such thrills, I picked up a couple of Shakespeare paperbacks and, in ninth-grade study hall, eagerly read the major tragedies, preferring *Hamlet* for its bitter, almost adolescent humor.

Not long thereafter, I shelled out some outrageous sum—could it have been $7.50?—to see a special filmed version of the tragedy starring Richard Burton and directed by John Gielgud. Burton had wowed audiences in *Cleopatra,* and his Prince—in black turtleneck—looked sexy, moody, and murderous. The production itself resembled a rehearsal—a nearly bare stage, the players in modern clothes—but the rapiers and rapier wit were there unbated. When Horatio wonders why Hamlet's mother Gertrude remarried so soon after the death of Hamlet Sr., Burton acidly replies: "Thrift, thrift, Horatio. The funeral baked meats / did coldly furnish forth the wedding tables." When Polonius asks what he is reading, the student prince answers, with the weariness of a Ph.D. candidate: "Words, words, words." Later, in the interview with his mother, Hamlet really begins to speak daggers, and his language sicklies o'er with graphic images of Gertrude's sexuality: "To live / in the rank sweat of an enseamed bed, / stewed in corruption, honeying and making love / over the nasty sty." That's entertainment!

And so, too, was the most exhilarating live Shakespeare performance I have ever chanced to see: Peter Brook's celebrated 1970 Stratford production of *A Midsummer Night's Dream.* The stage was surrounded with bare white walls that made it look like an antiseptic gymnasium; trapezes hung from the ceiling; scenery was minimal—a huge billowy feather represented Titania's bower. The actual performance combined drama, circus, and orgy. Just before the intermission, for instance, Bottom the weaver, who has been "translated" into an ass, and the beautiful fairy queen Titania, mad about him because of Oberon's magic, prepare to celebrate their nuptials. Bottom is hoisted up on the shoulders of some beefy fairies, one of whom sticks his arm up through the weaver's legs, like a gigantic phallus which he proceeds to thrust outward each time that Bottom brays forth his passion for the love-sick queen, who rapturously leads her donkey-eared inamorato into the darkness. Too, too sullied flesh, indeed. Only a few Thersites-like critics groused that such drunken carnival was hardly Shakespeare.

Hamlets

Hamlet—the Mona Lisa of literature, according to T. S. Eliot—is the most written-about secular work in the world (though *King Lear* has replaced it as the modern scholar's choice for greatest Shakespeare play). There even exists a biennial journal entitled, and solely devoted to, *Hamlet Studies*. As for its hero, forever will he mope, in the words of Holden Caulfield, as "a sad, screwed-up type of guy." But in just what way? While one critic maintains that the tragedy examines the effects of unhealed grief, another asserts that it is a profound meditation on death. To romantics the sensitive Hamlet hems and haws because of his poetic nature; to realists he acts with considerable dispatch, first to test the ghost's accusations and then to find a way to reach a heavily guarded king. Ernest Jones, following a note by Freud, diagnoses an obvious Oedipus complex: The young hero delays his vengeance because he identifies with Uncle Claudius, who has acted out Hamlet's own desire to kill his father and marry his mother. G. Wilson Knight proposes that Claudius seems a pretty good ruler and that his moody, murderous nephew is the actual source of the rottenness in Denmark. By contrast, several modern scholars emphasize that Elsinore has been so thoroughly corrupted by Claudius and his hangers-on that Hamlet hesitates because he despairs that anything can put things to right. Others feel he waffles because he cannot figure out how to accomplish his revenge without being himself tainted by it. In his edition Harold Jenkins stresses Hamlet's pivotal position: The would-be avenger of a dead father becomes himself the focus of a son's revenge, that of Laertes for the accidentally murdered Polonius. Perhaps too, as Eleanor Prosser concludes, the ghost really was a "goblin damned" come to lure the melancholy Dane to his own destruction. For at least one reader of studious bent, *Hamlet* teaches that the purpose of thought is not self-cultivation (no matter how unweeded or gone to seed one's inner garden) but action.

In *Hamlet* nothing remains single or simple, and every action mirrors another. Has anyone, for instance, noted that Hamlet's advice to his mother strangely echoes the rhythms of Polonius's advice to his son? Probably. It was to counter a lot of this sometimes burdensome sophistication that C. S. Lewis, in "The Prince and the Poem," stressed the tragedy's most basic elements: "I am trying to recall attention from the things an intellectual adult notices to the things a child or a peasant notices—night, ghosts, a castle, a lobby where a man can walk four hours together, a willow-fringed brook and a sad lady drowned, a graveyard and a terrible cliff above the sea, and amidst all these a pale man in black clothes . . . with his stockings coming down, a dishevelled man whose words make us at once think of loneliness and doubt and dread, of waste and dust and emptiness, and from whose hands, or from our own, we feel the richness of heaven and earth and the comfort of human affection slipping away."

Basic Bard Watching

There are demanding and specialized books about Shakespeare aplenty, but only a few good general ones for the common reader: Mark Van Doren's *Shakespeare,* Francis Fergusson's *Shakespeare: The Figure in the Carpet,* S. Schoenbaum's handbook *Shakespeare: His Life, His Language and His Theater,* perhaps A. C. Bradley's classic *Shakespearean Tragedy.* Those with access to libraries might also look through John F. Andrews's three-volume *Shakespeare: His World, His Work and His Influence,* a survey with contributions by divers hands covering every aspect of Bard biz. Another addition to this short list might be Maynard Mack's engagingly written *Everybody's Shakespeare,* a collection of the noted Yale scholar's essays, chiefly on the tragedies. The book includes several classic pieces: "The World of Hamlet," here retitled "The Readiness Is All," probably the best short essay on the play; the influential brief introduction to Jacobean drama, now renamed "What Happens in Shakespearean Tragedy"; and an illuminating survey called "Play and History," which talks of some of the social realities behind the works.

For readers particularly interested in *Hamlet,* I recommend the introductions and apparatus to some of the standard scholarly editions of the tragedy (e.g., those by G. L. Kittredge, John Dover Wilson, the Oxford edition by G. R. Hibbard, the New Cambridge by Philip Edwards). For fun, try a few of the works inspired by the play: Richard Curtis's unprintably funny "Skinhead Hamlet" (included in *A Shakespeare Merriment,* edited by Marilyn Schoenbaum); Michael Innes's leisurely mystery *Hamlet, Revenge!,* in which Polonius is actually murdered during the play; Laura Bohannon's irresistible "Shakespeare in the Bush," wherein an anthropologist attempts to retell the story of Hamlet to a group of African elders; and Tom Stoppard's *Rosencrantz and Guildenstern Are Dead,* which shows the familiar drama from the viewpoint of Hamlet's doomed schoolfriends. Of course, real Hamletophiles will find a kind of pained amusement, like that from the quills upon the fretful porpentine, in some of the more extreme examples of current scholarship: For one psycho-critic, the skulls in the graveyard scene are symbolic testicles. Good grief, sweet prince!

🐚

There is no villainy to which education cannot reconcile us.

　　　　　　　　　　　　　　　—Anthony Trollope

After Strange Books

Avid readers, along with certain connoisseurs of wine, women, or song, sometimes grow so refined in their tastes that these become eccentric, even bizarre. The typical novel, like *vin ordinaire,* the missionary position, and the so-so soprano, no longer offers enough kick: Hollow-eyed, we hunger after more exotic and piquant sensations. For readers this cry for "madder music and for stronger wine" may lead to antiquarianism—a passion for the odd, marginal books of the past—or to the cult of the new, the cutting-edge and the underground. Sometimes these two extremes even meet in certain strange books.

Consider, for example, the twentieth century's recurrent attempts to break away from the novel's confining linearity, the dominion of row after row of type. By cutting up steel engravings from melodramatic pulp fiction, Max Ernst created nightmarish collage novels, *La Femme 100 Têtes* (The Hundred-Headed Woman, 1929) and *Une Semaine de Bonté* (A Week of Kindness, 1934). Lion-headed gentlemen stare at languorous demimondaines in dishabille; bedsheets become swirls and eddies of water; "in the heart of Paris, Loplop, Bird Superior, brings nightly food to the streetlamps"; and throughout there shudders an air of menace, sexual transgression, and torture. As André Breton once said, these albums suggest "the meticulous reconstruction of a crime witnessed in a dream."

A similar technique, juxtaposing a clichéd text with engravings cut from the British equivalent of an old Sears catalogue, resulted in a comic masterpiece, *What a Life!* (1911) by E. V. Lucas and George Morrow. Depicting the life of Baron Dropmore, of Corfe, this annotated photo album gently pokes fun at the conventions of Edwardian biography: unhappy school days, raffish upper-class friends, a dastardly crime in a country house, heartbreak, travel, wartime service, and eventual family happiness. The humor depends, of course, on perfect pitch, as when a young woman wearing a ludicrous paper crown, advertising a product called Grapholine, earns the following comment: "The Duke's only daughter, who became Lady Grapholine Meadows, was never seen without her coronet, which was a masterpiece of the jeweler's art."

Much this same playful sensibility, but now deliciously warped, reappears in Edward Gorey's macabre keepsake albums. *The Hapless Child* (1961), with elegant periphrasis and Edwardian-style pictures, relates the non-stop misfortunes of a little girl who loses her parents, suffers abuse by her schoolmates, and is eventually sold to a drunken brute. When she finally runs away from her cruel tormentor, the now-blind girl is struck down and killed by a car driven by her own father, who, having been wrongly reported dead, has been desperately searching the city for her. In a final twist of the knife, the father never recognizes the thin and wasted creature as his own child.

All this, of course, would be horrifying were it not for the sheer bathetic excess of misery; the result sends up Victorian melodrama and any number of Shirley Temple movies. Gorey's prose, dry, precise, and formal, complements his pictures perfectly. In *The Unstrung Harp* (1953) he guys professional authorship and its ways: "The night before returning home to Mortshire Mr. Earbrass allows himself to be taken to a literary dinner in a private dining room of Le Trottoir Imbecile. . . . The talk deals with disappointing sales, inadequate publicity, worse than inadequate reviews, others' declining talent, and the unspeakable horror of the literary life."

Gorey is well known; but Milt Gross remains underappreciated. Gross's *He Done Her Wrong* (1930) is the book version of a silent movie melodrama. Using only black and white pictures (and not a single word), Gross's saga ranges from the polar gold fields to the big city, depicting the adventures of a prospector who is betrayed by his partner, a Snidely Whiplash who absconds with both the young man's money and his girl. The album is replete with haunting images: At one point the square-jawed hero and the now unhappily married heroine just barely fail to meet when a movie marquee sign is suddenly lowered onto the sidewalk, blocking their view of each other. It bears the words "Now Playing 'Fate'—Bryan Theater." A lovely, unique piece of Americana.

In these books one picture is worth at least a thousand words. But there are other means of breaking up traditional narrative. Borges transmuted the personal essay into metaphysical fiction (e.g., "Pierre Menard, Author of the Quixote," "The Aleph"). In "Tlon, Uqbar, Orbis, Tertius," the Argentine fabulist and his friend Bioy-Casares discover a single volume from a mysterious encyclopedia that appears to describe a world utterly different from our own. Employing his trademark smoke and mirrors, Nabokov turned the seemingly scholarly commentary on a 999-line poem, *Pale Fire* (1962), into a dizzying game of unreliable narration, madness, and murder. Georges Perec's *Life a User's Manual* (1978) unfolds the secrets of the inhabitants of a Paris apartment house; all the chapters are pegged to the various rooms in the building. Beckett's *How It Is* (1960) reduces action to the almost nonexistent: In short bursts of prose, without punctuation, the text follows the movement and memory of a character named Bom who does next to nothing but crawl through a kind of cosmic mud for 200 pages. For many, myself included, these improbable stories and novels are among the greatest masterpieces of our time.

But there are still other, less well known attempts to break away from the constrictive bonds of plot and narration, what E. M. Forster once summarized as "The king died, and then the queen died of grief." Michel Butor's *Niagara* (1965) bears the subtitle *A Stereophonic Novel,* which means that it presents several different narrative tracks simultaneously, all of them focusing on Niagara Falls. On any page one might find a half dozen different voices: an announcer who details, in the language of tourism, the beauties of the Falls; newlyweds on their honeymoon; an old married couple revisiting the site on their fiftieth anniversary; the black gardeners who work at the surrounding park; a gigolo and his rich inamorata; and high-flown passages from Chateaubriand glorifying the Niagara of the early nineteenth century. Each of these is clearly distinguished, so that the reader may "listen" to a single voice, or several, or even attempt to follow all of them at once.

The flight from authorial control reaches one apogee in Marc Saporta's *Composition No. 1* (1962), which was published as a set of loose sheets in a box. "The reader is requested to shuffle these pages like a deck of cards; to cut, if he likes, with his left hand, as at a fortuneteller's. The order the pages then assume will orient X's fate." Each page here must necessarily stand on its own; yet having read through one combination, I found the story of X's marriage, graphically described love affairs, and wartime memories consistently gripping. Stanley Crawford's *Some Instructions*—or, to give its full title, *Some Instructions to My Wife concerning the Upkeep of the House and*

Marriage, and to My Son and Daughter, concerning the Conduct of Their Childhood—does away with ordinary narrative by presenting a kind of marriage almanac—a succession of schedules, calendars, memos, and notes of husbandly advice. "The house is the Marriage, and thus to maintain and keep in good repair the house, tidy and well cleaned, is to keep the Marriage too in good repair, tidy, well cleaned."

J. G. Ballard has a story that consists solely of an index. The brilliant Steven Millhauser reveals a high romantic tragedy in "Catalogue of the Exhibition: The Art of Edmund Moorash 1810–1846" (in *Little Kingdoms,* 1993); the text consists of museum notes on a suite of paintings. Jerome Charyn's *The Tar Baby* (1975) reproduces an entire issue of an imaginary literary magazine. *Tar Baby*'s memorial number for Anatole Waxman-Weissmann (1931–1972) includes letters to the editor, advertisements, course offerings, an interview, and essays like "Auguries of Futility: The Misinventions of Anatole Waxman-Weissmann," by Seth Birdwistell, and editorials by W. W. Korn, Bret Harte Professor of Rhetorical Arts and Sciences at Galapagos Junior College. By reading through the issue, one learns about the improbable history, rivalries, and friendships of an intellectual security guard whose "lifework consisted of a trunkful of notes, an aborted biography of Wittgenstein and one elliptical essay endlessly revised."

Such fun with academics also characterizes Gilbert Sorrentino's mammoth *Mulligan Stew,* which parodies virtually every form of contemporary writing. The novel even reprints an entire chapbook of wonderfully bad confessional poetry, Lorna Flambeaux's "The Sweat of Love," and a short play, actually a masque, about baseball (and other matters) called "Flawless Play Restored." Sorrentino dedicates this book to Brian O'Nolan, better known as Flann O'Brien, whose *At Swim-Two-Birds* (1939) is itself a wellspring of literary playfulness and Irish humor. O'Brien's second masterpiece, *The Third Policeman* (1967), takes the idea of the unreliable narrator to one logical end: The hero turns out to have been dead throughout most of the book. *Peace,* by science fiction novelist Gene Wolfe, is another example of such post-mortem fiction. Wolfe enjoys narrative trickiness: in *The Shadow of the Torturer* (1980, first part of a series), the protagonist can forget nothing; in *Soldier of the Mist* (1987, with a sequel), the hero loses his memory each time he goes to sleep.

Henry Green's classic proletarian novel, *Living* (1929), avoids using the definite article ("the") throughout; Georges Perec's novel *La Disparition* (1969) never uses the letter E; William Gaddis tells *JR* (1975) and *A Frolic of His Own* (1994), both recipients of National Book Awards, almost entirely in speech and without identifying the speakers.

Of course, as all you "gentes and laitymen, full stoppers and semicolonials, hybreds and lubberds" know, the masterpiece of word magic remains James Joyce's *Finnegans Wake* (1939), that epic tale about "the farce of dustiny." No doubt its artificial language, built around the "abnilisation of the etym," encouraged Anthony Burgess to create his own Russified English for *A Clockwork Orange* (1962) and Russell Hoban to remake current speech and slang for *Riddley Walker* (1980). Both novels, set in grim futures, are serious moral fables made exhilarating through their poetic languages.

❧

To conclude this mini-survey of the wilder shores of fiction—and I have failed to mention William Burroughs's cutouts, William Gass's typographical experiments (*Willie Master's Lonesome Wife*, 1968), and many others—let me praise one of the most original and appealing artistic projects of our time: Tom Phillips's *A Humument* (1987). This "treated Victorian novel" relates "the sad story of Bill Toge" and his progress in love and heartbreak. What Phillips did was this: He took a late Victorian novel entitled *A Human Document,* by W. H. Mallock, and transformed its pages by blotting out unwanted text and overlaying various pictorial patterns to help link the words he wanted to retain. Phillips decorates each page with his own artwork but never adds any words; still he manages to create out of the template of Mallock's novel a strange and haunting poetry, based on "realities broken by quivering peculiarities." Several pages are playfully erotic; many comment on the vagaries of the artistic life; others approach prose poetry: "turn to serious syllables soft as your body in the blue film of the hush and whisper of your mind." Phillips, naturally enough, belongs to "a generation in love with chancy art."

Don't some of these experiments with narrative form resemble today's creative cutting edge, hypertext and CD-ROM? As is so often the case, the utterly new turns out to be very much like the unjustly forgotten. Though the next fifty years should see some startling developments in the art of electronic storytelling, I doubt whether any of them will come as a complete surprise.

❧

The splendid illustrations of novels and
children's books . . . intended for persons who
can scarcely read are among the few things
capable of moving to tears those who can say
they have read everything.
—André Breton

Awful Bits

All writing submits to certain constraints—sonnets have fourteen lines, and sentences end in periods—but sometimes authors voluntarily adopt a more constrictive form. Spenser's *Faerie Queene,* for instance, is knit together with complex numerical patterns. Both *Gadsby* by Ernest Vincent Wright and *La Disparition* by Georges Perec are novels in which the letter E never appears. Recently, while reading a life of Perec, I was carried away by a sudden desire to try one of his experiments. Never one to say no to temptation, I herewith present the world premiere of Act I of "Awful Bits," a gothic melodrama:

SCENE 1: *A 1930s Hollywood-style Frankenstein laboratory. Puttering about is Dr. Dee, a lineal descendant of the Elizabethan necromancer of the same name. Enter a lumbering Cockney factotum, Doolittle:*

DOOLITTLE: " 'ey, busy, Dee?"

   The doctor looks sharply about, pulls aside a curtain, where stands an inanimate zombie who closely resembles a B-movie Nazi mad scientist.

DOOLITTLE (*with a shock of recognition*): "E!"

DEE (*in a clipped efficient tone*): "Effigy."

The doctor then hands the servant a long list of what are clearly his next murder victims. Doolittle hesitates.

DEE (*with dramatic insistence*): "Each!"

DOOLITTLE (*looking down the list and obviously recognizing a name*): "I? Jay kill?"

The doctor stares into his hapless toady's face. Then slowly gives the thumbs down sign.

DOOLITTLE (*pauses, looks helplessly about*): "Amen."

SCENE 2: *Later that day. The bumbling Doolittle, having apparently failed to complete his deadly task, trades insults with his master.*

DEE: "Opaque, you are!"

DOOLITTLE: "Ass, t'you!"

SCENE 3: *Doolittle has been brought before Dr. Dee's dread master, the renegade Nazi scientist Johann Von Schmetterling, who has cloned a duplicate of himself and is obviously planning to create some kind of zombie army. Doolittle trembles before this demonic figure.*

VON SCHMETTERLING (*with an evil chuckle*): "Ve double you!" (*indicates a diabolical-looking machine. Then adds, with malice in a soft voice*), "Ask why?"

Before Doolittle can do just that, the madman opens a hidden door to reveal multiple copies of a complete household staff, lacking only a valet and a butler:

VON SCHMETTERLING (*points, then adds with his heavy German accent*): "Zee!"

SCENE 4: *The action shifts to the South of France. Doctor Dee and Von Schmetterling are sitting at a café, sipping Vichy water.*

DEE: "Why Aix?"

VON SCHMETTERLING (*with a suave SS-style estheticism, points to the azure sky and murmurs rapturously*): "Da blue!"

DEE (*his eyes suddenly open to natural beauty for the first time, mixes his words in a telling portmanteau coinage*): "View-teous!"

SCENE 5: *The red-light district in nearby Marseille. A waterfront bar crawling with sailors, whores, and transvestites.*

ONE SAILOR TO ANOTHER: "Are Kewpie, Owen"—*indicating two figures in the smoke-filled room*—"male?"

In the corner Rose, a nice Jewish girl from Long Island, has been reduced to selling her favors after being seduced and cruelly abandoned (by Dee, as we shall learn) while on her junior year abroad:

SAILOR (*drunkenly holding up a wad of francs*): " 'kay?"

ROSE (*nods and then adds*): "Chez"—*pauses trying to think of the French word, fails, and settles for the English,* "I?"

Sailor nods and the pair go off together, just as Von Schmetterling and Dee enter.

SCENE 6: *Doolittle—or his clone—is loading coffin-shaped crates, each identified by a letter of the alphabet. He is tired.*

DOOLITTLE (*letting out a sigh as he finishes box G and turns to its neighbor*): "H."

He pauses, then starts to lift the box. It's unexpectedly hard to budge, which puzzles him.

DOOLITTLE: "Gee, 'eavy."

Not too surprisingly, he drops the crate, which cracks open. In a flash a long arm, almost a tentacle, thrusts itself out and seizes the hapless Cockney by the throat.

DOOLITTLE (*gasping for air and help, tries to shout*): "Dee!"

He grows limp—is he dead or unconscious?—as the crate's top slowly opens further.

SCENE 7: *Later that same night, Rose is strolling the Vieux Port, when she looks up and sees the back of a prospective customer, another naval man.*

ROSE (*in a come-hither voice*): "Seabee!"

The seabee turns around and the girl recognizes her own brother.

ROSE (*aghast*): "Abie! . . . "

Curtain falls on Act I.

Should anyone be interested in hearing the conclusion of this modern Faust story, he or she may write to me privately. I should say that Von Schmetterling plans sordid things for Rose and Abie, while Dr. Dee, as the astute no doubt have guessed, has already taken the first steps on the road to redemption.

Turning 50

Invited to spend two weeks at the Atlantic Center for the Arts in New Smyrna Beach, Florida, teaching literary journalism. During the last half of January. Who could resist?

The Friday before I emplane—do people still say that?—Washington is pounded by a major ice storm, and much of the area suffers a blackout. Silver Spring flickers with ghostly candlelight. Naturally, I had planned to wash clothes that very evening. Sigh. Only late on Saturday morning is power finally restored, and, to my relief, I pack unexpectedly clean shirts and socks, along with a dozen or so classic novels, works of history, and similarly ambitious volumes. We are talking thousands of dense pages: John Cowper Powys's *Wolf Solent* ("the only book in the English language to rival Tolstoy," according to polymath George Steiner); a fat study of time travel in literature, philosophy, and physics; an even thicker one about modernism in the twentieth century. For recreation, I do take along Robert Barnard's *Death by Sheer Torture,* a mystery with a particularly witty opening paragraph:

"I first heard of the death of my father when I saw his obituary in *The Times.* I skimmed through it, cast my eye over the Court Circular, and was about to turn to the leader page when I was struck by something odd in the obituary and went back to it."

As it happened though, I never quite got around to reading any of these books, not even the Barnard. In fact, it was a very near thing that I didn't stay in Florida forever.

Reader, imagine turning 50.

We all know what a man of 50 is like: Stolid. Rotund. Favoring vests with watch-fobs. The embodied spirit of middle age. If we pick up a novel by Balzac or Dreiser, the man of 50 is always the dupe—the besotted fool who throws away his fortune on a showgirl and ends up committing suicide in a back alley. In Henry James, the man of 50 will usually glimpse the possibility of happiness—and then realize that he has waited too long, failed, with oh so absolute a certainty, to seize the moment when it was offered. For a woman it's no better, probably worse. Well into her forties a woman may feel beautiful, confident, sexually aware, provocative; but sound the knell of 50, and everything changes: She grows respectable, birdlike, obsessed with her bridge group or the Ladies' Garden Society. One day you're a smoldering Sophia Loren, the next you're wearing a babushka and playing bingo. Think of the mournful grocery shopper in Randall Jarrell's poem "Next Day":

> . . . Now that I'm old, my wish
> Is womanish:
> That the boy putting groceries in my car
> See me. It bewilders me he doesn't see me.
> For so many years
> I was good enough to eat: the world looked at me
> And its mouth watered.

The weather at the Atlantic Center was in the mid-70s, the sky so poetically blue one wanted to call it azure or cerulean, and the breezes wafted through the scrub oak and palmettos just enough to cool the cottage where I was staying. I unpacked my bags, dumped out fifty pounds of books, hooked up my borrowed laptop, and went for a walk. I had turned 50 last November.

In truth, a man of 50 would like to possess a philosophic calm, smile with Buddhist detachment at this mad, unimportant world of ours. In Plato's ideal republic, guardians take office at 50. Doubtless those serene philosopher-kings all look rather like the handsome bearded figures in Raphael's painting *The School of Athens,* the one where Aristotle points to the earth and his old teacher gestures to the sky. Instead I merely felt creaky, dull, set in my ways. At the oceanfront the waves rolled and curled, white caps billowing, as young men in wetsuits surfed toward the hard-packed shore. Like Prufrock, I padded slowly along the sand with my trousers rolled and thought about the mermaids: "I do not think that they will sing to me." Had I passed too much of my life in libraries? In the distance I could hear a jukebox in a seaside bar playing—and I gradually made out the voice of Patsy Cline breaking your heart with "Faded Love." Should I have spent more time in honky-tonks?

These are dangerous thoughts for a man just turned 50, the age of wistfulness and rash decisions.

That evening I met the six "associates" who were to study with me, the "master artist." Even the title bestowed by the Atlantic Center on its teachers made me feel like an ancient, wispy-bearded Chinese monk. Perhaps I should give up the laptop and write with a brush and ink on rice paper? Over the next several afternoons, my students—two university teachers, two columnists for small newspapers, an expert on Florida history and geography, the author of a forthcoming book on Japan—talked with me about writing. We sat in a room with the blinds drawn. One could, at the edges of the slats, make out the dappled sunlight on the pointed leaves of the palmettos.

In the evenings we took to going out for beer, glimpsing seabirds wading along the Indian River, watching the slow circling of hawks—or were they vultures? On the weekend we drove to a noisy barbecue joint near a fishing wharf. A stuffed alligator stood fiercely upright outside the entrance. Bikers had just left. In the darkness you could just make out the slapping of water against wood. The writer Anthony Burgess once said that the true function of poetry is to be memorized so that it may be recited aloud when drunk. "With rue my heart is laden / For golden friends I had, / For many a rose-lipt maiden / For many a light-foot lad. / By brooks too broad for leaping / The lightfoot boys are laid; / And the rose-lipt maids are sleeping / In fields where roses fade." After the Housman, out spilled bits of verse by Herrick and Frost, Yeats and Pope. Talismans. Charmed words. "Whenas in silks my Julia goes . . . No memory of having starred / Atones for later disregard . . . That is no country for old men."

The following week I was driven into Orlando to give talks on book reviewing, first to an association of the Atlantic Center's patrons, then to a group of students at the University of Central Florida. Somebody asked if I thought Florida's climate was "inimical" to creativity and scholarship. As I answered—"There are lots of eminent Florida writers, from Marjorie Kinnan Rawlings to Charles Willeford, from Zora Neale Hurston to Carl Hiaasen"—at the back of my brain I realized, with a start, that for the first time since I was 4 or 5, I had gone an entire week without reading a book. And I hadn't missed it at all.

Instead, I had been looking at marshlands and herons and pretty girls, had listened to a tropical storm hammer at my cottage, had lounged in outdoor restaurants, eating pork sandwiches and key lime pie. I told jokes after communal dinners, recounted strange anecdotes from my youth— "Did I ever tell you guys about the time a gypsy in France tried to sell me a human thumb?"—and during the day leisurely scribbled notes and *pensées* and stories on a pad of canary-yellow paper. My pile of books looked increasingly Northern and austere, about as inviting as Gregory the Great's commentary on the book of Job. Washington—with its work, ice, family obligations, doctor appointments, bills, and, above all, its relentless need to be doing, doing, doing—began to seem like a place I'd once read about, back in the days when I read books.

Before long, I started to identify with those characters in Conrad or Maugham who have slowly gone to seed in some sweltering backwater of empire. The whiskey-sodden doctor in the crumpled white linen suit. The plantation owner who has taken a native girl for his mistress. Surely I could find somewhere to play cards in the evening under a slow-turning ceiling fan? I stopped combing my hair; gradually lost my appetite. Perhaps malaria or dengue fever had set in?

I might have never read again, were it not for two circumstances. One night I wandered into a little building at the Atlantic Center, and noticed that it was lined with shelves. A library. As I retreated, my hand brushed against a table, and I knocked a small book onto the floor: *Quote Unquote,* by Jonathan Williams, a collection of favorite quotations, a commonplace book that I had read in what now felt like another life. I hesitantly glanced at a few pages: "Don't think—cook!"—Ludwig Wittgenstein. "He may be dead; or he may be teaching English"—Cormac McCarthy (hadn't I once reviewed some novels of his?). "Lives devoted to beauty seldom end well"— Kenneth Clark. As I read on, smiling, I could feel an ancient hunger starting to return.

But a few quotations could hardly retrieve a shattered reprobate, marooned on the shores of Tennyson's Lotos land. "Ah, why / Should life all labor be?" The Florida weather stayed perfect, after all, and the quiet desperation of being 50 still gnawed. No, what saved me, Dear Reader, was Mickey Mouse.

Naturally, once they had learned that I was going to Florida, my noisy offspring had reminded me, with some insistence, that theirs was the only family in the Western Hemisphere that had never visited Disney World, Epcot, and the MGM Studios—places held by their father to be roughly comparable to the outer circles of hell, but less interesting. Naturally, my protestations proved futile. So, at the end of my two weeks at the Atlantic Center, just when I was planning to inaugurate my new career as a beachside volleyball player, I was suddenly swept up into Amusement Park

Frenzy. Let me assure you that following a rugged day in the Magic Kingdom with children, I yearned for nothing more than to be in my hotel
room reading a good book. Any book. *Wolf Solent* suddenly looked irresistible. And I could hardly wait to start that 800-page study of modernism.
By the end of our Disney visit, I was daydreaming about being back in
Washington surrounded by my own bookshelves.

Though many 50-year-olds are called to be beachcombers, few are
chosen. Some of us, alas, are destined to find our escapes in novels, not life.
But for a short while the languorous existence of a lotos-eater was quite
wonderful—the feeling of a new dawn in a life that had grown routine.
With luck, a bit of that sunny paradise will never entirely abandon me. But
it was a near thing. I had heard the mermaids singing.

Blame It on Books

This morning, starting at around 7:30, I jogged around my neighborhood for forty minutes. Yesterday I lifted weights at the Silver Spring YMCA—presses, curls, squats, three sets each of ten or twelve repetitions. I alternate the aerobics and the strength training through the week. For most of the spring I've also taken an abdominal exercise class on Tuesdays and Thursdays. That's now down to only Thursdays, since my Tuesdays are given over to a swing dancing course. Three times a week I swim laps at our local pool. And this isn't all, by any means. Over the past five months I've lost thirty or thirty-five pounds. I now eat lots of vegetables and fruit, sip constantly on bottled water, ingest a multivitamin and a few other supplements daily, drink soy milk and nibble tofu, and no longer order dessert. Occasionally I do fantasize about glazed donuts, especially late at night.

As a result of this regimen, I've had to buy new clothes—a mixed blessing. It's astonishing to be able to wear a size 33 waist pair of pants again. Sometimes it even seems I could get away with a 32. When I look in mirrors I see a slightly strange face, thin, with unwelcome lines around my mouth, and slight hollows in my cheeks. An El Greco look, I suppose, and a little gaunt for my taste. Perhaps I will get used to it.

What has inspired this obvious midlife crisis, this madcap attempt to stave off the ravages of time and recapture a few remnants of fleeting youth?

Well, books, of course. Books and magazines. The initial impulse came from my trip last January to Florida's Atlantic Center for the Arts. There, as I walked along the beach, I felt like three of the lesser-known dwarves of Snow White—dumpy, creaky, and crabby. Ultimately, I resolved to amend my life and see what I could do to improve my physical well-being.

So, being a bookman, once I got home I went directly to the library. Now, I'm pretty familiar with my local libraries. I can find my way blindfolded to the children's and art shelves; I know where the classical CDs are kept; I regularly check out audio books. But I was nonetheless surprised—and ultimately pleased—to discover that the health/fitness section must be second only to general fiction in the sheer volume of material. In Wheaton virtually all the genre's classics were readily available: the masterworks of Jane Fonda, aerobic workout videos by Fabio-like hunks, guides to male sexuality, polemics about various herbal supplements guaranteed to extend life, oversized paperbacks on skin care, yellowing books on turning back the clock, pamphlets on becoming a vegetarian, an ancient John Travolta exercise manual, weightlifting bibles, and much, much else. Fortunately, I'd brought a good-sized cardboard box, and—don't you love libraries?—the front desk allowed me to check out twenty books and videos.

As a result, during the next week or two, I devoted my bedtime reading to these self-help guides. Nearly all of them proved as unputdownable as a Thomas Harris thriller. Here, after all, was a newfound land, an unexplored continent. In my adolescence I had pored over treatises on proper etiquette and effective public speaking and even the development of self-confidence, but those inspirational tomes had been directed primarily at mental change. Now the focus was the body, never a subject that I had felt particularly comfortable with. Like all self-respecting introspectives, I was mildly hypochondriacal, fearful of doctor visits, and ashamed of just about every part of my physical self. Locker rooms tended to fill me with envy, as I desired this man's lats and that man's pecs. On the rare occasions when I'd watch a baseball or basketball game on television, I'd admire the ease in Ripken's manner and the smile on Ripken's face, or the supernatural grace of a Michael Jordan. Having no recognizable athletic prowess myself, I had long tended to regard my body as a necessary evil, "the heavy bear that goes with me," the source of lifelong discontent—bowed legs, poor vision, bad molars, weak ankles, blemished skin.

But suddenly none of this really mattered. Through persistence that would eventually be transmuted into daily pleasure (or so my authorities assured me), I could rejigger my food intake and lose flab, sculpt my torso, and gradually acquire the all-round spiritual buoyancy that accompanies regular exercise. There was no need to settle for a decaying physical machine when I might transform myself into an Iron Man. Shaking my head, I called to mind—not for the first time—the motto of the library in John Bellair's juvenile thrillers: "Believe Half of What You Read." Still, why not give it a whirl? All these upbeat gurus had infected me with an unexpected exhilaration: I might discover the burn, the zone, the sweet spot in time. I might even go the distance, perhaps carrying a banner with a strange device: Excelsior! At the very least, here were new daydreams for a middle-aged guy.

Starting at the supermarket, I bought a vitamin book from the cashier and spent half a day carefully selecting groceries on the basis of their side-panels. Low sodium, low fat, high fiber. Reading has seldom been so utilitarian. No more Fruity Pebbles—bring on the Weetabix. Veggie burgers. Antioxidant green tea. Lean poultry. Enough kale, broccoli, and spinach to feed all the rabbits in *Watership Down.* Rice cakes. Wheat germ. Soy milk (vanilla-flavored, of course). Bananas and strawberries. Kiwi. Sweet potatoes. . . . My plump heroes, Falstaff, Stendhal, and Dr. Gideon Fell, would have roared with laughter.

Ignoring their imagined guffaws, I proceeded to the checkout counter and naturally passed by the magazine racks. Normally, I'd glance up, maybe even pause for a moment, hoping for a cover photo of supermodel Heidi Klum or a feature on this year's pretty brunette ("As dawn breaks, Coco stretches her tawny limbs, gently pushes aside the cat curled up beside her, and sleepily heads for her morning whirlpool . . . "). But this time my eye was caught by a picture of a big, tooth-filled smile affixed to a body flexing its even bigger biceps. There must have been at least a dozen periodicals, perhaps more, devoted to various aspects of physical culture. Such plenty. I tossed a couple into my cart. As my groceries were being totted up, I noticed one of those small, digest-sized magazines, promising fitness at any age. I bought that too.

Once home, I distributed my edible goodies into cupboard and fridge, blithely ignoring the "Yuck, what is this?" comments of my offspring, and then retreated to the bathroom.

There may be one or two greater sensual pleasures than reading magazines while soaking in a deep, hot bathtub, but none more reliable or innocent. As always, the ads in my magazines were at least as mesmerizing as the articles: Renova cream for wrinkles, the latest high-tech running shorts, sex videos guaranteed to transport my partner and me to hitherto unscaled heights of rapture, vitamins by mail, outfits from Hugo Boss or Giorgio Armani, sports cars and SUVs—all the stuff that midlife crises are made of. Aside from the regular features (a doctor answering questions about the prostate or the G-spot, a smiling Irish bartender proffering good advice about various moral dilemmas, e.g., whether to date the ex-girlfriend of one's best friend), most of the actual articles tended to address the same familiar, but perennially fascinating, questions: how to execute various classic exercises, how to buy a pair of running shoes, how to eat while training, how to dress with style, how to make love more thoughtfully, how to take care of the various parts of your ever-better body.

Now, the trouble with reading, an anonymous showgirl once observed, is that it just puts ideas into your head. As Emma Bovary and Don Quixote found out years ago, such modern "romances"—in book, periodical, and video form—soon made me increasingly dissatisfied with my bland, provincial self. Couldn't I be as cool as these wafer-thin guys in sunglasses, lounging by the pool in Cozumel? Couldn't I get as "ripped" and "cut" as these Arnold wannabes? Well, maybe not that thin or that musclebound, but somehow better than I was? I didn't want to look like a guy who spent most of his time turning the pages of books and writing about them. Instead of dusty antiquarian M. R. James, I could be debonair Mr. James . . . Bond. All I had to do was work at it. That seemed straightforward enough. Besides, I had all this printed matter to guide me.

And so I started, adapting various prescriptions to my own needs, ultimately settling on forty-five minutes to an hour of exercise a day and a fairly Spartan diet. A couple of weeks later, when I returned my first batch of material to the library, I remembered that one could check out old magazines, and left with past issues of *GQ, Runner's World, Men's Health*—as well as a selection of books from another section of the library hitherto unknown to me: the shelf reserved for guides to sartorial fashion. Soon I was learning that paisley goes with nothing, that one shouldn't wear button-down shirts with classy suits, that linen jackets are hard to care for, and that everybody should have a personal style. What was my style? Blue jeans, flannel shirts, and gym shoes. I had always vaguely aspired to be—as James Salter described the hero of his novel *Solo Faces*—a guy who looked good in old clothes. But maybe I could be a little more daring, a little sleeker . . .

And so it went. From body to apparel and then on to toys. Surely, the new me would require a new car. The family Dodge Grand Caravan just didn't fit the vision. Maybe a little emerald green Miata. Another stop at the library and newsstand was soon called for—and home I went with *Consumer Reports'* annual car issue, copies of *Road and Track,* etc., etc. In the end, a residual sense of practicality led me to settle on a Honda Accord. But still I got the V-6, not the smaller, less peppy four-cylinder. Never dies the dream.

Ah, books. They are so wonderfully various, whether you need a copy of Ariosto's epic *Orlando Furioso,* Virgina Woolf's historical jeu d'esprit

Orlando, or even a vacation guide to Orlando and Disney World. Recently, for instance, I've been thinking about my pool game and my half-forgotten poker skills. Surely, my suave transformed self should be able to run the table like Fast Eddie or make that inside straight like the Cincinnati Kid. . . . It's clearly time to visit the library again.

On the Road Not Taken

I didn't figure on missing my books. Family, yes (sort of); *Book World,* yes (sort of); noble hound Seamus, regarded by all privileged to know him as the world's finest yellow Labrador, most definitely. But, strangely, I thought I could get along without the bookcases in the living room, bedroom, study, and basement. Without the boxes, piled higgledy-piggledy, marked Plato, Beckett, Le Guin, O'Brian, Yourcenar, Christie and Carr, Classics, Shaw, Modern Firsts, To Read, Music, Fairy Tales, Hammett, and Shakespeare. But nearly every day I still find myself rising from my desk chair—in this well-equipped but airless office where I now write—to retrieve, say, *Cheri* in French or my copy of William Gibson's *Mona Lisa Overdrive,* only to realize that those titles are hundreds of miles away. Comes as a shock each time.

Who would have thought it? In fact, I arrived in Orlando—as a one-semester visiting professor at the University of Central Florida—with a dozen cartons of books, most of them intended for my two classes: a graduate writing seminar in literary journalism and an honors lecture course about publishing and book culture. So on the shelves in my office, Room 417-E in the Humanities and Fine Arts Building, I can look up and see volumes of the artful nonfiction of Joseph Mitchell, M. F. K. Fisher, Janet Flanner, Kenneth Tynan, Rebecca West, James Agee, Anthony Burgess,

Virginia Woolf, Desmond MacCarthy . . . Shouldn't these be enough? There are, besides, a dozen guides to book collecting, as well as Douglas McMurtrie's old standby *The Book* and S. H. Steinberg's Penguin classic, *Five Hundred Years of Printing.* And then I've also brought along a score of works by and about Nabokov, since I'm using *Lolita* in my "Adventures in the Book Trade" class, partly as a starting point for talking about various aspects of modern publishing, but secretly because I wanted my students to read at least one really good modern novel. "I am thinking of aurochs and angels, the secret of durable pigments, prophetic sonnets, the refuge of art . . . "

But I didn't transport just texts for work. I knew myself well enough to pack comfort titles too, those books one absolutely needs for spiritual refreshment—in my case the collected poetry of Whitman, T. S. Eliot, Wallace Stevens, Robert Frost, and W. H. Auden, supplemented by the irreplaceable *Faber Popular Reciter,* edited by Kingsley Amis. Where else can you find together Reginald Heber's "From Greenland's Icy Mountains" ("Though every prospect pleases / And only man is vile") and "Horatius at the Bridge" and "In Flanders Fields," not to mention, though we must, such hymns as "Abide With Me" and "Lead, Kindly Light"? Just now I picked up my sturdy paperback, and it fell open—really, it did—to "Young and Old" by the usually religiose Charles Kingsley:

> When all the world is young, lad,
> And all the trees are green;
> And every goose a swan, lad,
> And every lass a queen;
> Then hey for boot and horse, lad,
> And round the world away;
> Young blood must have its course, lad,
> And every dog his day.
>
> When all the world is old, lad,
> And all the trees are brown;
> And all the sport is stale, lad,
> And all the wheels run down;
> Creep home, and take your place there,
> The spent and maimed among:
> God grant you find one face there,
> You loved when all was young.

The whole anthology pulses with such stirring, mildly cornball stuff. You should hear me at parties when I start to recite Tennyson's "Tithonus" or Kipling's "Recessional." "Lest we forget—lest we forget!"

Of course, I also made room for some of those Books One Has Always Wanted to Read and Never Quite Gotten Around To, beginning with

Byron's *Letters and Journals,* picked up for $75 in a used bookstore a couple of years back. Editor Leslie Marchand gives each of the thirteen volumes its own title, a phrase from Byron, and these are captivating in themselves: *In My Hot Youth; Famous in My Time; Alas, the Love of Women!;* and *Wedlock's the Devil.* As a grad student eons ago, I treated myself to Jacques Barzun's *Selected Letters of Byron,* and ever since have wanted to lose myself in the Marchand edition for a few weeks. But so far the books remain, impressively, on my shelf here, untouched.

They're in good company. They stand next to the first four installments of Anthony Powell's *Dance to the Music of Time,* one of those modern classics that everyone just naturally assumes I'm crazy about, if only because of my passion for the somewhat similar Evelyn Waugh, Nancy Mitford, E. F. Benson, and Ronald Firbank (not to mention Proust, with whose *À la recherche du temps perdu* the *Dance* is frequently compared). But I haven't read any Powell except his memoirs. So I quietly squirm when the classicist Bernard Knox launches into a paean to the twelve-part series. And, of course, right now it looks as though I may have to keep squirming.

Because I've also resolved to really immerse myself in Faulkner and Eudora Welty. After all, I'm living down heah in the South for the first time in my life, and obviously should read beyond *The Sound and the Fury,* "No Place for You, My Love," and a few other famous novels and stories. Which also explains why I've carried down my perfect, dawn-bright copy of Marjorie Kinnan Rawlings's Florida classic, *Cross Creek.*

Alas, prepping for classes, writing columns and reviews, slipping away for a little booking (landed a near-fine English first of Wodehouse's *Ice in the Bedroom*), conferring with students, sipping coffee or sharing meals with faculty members, agreeing to judge essay contests, conducting my weekly on-line chat, and promising to visit colleagues or old friends in St. Petersburg, Fort Lauderdale, Gainesville, Jacksonville, and Miami seem to be eating up all the time I imagined spending poolside, under a beach umbrella, sipping a cool tall one and catching up on Byron's erotic entanglements and the nefarious doings of the Snopeses.

Not enough time. That sounds like almost everyone's dying words. So maybe I should send off for the collection of the world's 100 greatest books that I saw advertised in an airline magazine recently. Each classic is reduced to a forty-five-minute audiocassette presentation: "You'll learn about the author's life and the time in which he or she lived; you'll hear a description of the book's themes; an analysis of the characters; a detailed re-creation of the story with descriptive passages from the book; and a concise yet full discussion of the book's relevance." And not only that. "Despite their condensed presentation, the mood and richness of the original works have

been preserved to a remarkable degree. And, by reinforcing the audio presentation with printed Knowledge Maps, you can absorb the lessons of
great literature in the most efficient manner possible." Yet even that's not
all, folks. "If you were to read each of these 100 great books at the rate of 4
per year (an ambitious goal for most of us), it would take 25 years to read
the entire collection! But now you can absorb much of their knowledge,
wisdom and insight in just a few weeks of enjoyable listening. And, after
listening to the entire collection, you will have a depth of knowledge
achieved by only a few people who have ever lived."

Well, I don't know. I've been reading books for forty-five years now,
and I still don't feel I have much depth of knowledge. Does anybody ever?

My classes themselves seem to be going reasonably well, especially now
that I've stopped being saddened at how little the young have read. The
students are uniformly eager, earnest, and lively, like young Labrador pup-
pies, but the culture of our time has left them cut off from the literature
and art of the past. In my writing seminar I offered, in a fit of insanity, to
give an A for the course to any student who could quote a single line by
A. E. Housman. With rue my heart is laden, for I didn't have to pay up.

In my honors class, which draws on undergraduates from several majors, I hardly expected anybody to know much about Vladimir Nabokov.
One must be realistic, after all. But when I referred to Graham Greene—
who was instrumental in helping *Lolita* gain respectable literary attention
—nobody knew his name or work either. Ah, thought I shrewdly, searching for a pedagogic device, these kids love movies. I mentioned that Greene
had written the script for the classic film *The Third Man*. Only one person
had seen *The Third Man*. Well, I try not to be appalled. I can remember the
shock on my own English professors' faces when they realized that their
1960s students didn't recognize Latin tags or lines from Horace. They
shook their jowls in disbelief: How could you not know the classics? Well,
the world changes. *Sic transit gloria mundi.*

Today we read Caribbean literature and the poems of Sor Juana and
Emilia Lanier—thought by A. L. Rowse to be the Dark Lady of Shakespeare's sonnets—and captivity narratives and slave memoirs and all sorts
of worthy, hitherto neglected books. For young scholars, especially women
and people of color, such works are often exhilarating discoveries. We are
exploding the canon. And a large part of me welcomes just such a blow-up.
Make it new. But I sometimes feel too old to light out for these little-
explored territories, and I frequently long for the safety of the books I already know or want to know.

So, scanning the authors I've brought to Orlando, I occasionally wonder: What has Robertson Davies or Katherine Anne Porter or William

Empson to say to these bright-eyed, fit, and intelligent children of the new millennium? I am in the land of Disney and NASA—the twin poles of American civilization—and at times feel utterly superannuated. Superannuated. Who, these days, will even perceive that word as a feather-light allusion to Charles Lamb? Doesn't matter. That's just Dirda showing off again.

Oh, well. I do try to keep Hawthorne's observation in mind: "It is a good lesson for a man to step outside the narrow circle in which his claims are recognized, and to find how utterly devoid of significance, beyond that circle, is all he achieves, all he aims at." Sound advice. Still, here, amid the palmettos and the sunshine, surrounded by youth and beauty, supported by an amiable English faculty, at least one displaced literary journalist finds himself uncertain and afraid, as the clever hopes expire . . .

No, no, enough of such facile allusion. I am genuinely worried. Who will read the books I cherish? Who will keep alive the writers I revere? For three and a half months I can do my best to instruct, and—who knows? greater miracles have happened—inspire the young with the delights of world literature. My colleagues here will certainly be doing the same, as they have year after year. But still I worry. And I miss my books.

Excursion

I was fully prepared to be disappointed with New Orleans. Tacky voodoo dolls. Garish Mardi Gras floats. Anne Rice striking spooky poses in marbled cemeteries. Surely New Orleans would be the capital of kitsch, a painted jade of a city, Disney World for Levittowners on holiday.

And who couldn't imagine the bookshops in the Big Easy? Serried rows of the *œuvres complètes* of Frances Parkinson Keyes, that forgotten giantess of the bestseller lists of yore. Multiple book-club editions of *Dinner at Antoine's* and *Steamboat Gothic.* Worn copies of Lafcadio Hearn's lesser works, not to mention tattered firsts of James Lee Burke's more common mysteries.

But, shrewd reader, you can doubtless see what's coming: I fell in love with the place. We are talking major-league enchantment here. The belle of the bayou hath me in thrall.

Late in September I left O-Town—as the oldies deejay calls Orlando, where I'd been teaching in the fall of 1999—to spend three days at the annual Words & Music extravaganza, organized largely by the Faulkner Society. On a Thursday evening I strode purposefully off my plane, pen in hand, repp tie casually knotted, a serious journalist in a navy blue blazer, out for a story. But no character in Graham Greene ever went to seed faster than I did in the Crescent City.

The actual weekend passed in a fever-dream of heavenly irresponsibility. On Friday I woke a little after dawn at the Royal Orleans Hotel—pronounced "OrLeens," by the way; the city itself is a slurred "NuOrluns." The night before, Marty, the doorman, had greeted me with the state's most ingratiating smile, exhibiting the kind of Southern cheeriness that a natural-born melancholiac can only envy. Still preternaturally affable at 7 A.M., he pointed me to Chartres Street, which leads to St. Louis Cathedral at the edge of Jackson Square. From that moment on, everything grows a bit hazy. When you have drunk the milk of paradise, you tend to forget about taking notes.

After all, to saunter through the French Quarter for beignets and coffee on a perfect September morning, or to sip a Pimm's cup at Napoleon House, as the barman slices cucumbers and the Emperor himself looks down at you from a hundred pictures and posters on the wall—what could be more idyllic? Except, perhaps, to lounge at an outdoor café in Pirate's Alley, next to the Faulkner House Bookshop, and chat about modern fiction with Pulitzer Prize–winning novelist Oscar Hijuelos, as your wine glasses catch the slanted light of a fall afternoon. It might almost be a quiet corner of Paris or—as Hijuelos remarked—old Havana.

Decadent? Perhaps. New Orleans is a big modern city, with the usual urban complexities, and a visitor pampers himself, ignores the potholes, finds the decaying neighborhoods romantic. Still, a corner eatery like Mena's Palace, where I ordered seafood gumbo, possesses something I hadn't experienced in a long time: a European civility, coupled with an easygoing hedonism. As A. J. Liebling once observed (in *The Earl of Louisiana*), New Orleans is actually a Mediterranean city, lying "within the orbit of a Hellenistic world that never touched the North Atlantic. The Mediterranean, Caribbean, and Gulf of Mexico form a homogeneous, though interrupted, sea."

Big, Easy, and Bookish

Body should not be bruised to pleasure soul, said Yeats. He might have been thinking of New Orleans, where the life of the mind and the senses really might be one. Late that first afternoon, I stopped in Beckham's Book Store and discovered a beautiful hardcover of M. W. L. Laistner's classic *Thought and Letters in Western Europe, 500–900*, then strolled over to Felix's, where I plopped into a booth for a shrimp po-boy sandwich, washed down with a glass of beer—the local Abita amber, of course. Refreshed, I then wandered on to another bookshop, where I spied a neatly tied bundle of fifteen issues of *Arion*, a lively quarterly devoted to the Latin and Greek classics. A buck apiece. I bought them all—as who would not? On the shop's second floor I later picked up Gerard Manley Hopkins's correspondence with Richard Watson Dixon, which I've needed for years to fill out my Hopkins collection, and the volume of the Yale edition of James Boswell's letters concerning the creation of his *Life of Johnson.* Treasures, both. A good afternoon.

A good day. Earlier that sunny Friday, I had attended a luncheon/ seminar presented by Words and Music 99: "Walker Percy's Search for Meaning in a World of the Mundane." There I chatted with a former corporate wheeler-dealer, now the proud owner of a St. Charles Street cabaret called Le Chat Noir. Images of Sally Bowles flashed through my head. Willkommen. Bienvenue. Welcome. "Ride the streetcar," said my new friend, "and come visit my club." Talking about books, she recommended *Obituary Cocktail,* a picture album of the city's great saloons.

I told her about Susan Larson's splendid *Booklover's Guide to New Orleans.* Following lunch, Rosemary James—organizer of the conference— introduced the speakers, including Faulkner textual scholar Noel Polk, writers Tim Gautreaux, Stewart O'Nan, and Nancy Lemann, and Kenneth Holditch, an old friend of Percy's and an expert on Tennessee Williams. Holditch reminisced about the revered author of *The Moviegoer:* "Walker was terribly allergic to kiwi fruit. . . . He never missed *As the World Turns* and *The Mary Tyler Moore Show.* . . . It took a long time to decipher his handwriting." He also recalled Percy's one writing class at Loyola—students included Gautreaux, Valerie Martin, and journalist Walter Isaacson —at which the novelist read from the manuscript of John Kennedy Toole's rumbustious Pulitzer Prize–winner, *A Confederacy of Dunces.*

"No, Joe, I Don't Do That"

Which, according to Joseph DeSalvo of the Faulkner House Bookshop, is the quintessential New Orleans novel. Joe—everybody calls him Joe—also recommended *The Moviegoer* and *Decorations in a Ruined Cemetery,* by John Gregory Brown. Brown, an amiable New Orleans native now teaching at Sweet Briar College, just happened to be in the shop that day. It seems that everyone with any interest in literature drops by Pirate's Alley. A few weeks earlier, Cormac McCarthy came in. "I recognized him," Joe recounted, "and asked if he would sign a couple of his books." The famously reclusive novelist just said, "No, Joe, I don't do that anymore." Apparently McCarthy was spending some time here researching the lives of deep-sea divers on offshore oil rigs.

As one would expect, Joe keeps a large stock of Faulkner material; I bought a copy of the writer's youthful letters home, letters written while he was living in this very building during the mid-1920s and just starting out as a novelistic genius. But Joe carries a lot of contemporary literature, too: Sheila Bosworth, Shirley Ann Grau, Ellen Gilchrist. On the walls were numerous framed photographs—Hemingway, Welty, Shaw—and a holograph letter by Flannery O'Connor in which she writes a friend: "I hear that the NBC Catholic [radio] Hour that comes on Sunday afternoon is going to devote all this July's programs to the subject of Catholic literature."

Joe used to be a tax lawyer in New York, but book-collecting was his hook on sanity. He proudly showed me his cherished first edition of Boswell's *Life of Johnson*. Nine years ago Joe's wife, conference mastermind Rosemary James, discovered that the Faulkner House was on the market. It had been owned for the previous twenty or thirty years by a retired orthodontist who used it—only in New Orleans—to store and restore religious artifacts. Joe and Rosemary bought the building, moved in upstairs, and, feeling a sense of obligation to the house, opened the bookshop. At the same time, almost as a lark, they started the Faulkner Society. Even as I talked with Joe, writers kept coming by to say hello: Jayne Anne Phillips; local author Tom Franklin, whose story "Poachers" won an Edgar Award from the Mystery Writers of America. Then, just as I was about to leave, in sauntered Oscar Hijuelos. To my astonishment, Joe rushed away for a moment, then returned with a proof of *The Mambo Kings Play Songs of Love*, which he presented to its author. "I thought you should have this." Hijuelos was amazed. I was amazed—a bookseller giving away a modern first worth several hundred dollars. Later the novelist and I talked about publishing, the Irish comic genius Flann O'Brien, Hemingway: "If you're building cabinets," said Hijuelos of *In Our Time* and *The Sun Also Rises*, "you want to look at the work of a master cabinetmaker."

During my evenings I meandered around the French Quarter, past jazz clubs and strip clubs, past the Café du Monde, past mimes and horse-drawn carriages and Lucky Dog vendors, past trumpeters playing "Go Tell It on the Mountain." I even peered through the windows at Galatoire's restaurant, where the two strangers meet in Eudora Welty's wistful "No Place for You, My Love."

One night I stopped by the famous carousel bar at the Hotel Monteleone, outside of which once ran the even more famous streetcar named Desire. On my last day in paradise I drove up through the Garden District—a genteel neighborhood of pillared manors and elaborate iron grille work—to the Columns Hotel, where *Pretty Baby* was filmed. There I sat for an hour on the big front porch, sipping another Abita, and reading

Walker Percy's essay "New Orleans, Mon Amour": "Out and over a watery waste and there it is, a proper enough American city, and yet within the next few hours the tourist is apt to see more nuns and naked women than he ever saw before. And when he opens the sports pages to follow the Packers, he comes across such enigmatic headlines as Holy Angels Slaughter Sacred Heart. . . ." I remember looking up from my book, studying the giant live oak in front of the hotel, its trunk mottled with lichen, its branches spread out like Medusa's snaky curls. A latter-day Louise Brooks, with jet-black hair and severely cut bangs, sprawled at a table near me, smoking a cheroot in a long cigarette holder, sipping a drink that I hoped was absinthe. Later I went on to the Maple Street Bookstore, once a favorite haunt of Walker Percy's, and there, as a memento, paid $65 for a signed first of *The Thanatos Syndrome*.

That very Sunday, September 25, was William Faulkner's birthday. In the evening, pianist Quinn Peeper was scheduled to play the music of native son Louis Moreau Gottschalk, and the Faulkner medals for unpublished novella, short story, and essay were going to be presented. But late that afternoon I needed to be on my way back to Orlando, back to classes and book reviews, back to real life.

As my plane took off, I tried to decide whether to keep reading *A Confederacy of Dunces*. I couldn't, not with a class to teach the next day. Instead I opened my briefcase and pulled out a sheaf of exams that needed grading. "There are several reasons to make violence a comical act and many of these apply to the death of Clare Quilty in *Lolita*. . . ." I sighed and took another long sip of black coffee.

Millennial Readings:
December 5, 1999

Like most reasonable people, I have spent the past twelve months largely ignoring the advent of the year 2000. But now that we are only a few weeks away from Y2K, millennial thoughts have been troubling my usual readerly calm. Maybe I ought to be making thoughtful preparations for the UFO landings? Or steeling myself for Armageddon? Or examining the state of my soul before the Rapture or the Second Coming? Should I, in short, be taking this whole millennium business more seriously?

A quarter-century ago, I happened to read a medieval theological tract—ah, the dizzying joys of graduate school research!—which listed the various signs that will alert the wise to the impending biblical Apocalypse. Of the dozen or so sure indicators that the End was exceedingly Nigh, the only one I now recall is that during the last days rocks will split into four parts and begin to converse in strange tongues. So far as I am aware—and I feel reasonably confident that my colleagues on the *Maryland Weekly* would have covered this—geologists have yet to report any unusual seismic events, let alone conversations among the boulders in Rock Creek Park.

But perhaps I've been lulled into a false sense of security by the usual seasonal cheer. The bookstores glisten with crisp, oversized art books, spirited biographies, pushy bestsellers, and, best of all, those unexpected works of reference that once seen prove irresistible. I myself have squirreled away for wintry afternoons the new edition of *The Dictionary of Imaginary Places,* by Alberto Manguel and Gianni Guadalupi (brilliant short essays on Gondor, Gormenghast, Grand Fenwick, and Gont, to mention just some G spots); Frank M. Robinson's *Science Fiction of the 20th Century: An Illustrated History* (pulp graphics, paperback cover art, movie stills—sensational eye candy); and *Late Antiquity: A Guide to the Postclassical World,* edited by G. W. Bowersock, Peter Brown, and Oleg Grabar (11 survey essays; 500 encyclopedia entries—a *vade mecum* for anybody drawn to what we used to call the Dark Ages, that swirling, little-understood period from the third to the eighth centuries). Of course, such books encourage the illusion that we have all the time in the world for learning, reflecting on life, enjoying the works of the human imagination.

Yet for people of a certain age—that is, almost anyone past 35—this New Year's Day rings like a tocsin. *Dies irae, dies illa.* The millennium, after all, tolls for the middle-aged. Say 2000 and we can't help but calculate the number of years since our birth, and before long we contemplate sitting upon the ground to tell sad stories of the death of kings. Most of us try to resist such dire propensities toward old fogeyism. Hey, we think to ourselves, 45 or 51 or 60 isn't that old. Still feel pretty chipper inside; not too many aches; not that many pills. We can't complain—or rather can't complain much. Nevertheless, it grows harder and harder to keep up interest in a world that seems to be just escaping our grasp. Do we really care about e-books? DVD? Faster Internet access? Once we regarded even personal disasters as kind of exciting, something we would learn from, look back upon, possibly feel a certain nostalgia for one day. No longer. Instead we adopt a cautious hedonism: Not the fruit of experience but experience itself is what we wish to savor. And right now. *Carpe diem.* Seize the day. Seize the minute.

In Barry Targan's short story on this classic theme, "The Rags of Time," a college professor embarks on the familiar ill-advised affair with one of his students. Near the story's climax, the pair are discussing Marvell's "To His Coy Mistress," and the teacher asks his own young mistress what the poem is about. "Love," she ardently replies; no, he cries out despondently, "Death."

Both are right. And thus is it with a new millennium: for the young it signals hope, energy, passion, fresh beginnings; but for others, the end of something. A world. A way of life.

As a newspaper and book person, I might readily bewail the triumph of digital technology: With the close of 1999, *Book World*'s print version will no longer be available by subscription; readers in Oregon or Florida will have to peruse these pages on the *Post*'s Web site. This is not how I think of enjoying a book review section. Yet art and literature will certainly survive, mutate, and flourish in the next century. Universities have already shown us that the humanities and the hard drive can support each other.

My real regret lies elsewhere. More and more, I sense that focused reading, the valuing of the kind of scholarship achieved only through years spent in libraries, is no longer central to our culture. We absorb information, often in bits and pieces and sound bites; but the slow, steady interaction with a book, while seated quietly in a chair, the passion for story that good novels generate in a reader, what has been called the pleasure of the text—this entire approach to learning seems increasingly, to use a pop phrase, "at risk." Similarly, even a basic knowledge of history, classical mythology, and the world's literatures now strikes many people as charmingly antiquarian. Or irrelevant. Or just sort of cute.

"One of the more frightening things about our age," wrote the poet and critic Randall Jarrell, is "that much of the body of common knowledge that educated people (and many uneducated people) once had, has disappeared or is rapidly disappearing. Fairy tales, myths, proverbs, history— the Bible and Shakespeare and Dickens, *The Odyssey* and *Gulliver's Travels*—these and all the things like them are surprisingly often things that most of an audience won't understand an allusion to, a joke about. These things were the ground on which the people of the past came together. Much of the wit or charm or elevation of any writing or conversation with an atmosphere depends upon this presupposed easily and affectionately remembered body of common knowledge; because of it we understand things, feel about things, as human beings and not as human animals."

So there I go, starting to sound more wistful than the Ghost of Christmas Past. But, after all, 'tis the season for such melancholy.

The really great tragedy of life is that we are linear beings in a hypertext world, and we only get to play the game once. Robert Frost observed that "two roads diverged in a yellow wood," and he was sorry that he couldn't travel both. In fact, life is chockablock with intersections, and there are myriad roads we'd like to go down and can't. If you aim to become the greatest lover since Don Juan, you can't also live as a Buddhist sage; if you want to emulate Mother Teresa, you won't have time to dazzle as the finest soprano since Maria Callas. Life is made of choices. Yet people, alas, are made of yearnings. Most of them unfulfilled.

Yet through books we can augment our inherently limited selves, explore that achy solitude we all carry around within us. By turning the pages of James Salter's *The Hunters*, I know the exhilaration of a fighter pilot in Korea. By reading Annie Proulx's *Accordion Crimes*, I can relive the immigrant experience in America, among Italians, Slavs, Germans, and Mexicans. By plunging into Ben Okri's *The Famished Road*, I can enter a modern Africa haunted by ancient spirits. Books don't just open up the world to us, they open us up, too.

That sounds . . . altogether corny, I realize, but about reading I remain shamelessly, irredeemably sentimental. As this holiday and Y2K season runs its course, I fervently hope we will be opening up books on Christmas Day, receiving them as Hanukkah presents or Kwanzaa gifts, at least for a little while longer. Still, who knows? "The millennium which is about to end," wrote Italo Calvino, "has been the millennium of the novel." He may have only been partially right. Increasingly, it looks as though it may have been the millennium of the book too.

Oh, well. As much as possible, we must fare forward, hopefully. So, come New Year's Eve, I will tipsily welcome the millennium with John Dryden's once-famous lines:

> All, all of a piece throughout:
> Thy chase had a beast in view;
> Thy wars brought nothing about;
> Thy lovers were all untrue.
> 'Tis well an old age is out,
> And time to begin a new.

MICHAEL DIRDA is a writer and senior editor for the *Washington Post Book World*. For three years he was a board member of the National Book Critics Circle. His essays and reviews have appeared in numerous publications. In 1993 Dirda received the Pulitzer Prize for Distinguished Criticism.